Religion,
Politics,
and Social Change
in the Third World

Religion, Politics, and Social Change in the Third World

A SOURCEBOOK

Edited with Introductory Notes
by DONALD EUGENE SMITH

 THE FREE PRESS, NEW YORK
COLLIER-MACMILLAN LIMITED, LONDON

The Free Press
A Division of The Macmillan Company
866 Third Avenue, New York, New York 10022

Collier-Macmillan Canada Ltd., Toronto, Ontario

Library of Congress Catalog Card Number 73–143516

For my Father-in-Law
M. Josiah Ramanjulu

CONTENTS

PREFACE

For the vast majority of men in the Third World today, religion constitutes the core of traditional culture and the integrative value system of society. Four major religious systems, Hinduism, Therevada Buddhism, Islam, and Roman Catholicism, predominate over a vast geographical area: South and Southeast Asia, the Middle East and North Africa, and Latin America. In this book we seek to explore the dynamic relationships which link religion, politics, and social change in this vast area.

While the analytic categories which structure the book are ours, the exploration proceeds by examining the words of Third-World leaders themselves as they grapple with the problems of readjusting the relationships among religion, politics, and society. The readings selected include excerpts from authoritative religious pronouncements, political party manifestos, election campaign statements, parliamentary debates, political writings, government reports, constitutions, treaties, concordats, and press commentaries. The readings are preceded by introductory notes to place them in proper historical context. For the most part, however, the selections tell their own story, and the reader can savor for himself the richness of the material brought together from such diverse sources.

The comparative perspective has been maximized by the structure of the book. In Chapter I, for example, we find readings from Colombia, Burma, and Pakistan; in Chapter II, from Chile, Mexico, Indonesia, and Turkey. Most of the chapters include material relating to three major religions, and Chapter IX has sections on all four. It might be noted in passing that, were it not for the limitations of space, we might well have included some selections on Judaism, for the Israeli phenomena of religion-based nationality, religious law, and religious political parties are closely parallel to phenomena found in the Hindu, Buddhist, Muslim, and Catholic countries.

This book is the result of research interests which have engaged me over the past fifteen years, and further pursues questions raised in earlier books: *India as a Secular State* (1963); *Religion and Politics in Burma* (1965); an edited volume, *South Asian Politics and Religion* (1966); and *Religion and Political Development* (1970). Starting with a strong orientation toward the study of India, my interest in comparative questions has gradually taken me to other parts of the Third World. Three years of research in South Asia, with short stays in Southeast Asia and the Middle East, were followed by a summer in Latin America (Mexico, Colombia, and Chile) in 1968. The last-mentioned book, *Religion and Political Development*, is an attempt to deal comparatively with the major questions relating to the interaction of politics and religion; Hinduism, Buddhism, Islam, and Catholicism are considered in the analysis. The present volume contains many of the primary sources used in this study, as well as many others not known to me before I began the task of compilation.

It is my hope that this collection of readings will prove to be useful for study and research, but even more that it will serve to stimulate further social science research in an important area that has been too long neglected. Even to scan the table of contents is to become aware of the vast ramifications of this subject of religion, politics, and social change. I have sought to make the scope of this book comprehensive, in that the major problem areas have been at least touched on. However, the readings selected are at best illustrative and point to a large body of material which still awaits the attention of scholars with theoretical and linguistic tools adequate to the task of bringing it to light.

The languages in which the selections originally appeared include Indonesian, Burmese, Vietnamese, Sanskrit, Hindi, Urdu, Turkish, Arabic, Latin, English, and Spanish. English translations of most of the readings were available, but I have translated eighteen of the selections from Spanish. Throughout the book, a cross reference to another reading is indicated by an upper-case roman numeral corresponding to a chapter, followed by an arabic numeral. Thus IV.2, for example, refers to Chapter IV, selection 2.

A bibliography at the end of the book directs the reader to the most important scholarly studies of various aspects of this subject. Because of limitations of space, this list of secondary sources includes only books and monographs; many of these, however, contain bibliographies and footnote references to the extensive periodical literature.

I am very grateful to the various institutions which over the years have supported the research out of which this book has come. Included are the following: the U.S. Educational Foundation in India, the Council on Religion and International Affairs, the Carnegie Corporation of New York, and the Social Science Research Council. In particular, I am deeply appreciative of the award granted by the Institute of Advanced Projects of the East-West Center, Honolulu, Hawaii, which enabled me to carry out the work on this book during the 1969–70 academic year. To Dr. Minoru Shinoda, the Director, Mrs. Hazel Tatsuno, Administrative Assistant, and the entire staff go my warmest "Alohas" and thanks.

A number of individuals were most helpful in locating material which has been included in this collection. I wish to express my gratitude to: Father Renato Poblete, S. J., of the Centro Bellarmino, Santiago, Chile; Professor Lucy Behrman, of the University of Pennsylvania; Professor Daniel Crecelius of California State College, Los Angeles; Professor Frederick B. Pike, of the University of Notre Dame; Professor Hafeez Malik of Villanova University; Mr. Charles Ashton, of Washington, D.C.; and Mr. Michael L. Lohf, my research assistant at the East-West Center. A word of warm appreciation is extended to those who typed the manuscript of this book with great care: Miss Hannin Chun, Miss Karen Furuta, Miss Diane Koga, Miss Doreen Sugimoto, and Miss Lorraine Tani.

Philadelphia, Pennsylvania   DONALD EUGENE SMITH

Religion,
Politics,
and Social Change
in the Third World

Introduction:
Religion, Politics,
and Social Change

The interaction of Hinduism, Buddhism, Islam, and Catholicism with politics and social change in the Third World is so large and complex a subject that prudence suggests that it best be left alone. On the other hand, some of the most crucial problems of modernization are so involved in this interaction that the inherent importance of the subject compels us to leave prudence aside. While detailed knowledge of all the problems encompassed in South and Southeast Asia, the Middle East, North Africa, and Latin America is beyond the competence of any one scholar, some broad strokes may be placed on the canvas.

As each chapter, section, and reading in the book has an introduction (of correspondingly decreasing length), our purpose in this interpretive essay will be to provide the overview, to examine the parts in relation to the whole. For the framework of this overview, we shall use the three major parts into which the book is divided.

RELIGION AND POLITICAL AUTHORITY

At the beginning of the nineteenth century, a wide range of independent Hindu, Buddhist, Muslim, and Catholic kingdoms shared a basic notion of the sacral nature of government. In these traditional

1

religio-political systems, the ruler was either a god or an agent of a god, and the ideological basis of the state was provided entirely by religious ideas. The disruption of these traditional integralist systems produced by the intrusion of Western ideas and Western power had the effect of separating the religious and political components. This was the beginning of the long, uneven, and complex process of secularization.

Religions which in the traditional pattern had been strongly supported and regulated by royal authority suddenly had thrust upon them an autonomy for which they were ill prepared. And states which in the traditional pattern had been legitimized by religious ideas were suddenly faced by a crisis of legitimacy. Under Western rule, the colonial areas were held together by vastly superior military, technological, economic, and administrative power, but with its demise the new states of the Third World are faced with the full impact of the legitimacy crisis.

In the West, the breakup of the medieval Catholic synthesis was internally generated (the Reformation and Renaissance), unlike the experience of the Third World. The decline of European notions of sacral government led, in the seventeenth century, to the formulation of secular ideologies to assume the legitimizing functions of religion. Theories of a social contract, representative government, or other variations on the basic idea of democracy were most prominent, but there were also secular theories of authoritarianism.

Western notions of representative government were an important part of the external attack on Hindu, Buddhist, Muslim, and Catholic traditional religio-political systems in the early nineteenth century. However, these notions were more effective in discrediting indigenous traditions than in creating a legitimizing force of their own among Third World peoples. In point of fact, only a small elite exposed to Western education developed a real comprehension of and commitment to the secular political values in question. The masses remained steeped in traditional religious modes of thought, and in any event were far removed from the political process.

In Asia and North Africa, the continuing political potency of religious symbols and loyalties was demonstrated in anti-colonial nationalist movements. And independence was achieved in the 1940s and 1950s by peoples still divided into considerably secularized elites and largely traditional masses. The elites, who provided the political leadership at the national level, were here confronted with a cruel dilemma. Significant socio-economic change and modernization, as they saw it, depended in part on the continued secularization of society and culture. That is, essentially the same process which had made them into modern men would have to be repeated a thousandfold among their countrymen.

On the other hand, in an age which increasingly assumed mass participation in politics, how could an elite maintain its political leadership solely on the basis of secular ideals still foreign to the masses? Religion, that traditional legitimizer of social, economic, and political structures, once again presented itself as a qualified candidate for the job. The choice was between secular modernization of society and religious legitimation of polity.

Confronted with this choice, it is not surprising that strange neo-traditionalist compromises were struck. While the sacred ruler stood at the center of the traditional system, sacred *republics* (Catholic, Islamic, and Buddhist) now appeared on the scene. For many among the elite leadership, it was a question of strategy and timing. For while secular modernization was the long-term goal, political legitimacy was an immediate necessity, and if this meant concessions to traditional religious symbols, so be it. However, the secularization of the polity, like the secularization of culture and society, is a process which has moved inexorably since the breakup of the traditional religio-political system. It is doubtful that neo-traditionalist contrivances, such as sacred republics, can provide more than temporary, partial, and unsatisfactory answers even to the problem of legitimacy. For, the assumptions which have growing influence in the Third World today are not only that the common people are political participants, but that governments are responsible for their social, educational, and economic welfare. The growth of this instrumentalist assumption about government undermines all sacral regimes. The sacred ruler in the traditional system did not have to grapple with such problems.

The secularization of the polity has been associated with various kinds of modern ideologies. Liberalism has stressed individual freedom of religion; revolutionary nationalism has emphasized the sovereignty and integrity of the modern nation-state; Marxism has attacked the reactionary role of religion in society; and the very ideological pluralism of the modern world militates against the view that ultimate religious values are encarnated in states.

The secularization of the polity is in many respects a prerequisite for significant social change. For in the traditional Hindu, Muslim, and to some extent Catholic religio-political system, law was understood as divine command. The traditional polity, it must be remembered, was not a legislative state. As we shall see, the law of marriage, divorce, and related matters remains the last bastion of the religious concept of law.

And if changes in such laws are deemed essential in the interest of social reform, the modernizing state must intervene to substitute man-made laws which will better serve changing social needs.

RELIGION AND POLITICAL BEHAVIOR

The secularization of polities over the past century and a half is unquestionably the most fundamental process in the changing relationship between religion and political authority. This is true despite the frequently short-lived neo-traditionalist forms we have noted. However, as states become more secular, new religio-political phenomena arise.

Religious interest groups, religious political parties, and religious communal groups become prominent actors in the new mass activity known as politics. Individual religious leaders and clerical groups utilize sacred symbols to mobilize the masses for nationalist struggles, internal revolts, election campaigns, or even riots aimed at other religious communities. Even while Islamic states and Islamic law undergo extensive secularization, the *ulama* lead nationalist movements, Islamic political parties present significant challenges to their secular opponents, and a mobilized Muslim minority carves out a separate state for itself.

These new manifestations of religious consciousness now play an important role in transitional politics, but their prospects for the future seem dim. Politics has its own goals and its own "laws" and generates its own motivations. While religion, a mass phenomenon in traditional societies, can play a useful role in transitional societies in making politics meaningful to the apolitical masses, the general forces of secularization of culture and society will in the long run erode its political effectiveness also.

It may even be argued that participation in the political process itself, in the modern context, has an important secularizing effect. The political party with an Islamic ideology operates in a milieu of ideological pluralism and finds itself making deals which are politically expedient but which implicitly deny Islam understood in its own terms as a system of comprehensive divine commands, not something to be manipulated. In societies characterized by religious pluralism, the religious political parties find themselves watering down doctrinal distinctives in order to capture minority votes. In the long run, particularistic ideologies such as Islam give ground before universalistic ideologies such as socialism.

All of this, however, does not mean that the new political manifestations of religious consciousness are not important. They are very important at this point in time and merit careful study. We must start with the role of religion in anti-colonial nationalist movements, for here we find patterns which reappear in modified form after independence. The Asian and North African religio-political parties originated in these nationalist movements, and clerical groups first showed their potential for political leadership in this context. But above all, the enormous power of religious symbols to move masses of men to dangerous and self-sacrificial action was conclusively demonstrated. Nationalism itself, of course, acquired precisely the same kind of religious quality for many of the more secular nationalists.

Religion and nationalism tended to coalesce in the course of these freedom struggles. For Hindus and Buddhists, the coalescense created no sharp ideological problems; religious nationalism did create practical problems in Hindu and Buddhist societies with large religious minorities. Aggressive Hindu nationalism in India, for example, could only alienate the religious minorities, and when the Muslim minority constituted one-fourth of the population, the consequences were bound to be serious.

In predominantly Muslim countries, on the other hand, the relationship between religion and nationalism was more problematical. So long as nationalism meant only anti-imperialism there was no conflict, but sharp ideological cleavages developed over the compatibility of Islam with nationalism when nationalism was defined as the major principle for ordering political loyalties. The whole Islamic tradition of the supranational *ummah* ("Community of Believers") came into conflict with modern nationalism based on linguistic and ethnic group identity.

Religious factors have also been important in internal revolts against national governments. Thus, South Vietnam in 1963 witnessed the remarkable Buddhist crisis in which the monks mobilized opposition to the Diem government from their pagoda headquarters. The ritual self-immolation of Buddhist monks by fire provided the most powerful symbols of protest against the Catholic-dominated regime, and the agitation paved the way for the military coup a few months later.

Religious political parties have been powerful contenders in major elections in various parts of the Third World. Thus, the two major Islamic parties together won 39 percent of the seats in the parliamentary elections of 1955 in Indonesia. In the 1964 elections in Chile, political forces became polarized between the Catholic-oriented Christian Democratic Party and a Marxist coalition, FRAP, with victory going to the Christian Democrats led by Eduardo Frei.

In other cases, the major parties have had secular orientations, but religious issues have dominated the election campaigns. Thus in Ceylon, essentially secular parties contested the 1956 election on linguistic and religious issues; the victorious party was the one which promised to implement the Buddhist demand that Buddhism be restored to its "rightful place" in state and society.

In the three major elections cited above, clerical groups also played an important role in the campaigns. The *ulama* of the Indonesian Masjumi, an Islamic party, issued thundering condemnations of the Communist Party, declaring that anyone who voted for the Marxists was an infidel. The Chilean bishops condemned communism in similar terms, and their pastoral letter made excellent campaign literature for the Christian Democrats in 1964. And in Ceylon, the United Monks Front waged a hard-hitting and effective campaign on behalf of S.W.R.D. Bandaranaike's coalition in 1956. Religion has thus been an important factor in elections, and the dominant factor in some.

The politics of religious pluralism, already touched on, has been another form of religious influence on the political process. The competition and conflict of religious communities has sometimes erupted into communal violence. Separatist movements, such as the demand for the creation of Pakistan, have developed out of communal conflict. Political movements and political parties, based on communal ideologies which exalt the majority religion and culture and call for the suppression of the minorities, have also arisen out of communal conflict. For all Third World societies characterized by religious pluralism, national integration has been a major concern.

Thus, the relationship between religion and political behavior in the Third World has been both important and complex and is likely to remain so for a considerable time in these transitional societies. Secularization in its many forms both subtly erodes and frontally attacks these phenomena, but they are not going to disappear tomorrow.

RELIGION AND SOCIO-ECONOMIC CHANGE

The new Afro-Asian polities join the older Latin American republics as sovereign states at a juncture in history where vastly more is expected of governments than ever before. In the contemporary setting, the major function of Third World governments is to promote, direct, and effect fundamental socio-economic change. The effectiveness and even legitimacy of these governments is increasingly measured in these terms.

Can religion, which legitimized the largely static socio-economic and political structures of traditional societies, now be reinterpreted to provide ideological support for governments committed to modernization? Can the resources of the major religious systems now be tapped for the legitimation of change? In all four religions, important reform movements have emerged over the past century and a half. The impact of liberalism was a powerful catalyst in this process of redefining the sacred in more dynamic terms, but today the dominant idea which represents change is socialism. In various forms and with varying success, the religions are coming to terms with socialism, or at least the most salient values of socialism.

The traditional religious outlook tended to be predominantly otherworldly, although this was much less true of Islam than the other religions. Material values were deemed a threat to spirituality in this life and bliss, or at least karmic progress, in the next. The religious re-interpreters have thus had to establish material well-being as a religious value in its own right, no mean task of reinterpretation. Since land reform has been an almost universal concern in the Third World, religious social doctrine has had to develop a rationale for fundamental change in the countryside. This task was made doubly difficult by the fact that religious institutions themselves are among the largest landlords in many parts of the Third World. Finally, the religious legitimation of change included grappling with the population explosion, another difficult area in view of traditional attitudes, particularly in Catholicism.

As we have noted in the previous section, religion has been an important factor in bringing about *political* change; governments have been overthrown and elections won through the effectiveness of religious political parties, interest groups, issues, and symbols. With few exceptions, however, political change has not been translated into significant *social* change. The political activists identified with religion have generally not been motivated by a vision of social change.

Some of the political activists have been found in clerical groups seeking restoration of the influence they enjoyed in the traditional (pre-colonial) setup; this has been especially true of some of the political monks in Burma and Ceylon. Some clerical elements, particularly among the Muslim *ulama*, have been propelled into the center of politics by the desire to *oppose* social change. And many politicians, both clerical and lay, have undoubtedly found political power a sufficient end in itself, and religion an effective means to that end. This does not necessarily mean that their profession of religious commitment is insincere; they may simply regard it as a happy coincidence that what is religiously true is also politically effective.

To a considerable extent, the interpreters of the new "social gospel" in the various traditions and the political activists are two separate groups of people. In the Hindu tradition, Gandhi combined the two roles in a remarkable way, and Vinoba Bhave has followed in his steps, if we can regard the Bhoodan movement as having at least implications of a political character. However, Hinduism is so completely unstructured ecclesiastically that the efforts of great individual interpreters and reformers may have little effect on the system as a whole. For the best examples of evolving religious ideologies of social change, formulated and disseminated within a system-wide structure, we must turn to the Catholic church since Pope John XXIII and Vatican Council II. And for the best example of a religious ideology of social change integrally related to political activism we must look at the Christian Democratic parties of Latin America.

Building on the critique of capitalism found in the social encyclicals, Christian Democracy in Latin America arrived at what could be called Catholic socialism. However, since the formation of the first Christian Democratic government in 1964, in Chile, the vanguard of Catholic thought has become much more radical. Regarding the Catholic-oriented Chilean party now in power as the center of a "new Christendom," the Catholic radicals now press for a much more secular, pluralist, revolutionary, and to some extent, Marxist solution to Latin America's problems. The new Catholic left is committed to revolutionary social change and is quite prepared to make common cause with revolutionaries flying the Marxist banner.

Whether the revolution can be brought about peacefully is a major question, but decades of frustrated hopes increasingly incline the Catholic revolutionary to answer in the negative. The Catholic revolutionaries appear to be growing, particularly among the younger clergy, but not unrepresented even in the national hierarchies (for example, Archbishop Dom Helder Cámara of Brazil). It appears likely that in the next decade, some of the most dramatic developments in the relationship of religion to politics and social change will take place in this part of the Third World.

PART ONE

Religion
and
Political
Authority

I

State Religions and Religious States

At the beginning of the nineteenth century, the sacral nature of government was a fundamental conviction almost unanimously shared by Hindus, Buddhists, Muslims, and Catholics. In both the Hindu-Buddhist and the Judaeo-Christian-Islamic religious streams, *power* was regarded as an attribute of divinity. It is hardly to be wondered at, therefore, that government, which exercised such overwhelming power on earth, was regarded as divine. The ruler, in particular, was revered in all four religious traditions as either himself a god or an agent of a god. Religion answered the question of political legitimacy in the traditional polity, in the pre-modern West as well as in the Third World. While there were precursors, secular political theories which addressed themselves to the problem of legitimacy became important in the West only in the seventeenth century.

From the early nineteenth century, independent Hindu, Buddhist, Muslim, and Catholic kingdoms suffered a series of attacks — military, political, ideological — which spelled the end of traditional sacral government. Western imperialism absorbed many of these kingdoms; the Ottoman Empire contracted steadily; the ideas of the Enlightenment were responsible for the substitution of republics for the Spanish Empire in America. The frequently violent, forcible secularization of polities

11

may be regarded as an aspect of modernization which was necessary, but it created a major problem: states without legitimacy. The secular Western ideologies which were introduced were shared only by small elites and generally had little emotional appeal. It is not surprising, therefore, that long after the destruction of the traditional system, new religio-political amalgams were attempted.

These neo-traditionalist forms, whatever their weaknesses, had an answer to the major problem. The state achieved legitimacy by embracing religion. But the matter is really not so simple. Gone are the days when the religious world-view stood without competitors; today a whole array of secular ideologies are clamoring to be heard — and are heard. Some of the sacralized regimes have already fallen, and it is increasingly doubtful that religious ideologies will be convincing to Third World man as this century draws to a close.

In this chapter, we shall consider three neo-traditionalist constructs in which a religious ideology was superimposed on a *republic*, that most non-traditional form of constitution. "Sacred republics" were difficult to create, but there was really no choice; "sacred rulers" were *impossible* to create this late in the day.

UNION OF CHURCH AND STATE IN COLOMBIA

The neo-traditionalist polity constructed in Colombia after 1880 followed thirty-one years of Liberal anticlerical rule. During this long period of Liberal dominance, church and state were separated, ecclesiastical property was nationalized, and marriage law was secularized. Thus, not only were the Spanish monarchy and the divine right of kings dead ideas but no form of church-state union could claim authority based on the continuity of national tradition.

The constitution of 1886, however, constructed by President Rafael Núñez, declared that Catholicism was "an essential factor of the social order." A basic principle of the constitution, and of the Concordat with the Vatican ratified in 1887, was that church and state were the two pillars which upheld the entire Colombian society. Both constitution and concordat, in fact, incorporated principles found in the encyclical "On the Christian Constitution of States," issued by Pope Leo XIII in 1885. Church-state relations in Colombia, since then, could be described as a kind of bipolar balance of power. As we shall see in the 1953 Treaty on Missions, sometimes the balance strongly favored the church.

1. On the Christian Constitution of States

In this encyclical, frequently known by its Latin title, *Immortale Dei*, Leo XIII restated a Christian tradition that went back to Pope Gelasius' fifth-century theory of the "two swords." Note particularly Leo's explicit reference to the legitimacy conferred on states by religion.[1]

▷ ▷   (13) The Almighty, therefore, has given the charge of the human race to two powers, the ecclesiastical and the civil, the one being set over divine, and the other over human, things. Each in its kind is supreme, each has fixed limits within which it is contained, limits which are defined by the nature and special object of the province of each, so that there is, we may say, an orbit traced out within which the action of each is brought into play by its own native right. But, inasmuch as each of these two powers has authority over the same subjects, and as it might come to pass that one and the same thing — related differently, but still remaining one and the same thing — might belong to the jurisdiction and determination of both, therefore God, who foresees all things, and who is the author of these two powers, has marked out the course of each in right correlation to the other. "For the powers that are, are ordained of God." Were this not so, deplorable contentions and conflicts would often arise, and, not infrequently, men, like travelers at the meeting of two roads, would hesitate in anxiety and doubt, not knowing what course to follow. Two powers would be commanding contrary things, and it would be a dereliction of duty to disobey either of the two.

(14) But it would be most repugnant to them to think thus of the wisdom and goodness of God. Even in physical things, albeit of a lower order, the Almighty has so combined the forces and springs of nature with tempered action and wondrous harmony that no one of them clashes with any other, and all of them most fitly and aptly work together for the great purpose of the universe. There must, accordingly, exist between these two powers a certain orderly connection, which may be compared to the union of the soul and body in man. The nature and scope of that connection can be determined only, as We have laid down, by having regard to the nature of each power, and by taking account of the relative excellence and nobleness of their purpose. One of the two has

[1] From the translation published by the Catholic Truth Society, London. Reprinted in Etienne Gilson, ed., *The Church Speaks to the Modern World: The Social Teachings of Leo XIII* (Garden City, N.Y.: Doubleday Image Book, 1954), pp. 167–169, 172–173. Used by permission of the Catholic Truth Society.

for its proximate and chief object the well-being of this mortal life; the other, the everlasting joys of heaven. Whatever, therefore, in things human is of a sacred character, whatever belongs either of its own nature or by reason of the end to which it is referred, to the salvation of souls, or to the worship of God, is subject to the power and judgment of the Church. Whatever is to be ranged under the civil and political order is rightly subject to the civil authority. Jesus Christ has Himself given command that what is Caesar's is to be rendered to Caesar, and that what belongs to God is to be rendered to God.

(15) There are, nevertheless, occasions when another method of concord is available for the sake of peace and liberty: We mean when rulers of the State and the Roman Pontiff come to an understanding touching some special matter. At such times the Church gives signal proof of her motherly love by showing the greatest possible kindliness and indulgence.

(16) Such, then, as We have briefly pointed out, is the Christian organization of civil society; not rashly or fancifully shaped out, but educed from the highest and truest principles, confirmed by natural reason itself.

(17) In such an organization of the State there is nothing that can be thought to infringe upon the dignity of rulers, and nothing unbecoming them; nay, so far from degrading the sovereign power in its due rights, it adds to it permanence and luster. Indeed, when more fully pondered this mutual coordination has a perfection in which all other forms of government are lacking, and from which excellent results would flow, were the several component parts to keep their place and duly discharge the office and work appointed respectively for each. And, doubtless, in the constitution of the State such as We have described, divine and human things are equitably shared; the rights of citizens assured to them, and fenced round by divine, by natural, and by human law; the duties incumbent on each one being wisely marked out, and their fulfillment fittingly insured. . . .

(18) In political affairs, and all matters civil, the laws aim at securing the common good, and are not framed according to the delusive caprices and opinions of the mass of the people, but by truth and by justice; the ruling powers are invested with a sacredness more than human, and are withheld from deviating from the path of duty, and from overstepping the bounds of rightful authority; and the obedience is not the servitude of man to man, but submission to the will of God, exercising His sovereignty through the medium of men. Now, this being recognized as undeniable, it is felt that the high office of rulers should be held in

respect; that public authority should be constantly and faithfully obeyed; that no act of sedition should be committed; and that the civic order of the commonwealth should be maintained as sacred. [pp. 167–169]

(23) But that harmful and deplorable passion for innovation which was aroused in the sixteenth century threw first of all into confusion the Christian religion and next, by natural sequence, invaded the precincts of philosophy, whence it spread amongst all classes of society. From this source, as from a fountainhead burst forth all those later tenets of un-bridled license which, in the midst of the terrible upheavals of the last century, were wildly conceived and boldly proclaimed as the principles and foundation of that new conception of law which was not merely previously unknown, but was at variance on many points with not only the Christian, but even the natural law.

(24) Amongst these principles the main one lays down that as all men are alike by race and nature, so in like manner all are equal in the control of their life; that each one is so far his own master as to be in no sense under the rule of any other individual; that each is free to think on every subject just as he may choose and to do whatever he may like to do; that no man has any right to rule over other men. In a society grounded upon such maxims all government is nothing more nor less than the will of the people, and the people, being under the power of itself alone, is alone its own ruler. It does choose, nevertheless, some to whose charge it may commit itself, but in such ways that it makes over to them not the right so much as the business of governing, to be exercised, however, in its name.

(25) The authority of God is passed over in silence, just as if there were no God; or as if He cared nothing for human society; or as if men, whether in their individual capacity or bound together in social rela-tions, owed nothing to God; or as if there could be a government of which the whole origin and power and authority did not reside in God Himself. Thus, as is evident, a State becomes nothing but a multitude which is its own master and ruler. And since the people is declared to contain within itself the spring-head of all rights and of all power, it follows that the State does not consider itself bound by any kind of duty toward God. Moreover, it believes that it is not obliged to make public profession of any religion; or to inquire which of the very many religions is the only one true; or to prefer one religion to all the rest; or to show to any form of religion special favor; but, on the contrary, is bound to grant equal rights to every creed, so that public order may not be disturbed by any particular form of religious belief.

(26) And it is a part of this theory that all questions that concern

religion are to be referred to private judgment; that every one is to be free to follow whatever religion he prefers, or none at all if he disapprove of all. From this the following consequences logically flow: that the judgment of each one's conscience is independent of all law; that the most unrestrained opinions may be openly expressed as to the practice or omission of divine worship; and that every one has unbounded license to think whatever he chooses and to publish abroad whatever he thinks. [pp. 172–173]

2. The Concordat of 1887

This concordat between the Vatican and the Republic of Colombia has been in force from 1888 to the present day. It has frequently been praised by conservative Catholic clerics as setting forth a model pattern of church–state relations.[2]

▶ ▶ In the name of the most holy and indivisible Trinity, His Holiness the Supreme Pontiff Leo XIII and the President of the Republic of Colombia, His Excellency Señor Rafael Núñez, have named as plenipotentiaries respectively:

His Holiness, the most eminent Signor Mariano Rampolla del Tindaro, cardinal presbyter of the Holy Roman Church, of the Title of Santa Cecilia, and his Secretary of State, and

The President of the Republic, his excellency Señor Joaquín Fernando Vélez, Envoy Extraordinary and Minister Plenipotentiary before the Holy See:

Who, after presenting their corresponding credentials, have agreed to the following:

ARTICLE 1. The Roman Catholic Apostolic religion is the religion of Colombia, the public powers recognize it as an essential element of the social order, and they are bound to protect and enforce respect for it and its ministers, leaving to it at the same time the full enjoyment of its rights and prerogatives.

ARTICLE 2. The Catholic Church will enjoy complete liberty and independence of the civil power, and consequently there shall be no intervention of this power in the free exercise of its spiritual authority

---

[2] From the English translation by CEDEC Office of Information and Public Relations. From the Vatican text found in *Raccolta di Concordati su Materie Ecclesiastiche tra la Santa Sede e la Autoritá Civili* (Vatican City: Tipografia Poliglotta Vaticana, 1954), vol. II, pp. 1051–1061.

and ecclesiastical jurisdiction, its government and administration conforming to its own laws.

ARTICLE 3. Canonical legislation is independent of the civil law and forms no part of it; but it will be solemnly respected by the authorities of the Republic.

ARTICLE 4. The State recognizes in the Church, represented by its legitimate hierarchical authority, true and proper juridical personality and capacity to enjoy and exercise the rights that appertain to it.

ARTICLE 5. The Church has the right to acquire by legal title, and possess and freely administer movable and immovable property in the manner established by the common law, and its properties and foundations will be no less inviolable than those of citizens of the Republic.

ARTICLE 6. Ecclesiastical properties can be taxed in the same manner and to the same extent as private property; buildings destined for the use of the cult, conciliar seminaries, and episcopal and parish residences are excepted, however, and can never be burdened with contributions nor occupied or used for other purposes.

ARTICLE 7. The members of the secular and regular clergy cannot be obligated to perform public duties incompatible with their ministry and profession, and, furthermore, they will always be exempt from military service.

ARTICLE 8. The Government is obliged to incorporate in its laws of criminal procedure provisions to safeguard the sacerdotal dignity, wherever, for any reason, a minister of the Church figures in a process.

ARTICLE 9. The diocesan Ordinaries and the Parish Priests can collect from the faithful emoluments and ecclesiastical rents (proventos eclesiásticos) canonically and equitably established and based on either immemorial custom in each Diocese or the performance of religious services; and, in order that temporal authority shall lend its aid, the Ordinaries will act in agreement with the Government.

ARTICLE 10. Religious orders and associations of both sexes may be freely constituted and established in Colombia, always provided that their canonical foundation is authorized by the competent ecclesiastical authority. These will be governed by their own constitutions; and in order to enjoy juridic personality and be under the protection of the laws, they shall submit to the Civil Power the canonical authorization granted by the respective superior ecclesiastical authority.

ARTICLE 11. The Holy See will accord its aid and cooperation to the Government in establishing in Colombia religious institutions dedicated particularly to the exercise of charity, missions, education of the young, education in general, and other works of public welfare and beneficence.

ARTICLE 12. In the Universities and in the secondary schools, and other centers of learning, education and public instruction will be organized and directed in conformity with the dogmas and morals of the Catholic Religion. Religious instruction will be obligatory in such centers, and the pious practices of the Catholic Religion will be observed in them.

ARTICLE 13. Consequently, in said centers of learning, the respective diocesan Ordinaries, by themselves, or by special delegates, will exercise the right, respecting religion and morals, of inspection and review of textbooks. The Archbishop of Bogotá will designate the books which are to serve as texts for Religion and morals in the universities; and to the end of assuring uniformity of instruction in the indicated matters, this Prelate, in agreement with the other diocesan Ordinaries, will select the texts for the other public schools. The Government will prevent, in the conduct of literary and scientific courses, and, in general, in all branches of instruction, the spreading of ideas contrary to Catholic dogma and to the respect and veneration due to the Church.

ARTICLE 14. In the event that the instruction in Religion and morals, in spite of the orders and preventive measures of the Government, does not conform to Catholic doctrine, the respective diocesan Ordinary may deny such professors or teachers the authority to teach such material.

ARTICLE 15. The right of appointment to vacant Archbishoprics and Bishoprics belongs to the Holy See. The Holy Father, nevertheless, as proof of special deference, and with the intention of preserving harmonious relations between Church and State, agrees that, in the filling of archiepiscopal and episcopal Sees, the wishes of the President of the Republic take precedence. Consequently, for each vacancy he will recommend directly to the Holy See the ecclesiastics who in his opinion possess the necessary gifts and qualifications for the episcopal dignity. The Holy See, on its part, before making appointments will always reveal the names of the candidates it wishes to promote so that it may learn whether the President has reasons of a civil or political character to consider the said candidates as undesirable. Diocesan vacancies will be filled as soon as possible, and will not last longer than six months.

ARTICLE 16. The Holy See can establish new Dioceses and alter the territorial limits of those now existing when it regards this as useful and advantageous for spiritual welfare, consulting the Government previously and receiving any opinions from it that are just and advisable.

ARTICLE 17. The marriage of those who profess the Catholic Religion will produce civil effects with respect to the persons and property of the contracting parties and their descendants only when it is celebrated according to the provisions of the Council of Trent. The act of the ceremony will be witnessed by the functionary determined by law for the sole object of verifying the entry of the marriage in the civil register, providing it is not a marriage in *articulo mortis,* in which case this formality may be dispensed with, if it is not practical to carry it out, and replaced with supplementary evidence. It is the duty of the contracting parties to fulfill the requirements relative to the intervention of the civil functionary of the register, the duty of the parish Priest being limited to notifying them of the obligation which the civil law imposes on them.

ARTICLE 18. Concerning marriages celebrated any time in conformity with the provisions of the Council of Trent, and which should produce civil effects, the supplementary evidence of ecclesiastical origin should be admitted with preference.

ARTICLE 19. Causes affecting the bond of matrimony and the cohabitation of husband and wife, as well as those relating to the validity of betrothals, will be under the exclusive jurisdiction of the ecclesiastical authorities. The civil effects of matrimony will be regulated by the civil powers.

ARTICLE 20. The armies of the Republic will enjoy the exemptions and favors known as military privileges, which will be determined by the Holy Father in a separate agreement.

ARTICLE 21. After the Divine Offices the following prayer will be recited in all the churches of the Republic: *Domine salvam fac Republican: Domine salvum fac Praesidencius et supremas eius auctoritates.* . . .

3. The Treaty on Missions, 1953

This treaty between the Vatican and the Colombian government, signed during the proclerical dictatorship of Laureano Gómez, essentially placed three-fourths of Colombian territory, inhabited mainly by Indians, under the temporal control of the church. Note especially the provisions in Article 12 for the appointment and removal of civil servants in the mission territories.[3]

---

[3] From the English translation by CEDEC Office of Information and Public Relations. From the Vatican text found in *Raccolta di Concordati su Materie Ecclesiastiche tra la Santa Sede e la Autorità Civili* (Vatican City: Tipografia Poliglotta Vaticana, 1954), vol. II, pp. 79–83.

▶ ▶   ARTICLE 5. The Government of Colombia, as a just compensation for the sacrifice the Missionaries make in evangelizing the Indians has the obligation of providing the Missions of which this Agreement treats with the financial assistance determined in Articles Six and Seven.

ARTICLE 6. The Government of Colombia will contribute annually the sum of thirty thousand pesos ($ 30,000.00) for each one of the Vicariates and Prefectures Apostolic mentioned in the ordinals (a) and (b) of the Second Article of this Agreement. Furthermore, it will contribute annually the sum of three hundred sixty thousand pesos ($ 360,000.00), to provide for the extraordinary needs which the Missions may have.

The Payments here stipulated will be made semiannually in advance by the Government of Colombia, within sixty (60) days of the respective half-year period. Consequently, the total will be met in two (2) semi-annual installments, which will be paid to the Holy See through the Apostolic Nunciature in Bogotá.

ARTICLE 7. The Government of Colombia, without prejudice to the contributions indicated in the previous Article, will help with resources from its ordinary budget, as far as possible, with the construction of orphanages, schools, dispensaries, health centers, and other public welfare establishments in the Mission territories. At the same time, the Government of Colombia will seek ways of increasing the departmental and municipal assistance for education and public welfare in the same territories.

As a stimulus for the training of Colombian Indian clergy, according to the desires of the Holy See, the Government of Colombia will give effective help, to the extent of its possibilities, in the construction of seminaries in Mission territories and towards the maintenance of some scholarships in the seminaries already established in the future. . . .

ARTICLE 9. With the object of orienting education in Mission territories within the spirit and in accordance with the teachings of the Roman Catholic Apostolic Church, the Government of Colombia gives to the Chief Prelates of the Missions the following attributes of direction and vigilance in education:

(a) To create and move public primary, secondary, vocational-agricultural, and normal schools, in accordance with the standards of this Agreement.

(b) To appoint, promote, and dismiss teachers for said primary, secondary, vocational-agricultural, and normal schools, and to fix their salaries, all in accordance with the standards of this Agreement.

(c) To inspect and oversee the instruction in the educational centers of the respective Mission territories, including private institutions, to the end that it is oriented in conformity with Articles Twelve, Thirteen, and Fourteen of the Concordat in force. In cases where, for reason of Colombian legal procedure now in effect or which shall be established in the future, a license is required from some Colombian authority for the opening or functioning of private educational institutions, the respective Colombian authority will consult with the corresponding Chief Prelate of the Mission before reaching a decision. Nothing established in this ordinal will hold for private institutions established exclusively for the education of children of non-Catholic foreigners.

(d) To distribute utensils and to organize school restaurants for primary schools, according to the standards of this Agreement.

PARAGRAPH 2. The founding or moving of schools and the appointments, promotions and dismissals dealt with in this Article, as also the fixing of salaries, must be approved by the respective Colombian authority within the three (3) months following the date on which the corresponding Office receives the copy of the notification in which such measures are mentioned.

PARAGRAPH 3. Disapproval will have the effect of suspending the carrying out of the measure of the Chief Prelate of the Mission until an agreement is reached between the respective Colombian authority and the corresponding Prelate.

PARAGRAPH 4. The moving of schools, referred to in ordinal (a) of this Article and the dismissal of teachers referred to in ordinal (b), cannot be disapproved by the corresponding Colombian authority when they are based on motives of a religious or moral order, but in such cases the copy of the respective notification will be accompanied at least by an explicit declaration by the Prelate that there exists one or the other motive, or both.

ARTICLE 11. The Government of Colombia pledges itself to give, wherever required, and for the period of the duration of this Agreement, such lands from the public domain as may be required, in the opinion of said Government, for the service of the Missions, which lands shall be used for orchards, crops, pasture, etc. The concession of these lands shall have priority over any other concession except that destined for the construction of public roads or the exploitation of the subsoil, and will be made in conformity with the laws in effect at the time of granting.

The Government of Colombia will solicit the opinion of the respective Chief of Mission regarding the adjudication of public lands and the subdivision of reservations, in order to obtain better information regarding the rights acquired by the Indians.

ARTICLE 12. In order to avoid any danger of oppression of the Indians and persecution of the Missions, the Government of Colombia pledges itself to promote good understanding between its agent and the respective Chiefs of Missions, and to prevent by every means possible any disturbance. Civil functionaries for Mission territories will be appointed from among those who can be recommended from every point of view and who are known to be favorable to the Missions and Missionary religious. To the supreme authorities of the High Contracting Parties is reserved the solution of disputes which may arise between the civil authority and the Chief of each Mission because of measures taken by the latter in safeguarding the spiritual welfare and material interests of the Indians, or in exercise of the special functions assigned by Article Thirteen of this Agreement, and the complaint of the Head of a Mission shall be sufficient cause for the dismissal of employees of the Government, if the facts are proved.

ARTICLE 13. In order to stimulate the Indians to gather first of all in families and then to group themselves in reductions, and with the object of facilitating at the same time the performance of functions incumbent upon the civil authority, the Chief of the respective Mission will combine with the primary purpose of his charge, which is that of Christian civilization, that of promoting the material prosperity of the territory and of the Indians established in it. He will be careful, therefore, to study diligently the products of the region in his care, and will send reports to the Government of Colombia proposing adequate methods to derive greater benefits from these products. He will be careful, also, to spread among the Indians the most desirable industries. The Government of Colombia, for its part, pledges itself to help the Heads of the Missions in the development of agriculture and industry and effectively to support as much as possible the properties of the Indians.

BUDDHISM AS STATE RELIGION OF BURMA

The traditional Burmese religio-political system came to an end in 1886 when the British annexed Upper Burma and deposed King Thibaw. The European rulers applied their principle of the religious neutrality of the state, which had evolved in India, to the new territory to the east. While British rule imparted a secular orientation to the fields of government, administration, law, and education, the masses remained steeped in traditional Buddhist patterns of thought and behavior. The first nationalist impulses centered on religious themes, and the first major nationalist figure was a Buddhist monk, U Ottoma, whose influence was at its peak in the early 1920s.

After independence in 1948, Burma under U Nu's leadership steadily moved in the direction of neo-traditionalism. U Nu believed Buddhism to be compatible with and supportive of a modern ideology like socialism. Buddhism seemed to offer a powerful emotional element to cement national integration, and an ideological defense against communism. U Nu fought the 1960 election campaign on his pledge to make Buddhism the state religion, and the following year he redeemed his pledge. The new status of Buddhism was destined to be short-lived, however, for the constitution was abrogated by General Ne Win's coup in March 1962.

4. U Nu Proposing the State Religion Amendment

In this parliamentary speech, the prime minister adduced several interesting reasons for his desire to make Buddhism the state religion. In other speeches he also alluded to the common belief that he was a future Buddha, and that this great meritorious act would bring him closer to the goal. [4]

Mr. Speaker, Sir,

When the insurgent danger had subsided and breathing became easier we initiated the arrangements in early 1951 for the convening of the Sixth Great Buddhist Council. On the completion of these arrangements in 1954 we commenced the Sixth Great Buddhist Council. About three months before the closing of that Great Council I resolved for three reasons to urgently make Buddhism the state religion. May I explain each of these three reasons.

(1) I noticed that with each day of the Great Council there arose in me overwhelming generous faith. Through the stimulation of this great generous faith there arose in me the overpowering desire to perform urgently, after the great deed of merit of successfully and gloriously convening the Sixth Great Buddhist Council, another equally great meritorious deed of making it possible for Buddhism to become the

---

[4] From *The Guardian* (Rangoon newspaper), August 18, 1961.

State religion. This is the first reason for my resolution to make Buddhism the State religion.

(2) I believed that just as I had an overwhelming desire to make Buddhism the State religion so also would there be an overwhelming desire among monks, laymen and the Buddhist mass of people. This belief was the second reason for my resolution.

(3) I believed honestly that since the desire to make Buddhism the State religion was daily rising like a great tide in the hearts of monks, laymen and the Buddhist mass of people, if this matter were postponed for some length of time there would soon come a day when it would fall into the hands of fanatical political leaders and fanatical Buddhist monks and laymen. If this matter should fall into their hands I believed honestly that they would make laws which:

(a) would be inefficacious in the promotion of Buddhism,

(b) make the original suspicions of non–Buddhist citizens of the Union increase in respect of making Buddhism the State religion, and

(c) would be void of the three eternal laws of liberty, equality and justice.

If I undertook this matter I should be able to confront firmly these fanatics should they arise. And if I should reject their unreasonable demands they would not be angered to say: "He rejects our demands because he has no generous faith in the Sasana," but would say: "He rejects our demands because he firmly believes that they should not be accepted." Accordingly my decisions would be accepted graciously. This belief was the third reason for my resolution.

Mr. Speaker, Sir,

Because of these three reasons I invited the leaders of the then AFPFL and submitted to them my desire to make it possible for Buddhism to become the State religion. On receipt of their approval I declared [it] publicly, both as President of the AFPFL and as Prime Minister, for the first time, before 2500 monks and a huge crowd of laymen convened to celebrate the successful completion of the Sixth Great Buddhist Council and the 2500th Anniversary of the Sasana on Full Moon Day of Kason of the Burmese year 1314 or May 22, 1956. . . .

Mr. Speaker, Sir,

May I disclose with your permission, Sir, the arguments of some persons. . . .

These persons say: "In all activities good intention alone is not sufficient, the means too must be good. In making Buddhism the State religion, however well-intentioned the Government might be, the method is wrong. . . ."

According to the view, assumption and belief of these persons:

(1) The State and religion should be separate.

(2) The moment a religion is made the State Religion the State enters completely into the sphere of religion.

(3) It is wrong of the State to enter into the sphere of religion.

Mr. Speaker, Sir,

I have never accepted this view, assumption and belief. I do not accept it now, and will never accept it in the future. . . .

The persons who hold the above beliefs accept the view that Government should provide the leadership in the execution of health, education, social and economic works for the public. If this view is correct that Government should provide leadership in works which offer well-being to the public in the short span of one existence why should not the view be correct that Government should provide leadership in works which offer well-being in the inestimably long future existences?

Furthermore, Mr. Speaker, Sir, there is a factor which directly supports the contention that Government should provide the leadership in religious matters, *Guna vante passanti jana*. People take note only of those who have status and authority. If the Government encourages religion the people in the country too will encourage and support religion. Since this is clear should not the State assume leadership in the promotion of religion?

Mr. Speaker, Sir,

There is another matter which should receive the serious consideration of all who cherish religion. May I explain this. As the Honorable Speaker is aware the notion that religion is an opiate drug has spread in the world. The people who are propagating this notion are not ordinary people, they are Governments. They are Governments who believe in their bones that religion is a drug. They are threatening to replace the drug religion with their notion. These Governments are endeavoring day and night with a huge constellation of methods of persuasion and threat to realize their objective.

Mr. Speaker, Sir,

May I pose a question. Should this notion that religion is a drug propagated through various means by Governments be resisted alone by ordinary citizens who cherish religion? Should not Governments which cherish religion assume the leadership in resistance?

Mr. Speaker, Sir,

These questions I have posed should not be answered superficially nor lightly. As these questions pertain to matters which concern completely the well-being of the people of the world in their future existences they should be considered deeply and seriously, with due deliberation and accordance of priority. This I earnestly request you to do. Speaking for myself, as I have given them first consideration I have for long come upon the correct answers.

(1) If the Government can provide for the benefit of the people of the nation in the short span of life of this existence it should not only be able to provide for their well-being in the inestimably long future existences but should actually do so.

(2) Since it is the disposition of people to perform those acts which leaders of status have performed the Government will have to assume leadership in the promotion of religion and Sasana.

(3) Since Governments themselves are propagating the notion that religion is a drug all Governments which cherish and respect religion must assume leadership in religion in order to ably resist that notion.

5. U Raschid Opposing the Amendment

U Raschid, a respected member of the cabinet and a Muslim, opposed the state religion amendment. U Raschid posed the important question whether, in view of the religious pluralism which characterized contemporary Burmese society, the religion of the majority could serve to integrate and unite the nation. [5]

I am a Muslim. As a Muslim, I believe that there should be no compulsion in religion. Every one should be free to adopt and practice the religion he likes. As a Muslim I do not and indeed cannot object to or oppose anything that Buddhists and persons professing other religions may do for their own religions. All I can and do ask for is that as Muslims, we should have the same freedom.

Since Independence . . . we have had our problems. . . . But, on the whole, the situation in the country in regard to religion has been satisfactory. There has been a good deal of religious harmony. We have been proud of this situation. I have on many occasions spoken of this, in private and in public, not only in the country but also abroad.

During these years a great deal has been done for Buddhism in the country. Large sums of money from the Government Budget have been spent in support of Buddhist activities and institutions. This has been

[5] From *The Guardian* (Rangoon newspaper), August 18, 1961.

largely due to the leadership of our Prime Minister U Nu. A practice has developed that Buddhist judges of the Supreme Court and High Court go in their robes and worship at the Shwedagon Pagoda when the Courts open after the vacation. No non-Buddhist citizen has objected to these activities and expenses.

In 1956, shortly after Prime Minister U Nu made his submission to the Sayadaws that he would try to make Buddhism be adopted as a State Religion, I asked him whether any Government can do more than his Government had done since independence for Buddhism. He agreed that much more could not be done. Mr. Speaker, will the adoption of a State Religion improve matters? . . .

Mr. Speaker, it is to the credit of the Pyidaungzu Party and its leader Prime Minister U Nu that non-Buddhist members of the party have been permitted to oppose this Bill. Let me say that I have been against the idea of a State Religion from its inception in 1947 and have opposed it since the revival of the idea in 1956. While we were in the opposition in 1959, I opposed the matter in the Executive Committee of the Party as well as the Party Conference. The general election had not then been announced. But I secured permission at that time that if I was elected a Member of Parliament or appointed a Cabinet Minister I should be permitted to oppose this proposal. . . .

Mr. Speaker, I am apprehensive that the adoption of a State Religion will have a deep psychological effect upon the Buddhists in the country. They will begin to imagine that they have a special role in the administrative, economic, social and educational life of the country. The adoption of a State Religion will open the door to extremists to make more and more demands based on religion. We have already received some indications of these. Suggestions have already been made that this Bill does not go far enough, that there should be no equality of rights to followers of all religions, that in future the President of the Union of Burma, Cabinet Ministers, the Chief Justice of the Union, the Speakers of Parliament and the Commander-in-Chief should be Buddhists. It will not be easy for succeeding Governments to resist such demands.

Such a situation will lead to unnecessary conflicts between the various religious groups in the country. A situation of that type will not be good for the country. All religious communities will not then pull together. The country and the people as a whole will suffer. In this connection, we should bear the developments in undivided India in mind. Conflicts based on religion do not help the country. Any attempt by the religious majority to secure administrative, economic, social or educational advantages based on religion will be resisted by the religious minorities.

In regard to administration, I am not worried what the Ministers and top officers of Government will do. A narrow-minded Minister can do a lot of damage, but normally one can expect breadth of vision and understanding from Ministers and high officials. The bulk of the people, however, do not frequently come into contact with Ministers and high officials. They have to be in day to day touch with junior officers. What we are more concerned with is how these changes will affect the mentality and attitude of the junior officials. If so inclined, they can be a source of a good deal of annoyance to the religious minorities.

6. State Religion Promotion Act, 1961

The adoption of Buddhism as the state religion had symbolic importance, especially for the monks, and had a significant (adverse) effect on the minorities. But, as the text of this act shows, the practical evidences of the new status of Buddhism did not include any major restructuring of state and society.[6]

▶ ▶   It is hereby enacted as follows:

1. (1) This Act may be called the State Religion Promotion Act, 1961.
   (2) It shall come into force on such date as the President may, by notification, appoint.
2. (1) Buddhist Scriptures shall be taught to Buddhist students in all the State schools within the Union.
   (2) In all the State schools within the Union —
      (a) examinations in Buddhist Scriptures shall be held for Buddhist students;
      (b) certificates shall be granted to successful candidates in the said examinations;
      (c) prizes shall be awarded to those who have passed the said examinations with distinction.

Explanation — The purpose of holding the examination under this section shall be to grant pass certificates to those who are successful, but not to bar those who fail in the said examination from promotion.
3. In all the Universities and their constituent Colleges within the Union, if there is a sufficient number of students who are desirous of studying

[6] From *The Guardian* (Rangoon newspaper), August 1, 1961.

Buddhist Scriptures as a subject for examination they shall be allowed to do so in the same way as they are allowed to study other subjects for the same purpose.

4. The Government or Boards, Municipalities or other local authorities shall grant, in accordance with the rules made by the President in this behalf, those members of their services, who have made actual preparations to appear for any examination of Buddhist Scriptures to be held by any organization constituted by an Act, such as the Union Buddha Sasana Council, Pali Education Board, or Pali University Central Council, such leave as is admissible to them under the law for the time being in force, for the days on which the examination is held and for such days as are actually required for the journey to and from the nearest place where the examination is held.

5.   (1) In all State Teachers' Training Schools and Teachers' Training Colleges, Buddhist Scriptures shall be taught as a subject in order to enable students to teach the said Buddhist Scriptures.

      (2) This subject shall be compulsory for the persons who are Buddhists, and optional for the persons who are non–Buddhists, undergoing teachership training.

Explanation — The Teaching of this subject under this section is to grant pass certificates to those who pass in the said subject but the failure to pass therein shall not be a bar to promotion.

6. In cases where it is proposed to open new State primary schools, preference shall be given for the purpose to those monasteries which can provide suitable and adequate accommodation, and where a sufficient number of pupils is available and the presiding monk is willing to accept the conditions laid down by the Government.

7. The State Broadcasting Service shall broadcast on Buddhism for at least one hour either continuously or at different periods on Uposatha (Sabbath) days.

8. The Government shall have classes opened in prisons to enable prisoners to learn Buddhist Scriptures.

9. The Government or Boards, Municipalities or other local authorities shall —

      (a) close their offices within the Union on Uposatha (Sabbath) days,

      (b) close their schools also on Uposatha (Sabbath) days.

Provided that the President may from time to time, by notification, direct any other day to be a holiday in any office, if he is satisfied that because of the nature of business in such office it is inexpedient to close such office on Uposatha days.

10. (1) All ordinary shops licensed by the Government to sell toddy, fermented or distilled liquor or foreign liquor shall be closed on Uposatha days.

    (2) No liquor shall be sold or served in restaurants on Uposatha days.

    (3) In any hotel no liquor shall be sold or served on Uposatha days in rooms open to the public except that it may be sold or served in lodging rooms.

11. All State public libraries shall be provided with a complete set of Tripitaka Pali Texts, the Commentaries, Sub-commentaries and Burmese translations thereof and other suitable Buddhist literature.

12. (1) If there is a sufficient number of students who are desirous of studying Pali in all the State schools within the Union, arrangements shall be made in order to enable them to take Pali like other subjects beginning from the eighth standard and to provide a sufficient number of teachers for the said students.

    (2) It shall be open to any student to take Pali as a subject for all matriculation examinations held within the Union.

    (3) In selecting candidates for appointment to any post, whether by competitive examination or otherwise, the Public Service Commission shall give the same value to Pali as to other subjects.

13. (1) For the purpose of ensuring compliance with any provision of this Act or any order made thereunder, the President may issue instructions to any authority.

    (2) In Particular, and without prejudice to the generality of the foregoing power, such instructions may provide for the following matters:

    (a) installation of an image of the Buddha in a place easily accessible to the public for worship, either in a separate shrine room or in a separate Dhammarama in every Court building or group of Court buildings;

    (b) arrangement to be made in all State schools for the Buddhist teachers and students to pay their homage to the Buddha, to recite Buddhist Scriptures and to hear sermons on the teachings of the Buddha;

    (c) closing of the Government shops, the Municipal bazaars and the bazaars belonging to other local authorities on Uposatha days;

    (d) provision for the teaching staff and students in all State schools, Universities and their constituent Colleges with reading rooms;

(e)   provision of such reading rooms with Buddhist Scriptures, periodicals and papers;

(f)   assistance to be given by the Government to such public libraries within the Union as require assistance for providing themselves with the Tripitaka Pali Texts, the Commentaries, Sub-commentaries and the Burmese translation thereof.

THE ISLAMIC REPUBLIC OF PAKISTAN

The last of the Mughal emperors ceased to reign even in theory in 1858, but a century later Pakistan struggled to delineate, for itself and for the world, what a modern Islamic republic would be like. The movement for the creation of Pakistan, led by the highly westernized and secular-minded lawyer M. A. Jinnah, was based on the deep Hindu-Muslim cleavage in Indian society, and implied only a Muslim-majority state. The notion of *Islamic* state implied ideological and structural distinctives based on Islam.

After the emergence of Pakistan in 1947, the debate over the meaning of an Islamic state became a central ideological and political question. Those who stood in the tradition of Islamic modernism, like Prime Minister Liaquat Ali Khan, emphasized the universalistic ethical values of Islam: Equality, social justice, democracy, and respect for the worth and dignity of man. The traditionalist divines (*ulama*), on the other hand, spoke of the restoration of concrete institutional forms, and in particular, the enthronement of the *shari'ah* or Islamic law, a rigid and comprehensive code governing many aspects of social, political and economic life. The constitution of 1956, while primarily oriented toward the modernist view, did forbid the enactment of laws repugnant to the *shari'ah*.

7. A Modernist View of the Islamic State

The Objectives Resolution was moved by Prime Minister Liaquat Ali Khan and adopted by the Constituent Assembly on March 7, 1949; it was later incorporated with minor changes in the 1956 constitution. In his speech the prime minister interpreted Islam as a source of guiding principles and inspiration for the new state, not a rigid mold into which the state would have to be forced.[7]

---

[7] From *The Constituent Assembly of Pakistan Debates*, vol. 5, no. 1, pp. 1–7, 1949.

▶ ▶ Sir, I beg to move the following Objectives Resolution embodying the main principles on which the constitution of Pakistan is to be based:

"In the name of Allah, the Beneficent, the Merciful;

Whereas sovereignty over the entire universe belongs to God Almighty alone and the authority which He has delegated to the State of Pakistan through its people for being exercised within the limits prescribed by Him is a sacred trust;

This Constituent Assembly representing the people of Pakistan resolves to frame a constitution for the sovereign independent State of Pakistan;

Wherein the State shall exercise its powers and authority through the chosen representatives of the People;

Wherein the principles of democracy, freedom, equality, tolerance, and social justice, as enunciated by Islam, shall be fully observed;

Wherein the Muslims shall be enabled to order their lives in the individual and collective spheres in accord with the teachings and requirements of Islam as set out in the Holy Qur'an and the Sunnah;

Wherein adequate provision shall be made for the minorities freely to profess and practice their religions and develop their cultures; . . .

So that the people of Pakistan may prosper and attain their rightful and honored place amongst the nations of the world and make their full contribution towards international peace and progress and happiness of humanity."

Sir, I consider this to be the most important occasion in the life of this country, next in importance only to the achievement of independence, because by achieving independence we only won an opportunity of building up a country and its polity in accordance with our ideals. I would like to remind the House that the Father of the Nation, Qaid-i-azam, gave expression to his feelings on this matter on many an occasion, and his views were endorsed by the nation in unmistakable terms. Pakistan was founded because the Muslims of this subcontinent wanted to build up their lives in accordance with the teachings and traditions of Islam, because they wanted to demonstrate to the world that Islam provides a panacea to the many diseases which have crept into the life of humanity today. . . .

It is universally recognized that if man had not chosen to ignore the spiritual values of life and if his faith in God had not been weakened, this scientific development would not have endangered his very existence. It is God-consciousness alone which can save humanity, which means that all power that humanity possesses must be used in accordance with ethical standards which have been laid down by inspired teachers known to us as the Prophets of different religions. We, as Pakistanis, are not ashamed of the fact that we are overwhelmingly Muslims and we believe that it is by adhering to our faith and ideals that we can make a genuine contribution to the welfare of the world. Therefore, Sir, you would notice that the Preamble of the Resolution deals with a frank and unequivocal recognition of the fact that all authority must be subservient to God.

It is quite true that this is in direct contradiction to the Machiavellian ideas regarding a polity where spiritual and ethical values should play no part in the governance of the people, and, therefore, it is also perhaps a little out of fashion to remind ourselves of the fact that the State should be an instrument of beneficence and not of evil. But we, the people of Pakistan, have the courage to believe firmly that all authority should be exercised in accordance with the standards laid down by Islam so that it may not be misused. All authority is a sacred trust, entrusted to us by God for the purpose of being exercised in the service of Man, so that it does not become an agency for tyranny or selfishness. I would, however, point out that this is not a resuscitation of the dead theory of divine right of kings or rulers, because, in accordance with the spirit of Islam, the Preamble fully recognizes the truth that authority has been delegated to the people, and to none else, and that it is for the people to decide who will exercise that authority.

For this reason it has been made clear in the Resolution that the State shall exercise all its powers and authority through the chosen representatives of the people. This is the very essence of democracy, because the people have been recognized as the recipients of all authority and it is in them that the power to wield it has been vested.

Sir, I just now said that the people are the real recipients of power. This naturally eliminates any danger of the establishment of a theocracy. It is true that in its literal sense, theocracy means the Government of God; in this sense, however, it is patent that the entire universe is a theocracy, for is there any corner in the entire creation where His authority does not exist? But in the technical sense, theocracy has come to mean a government by ordained priests, who wield authority as being specially appointed by those who claim to derive their rights from their sacerdotal position. I cannot overemphasize the fact that such an idea is absolutely foreign to Islam. Islam does not recognize either priesthood or any sacerdotal authority; and, therefore, the question of a theocracy simply does not arise in Islam. If there are any who still use the word theocracy in the same breath as the polity of Pakistan, they are either laboring under a grave misapprehension, or indulging in mischievous propaganda.

You would notice, Sir, that the Objectives Resolution lays emphasis on the principles of democracy, freedom, equality, tolerance, and social justice, and further defines them by saying that these principles should be observed in the constitution as they have been enunciated by Islam. It has been necessary to qualify these terms because they are generally used in a loose sense. For instance, the Western Powers and Soviet Russia alike claim that their systems are based upon democracy, and, yet, it is common knowledge that their politics are inherently different. . . . When we use the word democracy in the Islamic sense, it pervades all aspects of our life; it relates to our system of government and to our society with equal validity, because one of the greatest contributions of Islam has been the idea of equality of all men. Islam recognizes no distinctions based upon race, color, or birth. Even in the days of its decadence, Islamic society has been remarkably free from the prejudices which vitiated human relations in many other parts of the world.

Similarly, we have a great record in tolerance, for under no system of government, even in the Middle Ages, have the minorities received the same consideration and freedom as they did in Muslim countries. When Christian dissentients and Muslims were being tortured and driven out of their homes, when they were being hunted as animals and burnt as criminals — even criminals have never been burnt in Islamic society — Islam provided a haven for all who were persecuted and who fled from tyranny. It is a well-known fact of history that, when anti–Semitism turned the Jews out of many a European country, it was the Ottoman empire which gave them shelter. . . . My friends from Bengal would remember that it was under the encouragement of Muslim rulers that the first translations of the Hindu scriptures were made from Sanskrit into Bengali. It is this tolerance which is envisaged by Islam, wherein a minority does not live on sufferance, but is respected and given every opportunity to develop its own thought and culture, so that it may contribute to the greater glory of the entire nation.

In the matter of social justice as well, Sir, I would point out that Islam has a distinct contribution to make. Islam envisages a society in which social justice means neither charity nor regimentation. Islamic social justice is based upon fundamental laws and concepts which guarantee to man a life free from want and rich in freedom. It is for this reason that the principles of democracy, freedom, equality, tolerance and social justice have been further defined by giving to them a meaning which, in our view, is deeper and wider than the usual connotation of these words.

The next clause of the Resolution lays down that Muslims shall be enabled to order their lives in the individual and collective spheres in accord with the teachings and requirements of Islam as set out in the Holy Qur'an and the Sunnah. It is quite obvious that no non-Muslim should have any objection if the Muslims are enabled to order their lives in accordance with the dictates of their religion. You would also notice, Sir, that the State is not to play the part of a neutral observer, wherein the Muslims may be merely free to profess and practice their religion, because such an attitude on the part of the State would be the very negation of the ideals which prompted the demand of Pakistan, and it is these ideals which should be the cornerstone of the State which we want to build. The State will create such conditions as are conducive to the building up-of a truly Islamic society, which means that the State will have to play a positive part in this effort.

You would remember, Sir, that the Qaid-i-azam and other leaders of the Muslim league always made unequivocal declarations that the Muslim demand for Pakistan was based upon the fact that the Muslims had a way of life and a code of conduct. They also reiterated the fact that Islam is not merely a relationship between the individual and his God, which should not, in any way, affect the working of the State. Indeed, Islam lays down specific directions for social behavior, and seeks to guide society in its attitude towards the problems which confront it from day to day. Islam is not just a matter of private beliefs and conduct. It expects its followers to build up a society for the purpose of good life — as the Greeks would have called it, with this difference, that Islamic "good life" is essentially based upon spiritual values. For the purpose of emphasizing these values and to give them validity, it will be necessary for the State to direct and guide the activities of the Muslims in such a manner as to bring about a new social order based upon the essential principles of Islam, including the principles of democracy, freedom, tolerance, and social justice. . . . It is, therefore, clear that this clause seeks to give the Muslims the opportunity that they have been seeking, throughout these long decades of decadence and subjection, of finding freedom to set up a polity, which may prove to be a laboratory for the purpose of demonstrating to the world that Islám is not only a progressive force in the world, but it also provides remedies for many of the ills from which humanity has been suffering.

8. Traditionalist Views of the Islamic State

Serious disturbances erupted in the Punjab in 1953 when orthodox *ulama* launched a violent agitation against the Ahmadiyya, a dissident Muslim sect which they regarded as beyond the pale of Islam. The agitation had very serious implications since Pakistan's Minister of External Affairs, Chaudhri Zafrullah Khan, was an Ahmadi. In seeking to understand the underlying causes of the disturbances, an official commission learned much about the *ulama's* notions of what it meant for Pakistan to be an Islamic state.[8]

▶ ▶   The point which must be clearly comprehended to appreciate the plausibility or otherwise of the [anti-Ahmadiyya] demands is that in an Islamic State or, what is the same thing, in Islam, there is a fundamental distinction between the rights of Muslim and non-Muslim subjects, and one distinction which may at once be mentioned is that the non-Muslims cannot be associated with the business of administration in the higher sphere. Therefore if the Ahmadis were not Muslims but *kaffirs* [infidels], they could not occupy any of the high offices in the State, and as a deduction from this proposition two of the demands required the dismissal of Chaudhri Zafrullah Khan and other Ahmadis who were occupying key positions in the State, and the third required the declaration of Ahmadis as a non-Muslim minority to ensure that no Ahmadi may in future be entrusted with any such position in the State. As this issue which the demands directly raised was fundamental, and of the greatest importance to the future of Pakistan, we have, with the assistance of the *ulama*, gone closely into the conception of an Islamic State and its implications which we now proceed to state. [pp. 200–201]

Sovereignty and Democracy in Islamic State

That the form of Government in Pakistan, if that form is to comply with the principles of Islam, will not be democratic is conceded by the *ulama*. We have already explained the doctrine of sovereignty of the Qur'an and the Sunnah. The Objectives Resolution rightly recognized this position when it recited that all sovereignty rests with God Almighty alone. But the authors of that Resolution misused the words "sovereign" and "democracy" when they recited that the Constitution to be framed was for a sovereign State in which principles of democracy as enunciated by Islam shall be fully observed. It may be that in the context in which they were used, these words could not be misunderstood by those who are well versed in Islamic principles, but both these words were borrowed from western political philosophy and in that sense they were both

---

[8] From *Report of the Court of Inquiry constituted under Punjab Act II of 1954 to enquire into the Punjab Disturbances of 1953* (Lahore: Superintendent, Government Printing, Punjab, 1954), pp. 200–201, 210–213, 218–219, 221, 231.

wrongly used in the Resolution. When it is said that a country is sovereign, the implication is that its people or any other group of persons in it are entitled to conduct the affairs of that country in any way they like and untrammelled by any considerations except those of expediency and policy. An Islamic State, however, cannot in this sense be sovereign, because it will not be competent to abrogate, repeal, or do away with any law in the Qur'an or the Sunnah. Absolute restriction on the legislative power of a State is a restriction on the sovereignty of the people of that State and if the origin of this restriction lies elsewhere than in the will of the people, then to the extent of that restriction the sovereignty of the State and its people is necessarily taken away. In an Islamic State sovereignty, in its essentially juristic sense, can only rest with Allah. . . .

Legislature and Legislation

Legislature in its present sense is unknown to the Islamic system. The religio-political system which is called *din-i-Islam* is a complete system which contains in itself the mechanism for discovering and applying law to any situation that may arise. During the Islamic Republic there was no legislature in its modern sense and for every situation or emergency that arose law could be discovered and applied by the *ulama*. The law had been made and was not to be made, the only function of those entrusted with the administration of law being to discover the law for the purposes of the particular case, though when enunciated and applied it formed a precedent for others to follow. It is wholly incorrect, as has been suggested from certain quarters, that in a country like Pakistan, which consists of different communities, Muslim and non-Muslim, and where representation is allowed to non-Muslims with a right to vote on every subject that comes up, the legislature is a form of *ijma* or *ijtihad*, the reason being that *ijtihad* is not collective but only individual, and though *ijma* is collective, there is no place in it for those who are not experts in the knowledge of the law. This principle at once rules out the infidels (*kuffar*) whether they be people of Scriptures (*ahl-i-kitab*) or idolators (*mushrikeen*).

Since Islam is a perfect religion containing laws, express or derivable by *ijma* or *ijtihad*, governing the whole field of human activity, there is in it no sanction for what may, in the modern sense, be called legislation. Questioned on this point Maulana Abul Hasanat, President, Jami'at-ul-Ulama-i-Pakistan says:

Q. — Is the institution of legislature, as distinguished from the institution of a person or body of persons entrusted with the interpretation of law, an integral part of an Islamic State?

A. — No. Our law is complete and merely requires interpretation by those who are experts in it. According to my belief no question can arise, the law relating to which cannot be discovered from the Qur'an or the *hadith*.

Q. — Who were Sahib-ul-hall-i-wal-aqd?

A. — They were the distinguished *ulama* of the time. These persons attained their status by reason of the knowledge of the law. They were not in any way analogous or similar to the legislature in modern democracy.

The same view was expressed by Amir-i-Shari' at Sayyad Ata Ullah Shah Bukhari in one of his speeches reported in the *Azad* of 22nd April, 1947, in the course of which he said that our *din* is complete and perfect and that it amounts to *kufr* to make more laws. Maulana Abul ala Maudoodi, however, is of the opinion that legislation in the true sense is possible in an Islamic State on matters which are not covered by the Qur'an, the Sunnah, or previous *ijma* and he had attempted to explain his point by reference to the institution of a body of persons whom the Holy Prophet, and after him the *Khulafa*, consulted on all matters relating to affairs of State. The question is one of some difficulty and great importance because any institution of legislature will have to be reconciled with the claim put forward by Maulana Abul Hasanat and some other religious divines that Islam is a perfect and exhaustive code wide enough to furnish an answer to any question that may arise relating to any human activity, and that it does not know of any "unoccupied field" to be filled by fresh legislation. . . .

Position of Non-Muslims

The ground on which the removal of Chaudhri Zafrullah Khan and other Ahmadis occupying key positions in the State is demanded is that that the Ahmadis are non-Muslims and that therefore like *zimmies* in an Islamic State they are not eligible for appointment to higher offices in the State. This aspect of the demands has directly raised a question about the position of non-Muslims in Pakistan if we are to have an Islamic Constitution. According to the leading *ulama* the position of non-Muslim in the Islamic State of Pakistan will be that of *zimmies* and they will not be full citizens of Pakistan because they will not have the same rights as Muslims. They will have no voice in the making of the law, no right to administer the law and no right to hold public offices. A full statement of this position will be found in the evidence of Maulana Abul Hasanat Sayyad, Muhammad Ahmad Qadri, Maulana Ahmad Ali, Mian Tufail Muhammad and Maulana Abdul Haamid

Badayuni. Maulana Abul Hasanat on being questioned on the subject stated as follows:

Q. — If we were to have an Islamic State in Pakistan, what will be the position of the *kuffar* (non-Muslims)? Will they have a voice in the making of laws, the right of administering the law and the right to hold public offices?

A. — Their position will be that of *zimmies*. They will have no voice in the making of laws, no right to administer the law and no right to hold public offices.

Q. — In an Islamic State can the head of the State delegate any part of his powers to *kuffar*?

A. — No. [pp. 210–213]

Apostasy

Apostasy in an Islamic State is punishable with death. On this the *ulama* are practically unanimous (vide the evidence of Maulana Abul Hasanat Sayyad, Muhammad Ahmad Qadri, President, Jami'at-ul-Ulama-i-Pakistan, Punjab; Maulana Ahmad Ali, Sadr Jami'at-ul-Ulama-i-Islam, West Pakistan; Maulana Abul Ala Maudoodi, founder and ex-Amir-i-Jama'at-i-Islami, Pakistan; Mufti Muhammad Idris, Jami' Ashrafia, Lahore, and Member, Jami'at-ul-Ulama-i-Pakistan; Maulana Daud Ghaznavi, President, Jami'at-i-Ahl-i-Hadith, Maghribi Pakistan; Maulana Abdul Haleem Qasimi, Jami'at-ul-Ulama-i-Islam, Punjab; and Mr. Ibrahim Ali Chishti). According to this doctrine, Chaudhri Zafrullah Khan, if he has not inherited his present religious beliefs but has voluntarily elected to be an Ahmadi, must be put to death. [pp. 218–219]

Propagation of Other Religions

Closely allied to the punishment for apostasy is the right of non-Muslims publicly to preach their religion. The principle which punishes an apostate with death must be applicable to public preaching of *kufr* and it is admitted by Maulana Abul Hasanat, Ghazi Siraj-ud-Din Munir and Master Taj-ud-Din Ansari, though the last subordinates his opinion to the opinion of the *ulama*, that any faith other than Islam will not be permitted publicly to be preached in the State. And Maulana Abul Ala Maudoodi, as will appear from his pamphlet, "Punishment in Islam for an apostate," has the same views on the subject. . . .

The prohibition against public preaching of any non-Muslim religion must logically follow from the proposition that apostasy will be punished with death and that any attack on, or danger to, Islam will be treated as treason and punished in the same way as apostasy. [p. 221]

We have dwelt at some length on the subject of Islamic State not because we intended to write a thesis against or in favor of such State but merely with a view to presenting a clear picture of the numerous possibilities that may in future arise if true causes of the ideological confusion which contributed to the spread and intensity of the disturbances are not precisely located. [p. 231]

9. Compromise in the 1956 Constitution

The document which finally emerged in 1956 reproduced the Objectives Resolution in its Preamble and contained various other provisions to justify the title, "Islamic Republic of Pakistan." The most significant related to the "repugnancy clause" found in article 198.[9]

▶ ▶ 24. The State shall endeavour to strengthen the bonds of unity among Muslim countries, to promote international peace and security, to foster goodwill and friendly relations among all nations, and to encourage the settlement of international disputes by peaceful means.

25. (1) Steps shall be taken to enable the Muslims of Pakistan individually and collectively to order their lives in accordance with the Holy Qur'an and Sunnah.

(2) The State shall endeavour, as respects the Muslims of Pakistan, —

(a) to provide facilities whereby they may be enabled to understand the meaning of life according to the Holy Qur'an and Sunnah;

(b) to make the teaching of the Holy Qur'an compulsory;

(c) to promote unity and the observance of Islamic moral standards; and

(d) to secure the proper organization of zakat, wakfs and mosques.

197. (1) The President shall set up an organization for Islamic research and instruction in advanced studies to assist in the reconstruction of Muslim society on a truly Islamic basis.

(2) Parliament may by Act provide for a special tax to be imposed upon Muslims for defraying expenses of the organization set up under clause (1), and the proceeds of such tax shall not, notwithstanding anything in the Constitution, form part of the Federal Consolidated Fund.

[9] From *Constitution of the Islamic Republic of Pakistan*, 1956, articles 24–25, 197–198.

198. (1)   No law shall be enacted which is repugnant to the Injunctions of Islam as laid down in the Holy Qur'an and Sunnah, hereinafter referred to as Injunctions of Islam, and existing law shall be brought into conformity with such injunctions.

(2)   Effect shall be given to the provisions of clause (1) only in the manner provided in clause (3).

(3)   Within one year of the Constitution Day, the President shall appoint a Commission

(a)   to make recommendations —

(i)   as to the measure for bringing existing law into conformity with the Injunctions of Islam, and

(ii)   as to the stages by which such measures should be brought into effect; and

(b)   to compile in a suitable form, for the guidance of the National and Provincial Assemblies, such Injunctions of Islam as can be given legislative effect.

The Commission shall submit its final report within five years of its appointment, and may submit any interim report earlier. The report, whether interim or final, shall be laid before the National Assembly within six months of its receipt, and the Assembly after considering the report shall enact laws in respect thereof.

(4)   Nothing in this Article shall affect the personal laws of non-Muslim citizens, or their status as citizens, or any provision of the Constitution.

Explanation — In the application of this Article to the personal law of any Muslim sect, the expression "Qur'an and Sunnah" shall mean the Qur'an and Sunnah as interpreted by that sect.

II

The Secularization of Polities

The secularization of the polity is one of the most fundamental ideological and structural changes in the complex process of political development. Since the early nineteenth century, virtually all the countries of what is now called the Third World have been subjected to powerful secularizing forces of foreign (Western) origin. And in the twentieth century, a number of independent nations have voluntarily opted for some version of a secular state. Despite the problem of legitimacy, which secularization in some ways intensifies, these states spurned neotraditionalist religio-political constructs, convinced that meaningful national progress could only proceed on secular lines.

The secularizers, however, have been motivated by very different ideologies and perceptions of the world. Some, represented by President Arturo Alessandri of Chile, operated on moderate, liberal, and democratic assumptions. This liberalism stressed the freedom and equality of the individual citizen, rights which were undermined by the state's constitutional tie to a church which might not receive the willing allegiance of the citizen. Secularization in this liberal tradition came about peacefully, as a result of parliamentary debate and decision. Radically opposed in spirit and method was the separation of church and state brought about by the Mexican Revolution, motivated in part by a militant anticlericalism which assumed that the church could be put in its proper place only by violent frontal attacks. During certain periods of this Revolution, atheism was officially promoted, and the government's policy toward the church could only be described as one of persecution. While Chile approximated the American pattern in achieving church–state separation, Mexico followed France's revolutionary example.

Somewhat similar differences can be found in the recent history of the Muslim world. In Indonesia, Sukarno had argued as early as 1926 that in the struggle for independence from the Dutch, the three main ideologies, nationalism, Islam, and Marxism, should all be recognized as valid. (See reading VI. 4.) After independence, he continued to insist that the reality of this ideological pluralism made an Islamic state impossible. The Indonesian Revolution, unlike the Mexican, accorded religion an honored place from the beginning, with the understanding that religion not be made the exclusive ideological basis of the state. In Turkey, on the other hand, the ideological hostility to Islam was considerable, although carefully disguised part of the time. There was, however, no lack of decisiveness, and the abolition of the caliphate (and later of the *shari'ah*) struck massive blows at a tradition of Islamic polity which went back to the times of the Prophet.

LIBERALISM AND SECULARIZATION IN CHILE

In Chile, as in most of Latin America, proposals to separate church and state were seriously debated in the latter part of the nineteenth century. *Reformas teológicas* were in fact enacted by the Congress in 1884 which secularized cemeteries and made the civil ceremony compulsory to give legal effect to a marriage. But clerical forces rallied in time to stave off the constitutional amendment to separate church and state. By the end of World War I, a general climate of tolerance and considerable religious indifference characterized the Chilean people. President Arturo Alessandri in his 1923 proposal argued that separation would benefit the church as well as the citizen and the state. While the archbishop of Santiago denounced this as tantamount to an act of national apostasy, he later reconciled himself to the fact, if not the principle, of church–state separation, and this was peacefully effected in 1925.

1. Alessandri on Freedom of Citizen, State, and Church

In this historic speech Alessandri summed up the arguments for a religiously netural state as the best guarantee of religious liberty.

Catholicism would also benefit by being freed from dependence on the fortunes of particular political parties. [1]

▶ ▶   The union between Church and State established in our Fundamental Charter, and the recognition of the Apostolic Roman Catholic religion as the religion of the State to the exclusion of all other faiths, should in my judgment no longer remain in our institutional setup.

The State is a juridical person; religion is a sentiment, a psychological manifestation solely of a natural person.

The State with a determined and compulsory religion is contrary to the physical nature of things; it is antiscientific. For this reason, the great majority of the civilized peoples have suppressed official religion from their fundamental laws, replacing it with the absolute freedom of all religions which do not go contrary to morality or sound customs. Tolerance has replaced sectarianism, definitively establishing as a milestone of progress the sacred and solemn respect for the free conscience before the civil authority.

We cannot forget, either, that the government of a people represents the collectivity of the citizens; consequently, it owes identical respect to the consciences of all, without taking into account that the believers might form large or small groups.

When our Constitution was written, it was understandable that the present article 4, and other corollary provisions, be included in it, because in that period the unanimity of our fellow citizens was almost surely in communion with those doctrines. But the passing of years, the diffusion of ideas, the natural movement of civilization, have made to prosper in the country numerous citizens who profess other religious communions and who also have a perfect right to be respected in the sanctuary of their consciences.

I do not accept hostilities or persecutions against any religion; I only ask tolerance and equality for all, and the exclusion of the privileges that always contain an injustice.

There is a clear and evident advantage in demarcating frankly the area in which the activities of civil life take place from that in which the respected inspirations of religious sentiment abide and act.

Experience teaches us that every measure directed to the secularization of instututions, while resisted initially, later becomes strongly rooted

---

[1] From *Legislatura Ordinaria de Cámara de Senadores*, vol. I, pp. 12–14, June 1, 1923. Translated by the editor.

in national life with the approval and applause of all. It is the natural consequence of the reestablishment of normality within the basic principles that sustain human organizations. In our own political history of the last half-century, we have seen the successive abolition of special tribunals and the ecclesiastical courts (*fuero eclesiástico*), the creation of secular cemeteries, and the laws of civil registration and marriage. Great agitations, true storms of inflamed protest, shook the country when these reforms were initiated; nevertheless, they were carried out; today they are accepted by unanimous opinion, and no one can question their usefulness and supreme importance for social progress. To resist them today would be absurd. The same thing would occur the day we reach the desired goal in the ascending order of these reforms.

Under the administration of the eminent Prelate, honor of our country and of the entire continent, who today directs the destiny of the Church, we have advanced far toward the prudent equilibrium of the separation that should mediate between the spiritual and the material.

Thanks to him, in large part, the activities of the temporal order have not been disturbed by undue interventions of the Church or of the clergy. It is loyal to recognize it, and it has been loyal to repay it. This attitude has eliminated possible reprisals, at the same time making disappear (may it be forever!) the bitter and passionate struggles that such frictions engender. This is experimental proof of the good fruits which are gathered when religious activities are circumscribed to the spiritual field which is proper to them.

But the life of a man is always an instant in the history of peoples, and it is therefore desirable to translate into law that which has already been evidenced in practice.

Thinking surely of this very thing, one of the most eminent and respected prelates of the Chilean Church, Don Rafael Valentín Valdivieso, in a memorable discourse delivered in the Faculty of Theology and Sacred Sciences on April 30, 1859, declared: "The supreme interest of the Church is that, in midst of the vicissitudes and agitations through which peoples pass, religion not suffer harm. But once its ministers organize themselves in political bands, they already compromise the sacred interests in their charge. In the eyes of their adversaries religion and politics become identified."

Immediately he adds: "The future of the Church, the most precious interests of religion, would remain, then, linked to the fortune of a party. When this party is defeated, the Church will be one of the first victims of the hatred and revenge of the victorious faction. If, on the contrary, it maintains a prudent neutrality toward all the parties, the Church is respected by all, and if it gains nothing by the triumph of one, neither does it lose anything by the fall of the other. Its action is always forthright, and its voice is everywhere heard without distrust or suspicion."

This is what I fervently desire for my fatherland: the Church, religious communions of whatever dogmas and beliefs, dedicated exclusively in their action to the sphere of consciences, the peculiar and proper sphere of the spiritual order; the neutral and equalitarian State, without privileges or exceptions, giving an example of respect for all consciences and upholding the guarantees which in religious matters, as in everything, correspond equally to the totality of the inhabitants.

These ideas concentrated in my spirit are the basis of a bill of constitutional reform which, according to reiterated promises, has for some time been studied and drafted. . . . I shall choose the opportune moment to present the bill, when the sovereign will of the nation, manifested in the form prescribed by law, indicates to me that there is a possibility of its being considered and acted on.

2. Objections of the Archbishop of Santiago

In this pastoral, the head of the Chilean hierarchy argues that separation of church and state is contrary to Catholic principles (see I.1, the encyclical "On the Christian Constitution of States") and would represent an act of national apostasy; he calls on the clergy and laity of Chile to oppose the constitutional reforms which include this act of secularization. [2]

▶ ▶   PASTORAL ON THE SEPARATION OF CHURCH
AND STATE

We, Crescente Errázuriz, by the grace of God and of the Holy Apostolic See, Archbishop of Santiago de Chile, etc.

To the clergy and faithful of the archdiocese, health and peace in the Lord.

A powerful political grouping declares itself to be committed to the separation of church and state and asks the ministers of their party that they present to the Congress a bill of constitutional reform to this effect. The Catholic, then, finds himself placed in a situation in which his adversaries drag him to the struggle, and he must therefore take all precautions to defend himself to the best advantage. Because, if it is true

[2] From "Pastoral sobre la Separación de la Iglesia y el Estado," *La Revista Católica* (Santiago, Chile), no. 522 (May 5, 1923), pp. 643–646. Translated by the editor.

that such a separation can be accepted as a lesser evil where the enemies of the Church persecute it openly, the Chilean Catholics, who are in an overwhelming majority and protected by the Constitution, have a strict duty to reject it absolutely, because it embodies an impious outrage toward God, unmitigated ingratitude toward the Church, and would bring in its train the saddest social consequences.

Separation between church and state signifies a public and solemn denial of God, a true and terrible national apostasy; the state proclaims that it does not know God; that in nothing will it take Him into account, nor will it respect His laws or listen to His voice, and that the Infinite Being, on whom all depends and to whom we owe all and on whose mercy our hope is built, does not even exist for our fatherland; the Christ who, emblem of peace and union of two fraternal peoples, dominates the heights of the Andes [at the border of Chile and Argentina] ought not to send His blessing to Chile, because Chile, imitating the Jews who asked for His crucifixion, says of Him: "We do not want Him to reign over us."

Since its birth, almost four hundred years ago, Chilean society has lived and has been nourished from the life and teachings of the Church, to such an extent that to suppress this fact for an instant, in the history of that society, would be to leave the most obvious events without explanation.

And they would have us ignominiously cast far away that Catholic Church which in Chile, as everywhere and more here perhaps than anywhere else, has inspired the most beautiful works, encouraged so many noble hearts, taught self-denial to their sons, pacified disputes, consoled afflicted souls, and relieved so many misfortunes.

She, who for four centuries has taught our fathers high-minded dignity, whose memory gives us pride, and formed Christian mothers whose virtues we venerate, should now disappear from society and her name be erased from the laws, from the homes, from the schools, from everywhere.

Has perchance the teacher of divine morality been converted into the corruptor of consciences and destroyer of the social order? What great evils is it intended to avoid with a similar upheaval? When solutions should be sought among the citizens for the arduous economic and social problems which oppress us, is it politic, prudent, even acceptable, to create the profoundest divisions among souls?

Never — all proclaim — has there reigned in Chile greater harmony between the Church and the State. Why, then, is it intended to wound deeply the Catholic people?

Whatever be the conditions on which the separation of church and state be proposed — understand it well, beloved sons and daughters — whatever be the ideas and the purposes that inspire the proposal, it carries within it the denial of God and must be combated and rejected by the Catholic.

The state without God will take care that that most holy name not reach the child's ear and will make it an offense for a teacher to teach respect, love, gratitude and obedience to the Supreme Maker and His holy laws. The child in that school, the youth in the high school and university, ignorant of and despising religion, if they rise in life will one day come to make laws and govern our Catholic people; if they remain in the multitude, they will form part of the enemies of the social order.

With regard to domestic society, the denial of God is its loss. Already we see no few evils in the law's lack of acknowledgment of the validity of the sacrament of marriage, and wherever the church is separated from the state, the legal dissolution of the tie leads the family to the degradation in which paganism had left it.

However great those evils, it is among the poor working people that the sad effects of the state without God will manifest themselves most clearly.

The Church, as you well know, does not see a single need without hastening to lend help, and it would be very difficult to enumerate the institutions that have multiplied to found thousands of establishments and to gather in them the unfortunate woman who desires to return to the path of virtue, the crippled child, the feeble old man, the sick, the mentally ill; in the institutions which offer asylum to her who is in danger of being lost or who is abandoned by her parents, a home for the widow, education for the poor, instruction for countless children and youth, practical means for earning a living for the worker; in sum, everything which can be imagined by the ardent love of him who sees a brother in every unfortunate man.

And to serve their neighbor thus, innumerable holy women and generous men abandon comforts, prospects of wealth and pleasure, family and even country to dedicate themselves completely and for life to the service of those who suffer.

Seek, beloved sons and daughters, outside of the Catholic Church similar self-denial and calculate, on one hand, the value of such services made to the state, and on the other, the ingratitude of the response to it which denies the God who strengthens those heroic souls and which breaks the heart of those who thus sacrifice themselves to do good.

May God turn away the danger which threatens our country; may God spare us the pain of witnessing such mournful days at the end of our long lifetime; may the country not see, may we not see the great calamity of a religious struggle: it usually commences with relative moderation; but very quickly excitement builds up and passions are inflamed; all see the beginning and no one can foresee the end, which ordinarily becomes the ruin of the country.

But now that a powerful political party, whose constituent principles are contrary to those of the Church, intends to erase all idea of God from our Constitution, it is necessary that the Catholics strive with might and main to stop it: strive by all licit means so that only those are elected to the Congress who will defend Catholic principles, and among those principles is the fundamental one of the union of Church and State. Let not the Catholics be deceived by the illusion of what some call "friendly separation." There is no friendly separation in doctrine, when one says: "I believe in God and worship Him," and the other, "God does not exist for me." In Chile we the Catholics are the immense majority, and it would be a profound error, and unworthy cowardice, to allow our Fundamental Charter to make, in the name of the nation, a profession of atheism.

The parish rectors and priests in general should explain the preceding lessons to the faithful, encourage them to defend the holy Catholic principles and to contribute through their efforts to the legal triumph of those principles.

ANTICLERICALISM AND SECULARIZATION IN MEXICO

The Catholic Church in Mexico wielded vast economic and political power in the past. When independence from Spain was achieved in 1821, the church owned one-half of the productive land in the country. In 1855, the Liberals under Benito Juárez initiated a series of reforms which eliminated ecclesiastical privileges, nationalized church lands, and secularized education. The Constitution of 1857 made no mention of an official religion, and two years later church and state were separated by decree. With the French intervention, however, the impetus of the Reform was broken. In the long dictatorship of Porfirio Díaz (1876–1910), the laws of the Reform were ignored, and the church gradually regained much of its power.

The Mexican Revolution, which erupted in 1910, was strongly opposed by the clergy who feared the revolutionary program of agrarian reform. In the long struggle which ensued, anticlerical measures were adopted by the government which in some cases virtually eliminated any right of religious liberty. As the following reading makes clear, the men of the Revolution sought vastly more than separation of church and state. They were convinced that a modern society could be built only by destroying the sources of church power, in the *spiritual* as well as in the social, economic, and political spheres. An accommodation with the church was reached after 1940, however, as more moderate positions were taken on both sides.

3. Subduing the Socio-Political Power of the Church

In this official publication, written by Emilio Portes Gil, Attorney General of the Republic, the Catholic Church is indicted for its long struggle against the principles of the Mexican Revolution. The document reveals the bitterness of the clerical-anticlerical conflict which has existed until recently.[3]

▶ ▶ The stand taken by the Catholic clergy, and its seditious, visionary and unpatriotic activities, induce it to believe that it will thereby achieve the restoration of inordinate power like that wielded by it in the past, and it fails to take into account the fact that it has at the present day broken down in the presence of the new organization of the modern state, which no longer circumscribes its functions to the creation of law, but on the contrary extends its action much farther and embraces all matters connected with economic, political, and cultural administration, and which has set for itself as one of its specific objects, the extirpation of fanaticism. This is why in the Mexican State the men of the Revolution cannot allow the people to remain sunk in ignorance and sloth; in the former, because it converts man into a member of a herd and because it surrenders, in a spirit of slavish submission everything in the way of scientific knowledge and of truth drawn from the real founts of experience. We here refer to religious activities with the entirely selfish aims of swelling the fortunes of the clergy, of enhancing their political power, and of freely allowing undue traffic in the acts of religion. As regards sloth, because when capital is accumulated in the hands of the clergy it is disastrously exported from the country to uphold an alien sovereign; besides which convents, seminaries and other similar institutions are centers of indolence, idleness and the repetition of useless acts, and places

---

[3] From Emilio Portes Gil, *The Conflict between the Civil Power and the Clergy* (Mexico City: Ministry of Foreign Affairs, 1935), pp. 4–7, 105–106, 110–111.

where those superstitions and falsehoods that darken the soul of child-hood, the teaching of youth and the judgment of grown men are fostered.

The reasons for the lack of conformity of the clergy in Mexico may in general terms be said to lie in the immense fortunes and enormous areas of landed property in the hands of the Church, from colonial times down to our own day, but since vigorously counteracted by the Reform Laws, the Constitution of 1913, the statutes emanating therefrom and the efficient action of revolutionary governments; the termination of a regime of privilege and undue concessions; the freeing of man's con-science darkened by an oppressive regime of material power, dogmas, threats and falsehood, all together making up an obscuring and stupid fanaticism, which prevented a dispassionate study of the problem of the Cosmos in accordance with the knowledge contributed by natural and social science; the recognition of the fact that only to the State falls the task of exercising those activities that tend to achieve the ends sought by the peoples, and the prevention of all interference by bishops, priests and other religious, in matters only coming within the province of the Nation's representatives; and lastly, the intervention of the State in the way of guiding the consciousness of the masses, in shops, in the fields, and in schools, by systematizing the study of human attainments for the better utilizations of natural resources and the fuller satisfaction of human needs, by unfolding the idea of public service and of duty so that every human being may contribute to the fulfillment of individual and social aims and not constitute an obstacle in the way of the achievement of the longed-for ideal of a society that shall be better organized, more humane and altruistic and with a fuller sense of responsibility; in few words, a noble effort of the Mexican Revolution, which all the peoples of the earth will deem just, to dignify and improve the lives of its citizens and to bring a breath of liberty and well-being, and a piece of land and a free conscience to the humble peasant dwelling far away in the mountains or lost in the limitless horizons of the fields. . . .

Our political code expressly defines the main principles governing the organization of the State; and consequently, the principle that the religious groups must necessarily submit to regulation by the political department, constitutes one of the bases of our constitutional system. A Mexican publicist asserts: "The struggle with the clergy is to such an extent identified with the essential principles of the Mexican Revolution, that we cannot, during the last twenty years, find any transcendent moment of our public life or far-reaching action of our regime, not connected to a greater or lesser degree with the fight against the Church, its economic power and control over people's consciences, achieved over four centuries of almost absolute supremacy." [pp. 4–7]

We shall . . . teach childhood how dangerous is that belief taught by the Clergy over so many centuries, according to which the poor and downtrodden have nothing to expect in this world and can but await their redemption in the next. Mexico does not desire such teaching; it rejects it, the more as it is presented by the Clergy to suit its own ends. If the children of Mexico are to be Christians, let them learn Christian doctrine from the very fount, and lips of the Master, as taught by the Gospel. . . . How is it possible that the disciples of such a Master could fight for centuries to recover unjust privileges enjoyed by them? Mexico applauds the doctrine, making for equality of all, of Him who treated the rich with harshness and the poor and weak with tenderness and brotherly love. We applaud Him who yielded the first place to the humblest; He who exposed the maneuvers of the priests called by Him a "race of vipers" and "whited sepulchers" and we likewise applaud Him because He was able to drive out of the temple, whip in hand, both Pharisees and merchants. . . .

We believe furthermore, that the new methods are certainly better than those of the past, and preferable to those of religious associations; first and foremost because they are not nourished on prejudices and lies but on the contrary study the phenomena of the Universe from a scientific standpoint, and because these rational methods of today will serve to lay the foundations of a strictly socialistic and vital concept of life. [pp. 105–06]

The Crown of Spain found itself compelled to limit the temporal power of the Church; the State likewise found itself compelled, when Mexico threw off the Spanish yoke, and found herself lacking in resources and burdened with obligations, to fight against a rich and powerful clergy with all its resources intact and ever increasing; out of necessity and as a patriotic duty the men of the Reform, with the support of the proletarian masses, had to combat the clergy while suffering the pressure of political, economic and social forces brought to bear from abroad, struggled to establish an integral State and to seek a new alignment of the former dominating classes.

In the same manner, and for identical reasons, the Revolution that began in 1910, when it found the Church and the clergy in full activity and reunited with the conservative class, composed of those remains of feudalism not yet totally eliminated, . . . has found it necessary to restrain and repress its temporal functions so that the Civil Power on its onward march might achieve the formation of nationality. . . .

We thus find always in the history of Mexico that same effort on the part of the Civil Power to impede the existence of the Church as a temporal power, that is, the State preventing, on grounds of social reality, of biological defense almost, the existence of another State.

The Mexican State is not now, as it was early in the last century, in a position of material inferiority opposite the Catholic Clergy, but it does occupy the same defensive and repressive attitude, in order to diminish or destroy that adverse force that attempts to lessen its power. [pp. 110–11]

IDEOLOGICAL PLURALISM AND SECULARIZATION IN INDONESIA

Islam was deeply involved in the Indonesian nationalist movement from its very inception. The first major nationalist organization was the religiously based Sarekat Islam, founded in 1912. However, secular nationalists such as Sukarno and Sjahrir, and Marxists such as Aidit, all participated in the struggle which led to independence in 1949. In a manner reflecting his own background of Javanese syncretism, Sukarno sought to define a common ideological base on which all together could build the new state: the *Pantja Sila*, or Five Principles. Belief in One Supreme God was the first principle, but as Sukarno explained it the concept had nothing of specifically Islamic content.

Sukarno's talent for ideological syncretism later led him to coin the slogan NASAKOM, an acronym using the first letters of the Indonesian words for nationalism, religion (*Agama*), and communism. These three ideological streams, he believed, could merge and flow together. Implicitly, Sukarno refused to accept Islam on its own terms, as a revealed total way of life, individual and collective.

4. State Based on Pantja Sila, Not Islam

H. Roeslan Abdulgani, a prominent cabinet minister under Sukarno, made two major speeches in the Constituent Assembly in 1957 on the ideological foundations of the Indonesian state. In the following passages Abdulgani shows the diverse ideological streams in Indonesian nationalism, and the consequent impossibility of building the state on Islam alone. [4]

---

[4] Reprinted from H. Roeslan Abdulgani, *Pantjasila: The Prime Mover of the Indonesian Revolution* (Jakarta: Prapantja [n.d.]), pp. 63, 66–73, 97. Used by permission.

▶ ▶ The Constitution which is to be drawn up must contain, beside provisions on the apparatus of the State, basic principles on the policy of the State regarding the various aspects of our life. And, what is fundamental, it must contain our political and social philosophy which must be in harmony with the demands of the present time and of future generations.

The philosophy of our political and social life, or the ideology of our State, must constitute the foundation on which the house of our nation will be built. The ideology of the State is the source of the philosophical outlook which will shed its light on the whole apparatus of the State and our social life. . . . [p. 63]

In this Constituent Assembly the Indonesian nation is passing through the ambitious process of formulating its political and social philosophy, or its *Weltanschauung*, which will be made into the foundation for the ideology of its state.

In the search for a definition of our State ideology, we should take the realities around us into account. Within the realm of the Asian-African continents, we come face to face with the following three facts:

(a) the existence of states founded on socialist/communist ideologies;

(b) the existence of states explicitly founding their forms of government on the teachings of Islam;

(c) the existence of states based on liberalist/capitalist ideologies. . . .

Can we use liberalism/capitalism as the basis of our State philosophy? The answer to this question is definitely in the negative.

Our revolution, our national struggle, is fundamentally a struggle of the people against colonialism. On the other hand that selfsame colonialism can historically be likened to a child of capitalism and a grandchild of the concept of liberalism.

To use this concept will, in point of fact, amount to denying the basic principle of our own struggle. Therefore, it will not concur with the historical course of our struggle.

Further, our experience as a nation which has lived under a colonial yoke has bolstered and strengthened our consciousness that the concept of liberalism will take us, in its further development, into the system of capitalism and colonialism — the very system we fought against in our struggle for independence.

Liberalism/capitalism teaches about equal opportunities in life, and permits free competition. In actual fact, however, this awareness only exists in the political field. In the economic and social fields, this concept produces economically weak and economically strong groups, which results in an ever-widening gulf between the two groups. . . .

Can we use the concept of socialism/communism as the basic pattern for our governmental structure?

One of the striking features of the governmental system in present-day communist countries is the constitutional position of one party. This brings forth its dictatorial character, whatever name or pretext may be given for its existence. It is hard for our people to accept this feature, since *musjawarah* (deliberation to arrive at a unanimous opinion), *mufakat* (unanimous decision) and *gotong rojong* (mutual assistance) constitute features of the utmost importance in our daily social life and in our political life. Whereas the dignity of man is not given the best possible scope to develop in a dictatorial system, our system of *musjawarah* and *mufakat* verily reflects the high value the dignity of man is given in our social life.

To be sure, the communist concept possesses most valuable standards to gauge economic life. *However, its cultural aspects do not, or insufficiently, give scope for a religious life. Whereas we know that the greater part of our nation adheres to one religion or another, the communist concept clashes with the religious character and disposition of our nation.*

What about the ideology of Islam as a basis for our political and social life? Before I set forth my opinion, permit me to advance a few matters so as to remove any misunderstanding, and thus enable a more matter-of-fact consideration.

As Muslims we keep up the teachings of Islam as a solid spiritual and physical guidance in our daily lives. Further, it is an un-disputable fact that the greater part of the Indonesian people adhere to Islam, so that Islam indeed is strongly rooted in our society. How-ever, in view of the experiences our nation as well as other nations have had in the course of history, I feel obliged to put forth the other facts with regard to political and social affairs.

At present, we have not yet come across a political pattern which, while based on the ideology of Islam, has succeeded in solving the problems confronting a modern state.

The ideology of Islam is also felt to be an inadequate guide to go by, because it still provides room for a monarchical system, as our examples above show. In circles of Islamic political scientists themselves, this question is not yet considered solved.

Any explicit provision in the Constitution that a certain religion is the one and only official religion will, in my opinion, give rise to the probability that other spiritual or religious beliefs will get less room for development. Besides, such a provision in our Constitution will be contradictory to the basically multi-religious feature of our society. Diverse spiritual convictions are to be found in our nation.

In the economic field, too, we have not yet come across an example where a country which has adopted Islam as its basis has succeeded in spreading justice and prosperity evenly among the people.

Therefore, we may well take our lessons from the above facts. . . .

The idea which underlay our proclamation, and underlies our national revolution, is the very thing which has inspired our Republic.

That idea is Pantja Sila. It is because of Pantja Sila that Indonesia has acquired its national identity. *Pantja Sila not only puts Indonesia's identity on record, but also enables directions to be indicated for the future.* To deny the ideals of Pantja Sila is tantamount to denying the true substance and objective of our proclamation and national revolution. [See Sukarno's 1926 statement, reading VI.4. Ed.]

An idea which has been able to inspire the struggle of a nation toward the attainment of its independence cannot but be deeply rooted in the life of that nation.

Our Pantja Sila answers the challenge to the life of our nation, which has lost its national identity since the fall of Madjapahit.

The concept of Belief in the One, Supreme God, which constitutes the first *Sila* (principle) of Pantja Sila, is a solid basis on which to afford free scope to the religious traits of the Indonesian nation. This principle guarantees the existence of freedom of religion.

The concept of humanity clearly depicts the character of the Indonesian nation, which loves peace and freedom, and also wishes peace and freedom for the other nations. The principle of humanity guarantees that the Indonesian nation values highly the dignity of man, and does not discriminate on account of race, sex and descent.

The concept of nationalism is a reflection of the 20th-century struggle of the Asian-African nations toward the attainment of independence, sovereignty and national identity.

The concept of sovereignty of the people expounds the system of our national life, which is based on *musjawarah* (deliberation to arrive at a unanimity of opinion), *mufakat* (unanimous decision) and *gotong rojong* (mutual assistance) and led by the desire to serve common interests.

The concept of social justice, which is a revolt against the pauperization process we went through in the past, and which is basic to the realization of prosperity for the people, wishes to see prosperity justly and equally spread among the people.

Thus I have reiterated the principles of Pantja Sila. Pantja Sila has been an inspiration to our revolution, and constitutes a strong basis for guiding our State and society in the future. [pp. 66–73]

Now, I would return to the question: Does the existence of a Ministry for Religious Affairs in our Pantja Sila-based State automatically make our State a theocracy?

The answer is decidedly in the negative. Viewed from the point of Islam, which has no priesthood — or from the Christian point, which wishes a separation of Church from State — the qualification of theocracy does not at all apply to our State.

On the other hand, it is *equally false* to qualify our Pantja Sila-based State as a state which is based on atheism or solely on the doctrine of materialism, since it is beyond doubt that our State actively and dynamically "guides, supports, preserves and develops religion."

Is our Pantja Sila-based State a secular one?

If secularity is understood to mean the opposite of theocracy, of a government by priests, then the Pantja Sila State may be described as secular.

However, if the application of the term secular to our State is understood to mean that Religion and State are entirely unrelated, are *absolutely* separated from each other in our Pantja Sila-based State, then our State is definitely not secular. [p. 97]

NATIONAL SOVEREIGNTY AND SECULARIZATION IN TURKEY

In an organic religious system like Islam, which tends to equate religion and society, there is no autonomous ecclesiastical structure (church) to be separated from the polity. In the Turkish Revolution led by Mustafa Kemal after World War I, the major thrust of the secularization process was the elimination of two institutions, both of which fused the spiritual and temporal regulation of society: the caliphate, and the Islamic law (*shari'ah*). The caliphate was abolished in 1924, and two years later the *shari'ah* was rejected entirely in favor of a secular civil code based on the Swiss model. It was not until 1928 that the constitution was amended to delete the clause recognizing Islam as the state religion, and this step had symbolic significance only.

For five centuries, the caliph of the Ottoman Empire symbolized the religious and political unity of the Islamic Community (*ummah*). European threats to the caliphate agitated Muslims, thousands of miles away, in India and Indonesia. Atatürk, however, rejected the Islamic Community and exalted the Turkish Nation as the new focus of loyalty. As the caliph symbolized the old ideal, the republic symbolized the new.

5. Caliphate Not Essential to Islam

On March 1, 1924, Mustafa Kemal inaugurated the fifth annual session of the Grand National Assembly with a speech in which he argued the necessity of "lifting and detaching the Islamic religion, to which we are happy to belong, from the political situation in which it has been embedded for centuries." On the following day, in a speech to the Party of the People, Seyyed Bey, Kemal's Minister of Justice, suggested the possibility of abolishing the caliphate. Seyyed Bey's historical and doctrinal arguments are found in the following selections from this speech. [5]

▶ ▶ Gentlemen! The *Shari'ah* considers the Caliphate from two points of view; one concerns religion, the other politics. The political side is a different thing, with which I do not wish to concern myself. I intend to explain how the Islamic religion should consider the question of the Caliphate. If for this we consult the Qur'an, we find that there is no passage regarding the constitution of the Caliphate, which we are discussing today. In the Qur'an there are two divine precepts on the government and administration of the country; one says, "The Muslims administer their business among themselves"; the other teaches, "obey God, his Prophet and those who retain the command." The first precept indicates the principle of consultation, the second recommends obedience to the government and the commanding officers. In the Qur'an the terms "Caliph" and "Imam" are found, but they are not applied to our Prophet nor to our Caliphs. In the divine concept the principle of the Caliphate is the confirmation of that which is just and the annulment of that which is unjust; in other words, the administration of justice. In one passage there is included a talk between God and Abraham. God says to Abraham, "I will give you Imam [leader] for [all] men," and Abraham asks, "And [will you also make any Imam] of my descendants?" And God answers, "The condition will not be extended to the overbearing." Therefore one can see that various Prophets were designated with the term of Imam and Caliph. In regard to the meaning of these words, Caliph means "successor" and Imam means "model.". . .

From what I have declared up till now, it follows that in the Qur'an there doesn't exist any precept regarding the question of the Caliphate,

---

[5] From *Oriente Moderno* (Rome), vol. 4, no. 3, pp. 172–173, 1924. Translation courtesy of Institute of Advanced Projects, East–West Center, Hawaii.

which we are in the process of dealing with. At least I have found nothing in the Qur'an.

Of the *hadith* [traditions], then, only two or three are concerned with the Caliphate; but in them it is not said what is the Caliph, nor what are his qualifications; nor can one derive from them that "the Caliph is necessary." Our Prophet, dying, did not give any explanations of this view. He left the problem to the Nation, as something that concerned the administration of the country. After the death of the Prophet, his illustrious Companions elected Abu Bakr as Caliph. Abu Bakr designated Omar as his successor at the end of his life. Even the Companions themselves were in doubt as to the title to be given to Omar upon his succession. Some thought of calling him "Caliph [successor] of the Caliph of the Prophet"; but to the fifth and sixth Caliph, the series of additions having become too long, they left out this expression and finally said "Caliph" without anything else. Some then said *amir al-mu'minin* ("Prince of the Believers").

Omar at the end of his life did not nominate a successor, not having found anyone worthy. The problem was referred to a council of six, who nominated Caliph Othman. Therefore it can be seen that the Companions themselves have not clarified in detail the problem of the Caliphate.

The Doctors (*ulama*) who followed differentiated two aspects of the Caliphate: real and formal. The real Caliphate is the true Caliphate and they call it "Caliphate of the Prophet" (*khilāfah nabawiyyah*). The Prophet Mohammed in one *hadith* [tradition] said, "the Caliphate will last 30 years after me. . . ." Therefore the great *ulama* maintain that the real Caliphate lasted until the death of Ali, or until the abdication of al-Hasan which occurred six months later, and that the Umayyad or Ommiad Sovereigns as well as the Abbasid were not true Caliphs. Some Hanafi jurists do not call him Caliph, but rather Sultan, the government of Mu'āwiyah. The Sadr ash-Shari'ah, whose competence is recognized by the *ulama* of the various rites, in the book entitled *Ta'dil al-'ulum* enumerates the qualifications that by law are required in the Caliph and affirms that whoever does not have them cannot be called Caliph. Kemal al-Din ibn al-Human, a Doctor, says that "the Imam has the right of full authority over the Muslims." That means command, and the command in other words, is the government. That which by law the Muslims have to undertake is the establishment of a government, because it is not lawful to be without government; the function of the government is to insure the union of the country and to establish justice and order.

Therefore it is not obligatory to take one person and to entrust to him the office of Caliphate with the name of Caliph. In the past the word Government was not used and that of Caliphate was employed. Here one can observe that the *ulama* unanimously say to the Muslims, "You have to elect an Imam for yourselves." But we can answer with Adud ad-Din, author of the book al-Mawaqif, "When an Imam who meets all the requirements cannot be found, there is no obligation to elect an Imam."

The opinion that for the validity of the Friday prayers and of the Bairan [ceremony] the permission of the Imam is necessary, is wrong. There is no obligation of authorization by the Imam. The permission of the Imam consists [only] in making sure that the doors of the mosques are open to the Muslims. Also the opinion that the leaders of prayers and preachers have to be nominated by the Caliph is wrong. The nomination of the preachers by the Sultan was a provision taken at the right moment in order to avoid disputes derived from the desire of every individual to have sermons to his liking. For the past year the nominations have been made [in Turkey] by the Minister of Shari'ah.

Not even the nomination of the "Leader of the pilgrimage" is an attribute of the Caliph; the function of the "Leader of the pilgrimage" is that of insuring the order of the pilgrims, therefore it is something that belongs to the government.

This is what the *shari'ah* says in regard to the Caliphate; that the Caliphate is a political and administrative problem and that it has the direct duty of establishing government in the Muslim world. Now it is a political matter to judge whether in our times a Caliph is necessary or not. The solution of this problem belongs to the Assembly; as for me I think that my declarations are sufficient to illustrate the views of the Islamic religion on the subject.

6. The Demise of the Caliphate

The abolition of the Caliphate by the Turkish Grand National Assembly in 1924 sent a shock throughout the Muslim world. However the full import of the secularization process did not become clear until two years later when high-ranking *ulama*, assembled in Cairo, reluctantly but realistically concluded that the Caliphate, the key institution which embodied (or at least symbolized) the classical Islamic polity, was truly dead and could not be resurrected.[6]

[6] Memorandum printed in *Oriente Moderno* (Rome), vol. 6, no. 5, pp. 272–273. From *Survey of International Affairs, 1925 (volume 1)*, pp. 578–581, by Arnold J. Toynbee, published by Oxford University Press (London, 1927) under the auspices of the Royal Institute of International Affairs. Used by permission.

► ►
MEMORANDUM SUBMITTED BY THE THIRD COMMITTEE OF THE CALIPHATE CONGRESS HELD AT CAIRO ON THE 13TH TO 19TH OF MAY, 1926

The Committee entrusted with the study of the last three points on the program of the Congress has the honor to submit its report on the considerations which have led it to take the decisions set forth in its foregoing report — leaving it to the honorable assembly to take whatever decision it may think fit in this matter.

The Caliphate possesses supreme importance in the eyes of Muslims, and this importance manifested itself in all the glory and prestige with which the Caliphate was surrounded in the age of the first Caliphs, when Muslims were united in the pursuit of a single end, namely, the glorifying of the Word of God, the defense of his religion, and [the maintenance of] the greatness of Islam. When, however, the strength of the Muslims declined and the influence of the Caliphate tended to disappear, the Caliphate became a heavy burden — so heavy that the Turks abolished it instead of making of it the foundation of their glory and power. Consequently, the leading *ulama* of Egypt met as a body and published the well-known decision in regard to the Caliphate which raised the question of examining the Caliphate under all its aspects.

In this decision it is affirmed that the Imam defends the Faith, applies its precepts, and administers mundane affairs as the Islamic Law provides and on the understanding that the Caliph has absolute discretion to dispose of his subjects' affairs and that all powers derive from him.

It follows that the most important requirement in the Caliph is that he should carry sufficient authority to give execution to his decisions and ordinances and to defend the territory of Islam and the property of Muslims in accordance with the precepts of religion.

Is it now possible for a Caliphate of this character to exist? As has been stated above, the Caliphate in accordance with the Islamic Law, in the true sense of the term, only existed in primitive Islam, when Muslims were of one mind and when the countries had been united by Islam into a single *bloc* obeying the same orders and subjected to the same organization. Now, however, this union has been dissolved; the countries and peoples of Islam have been divorced from one another in government, administration, and policy; and many of their inhabitants have been possessed by a nationalistic agitation which prevents one group from accepting the leadership of another, not to speak of submitting to being governed by it and permitting it to interfere in its public affairs.

In these circumstances it is difficult for the Caliphate, as defined above, to be realized.

This, moreover, is on the assumption that all Islamic peoples are independent and self-governing, whereas the reality is very different, seeing that the majority of these peoples are actually subject to alien Governments. This still further complicates the difficulty of a Caliphate according to the Islamic Law, owing to the delicate ties of relationship which link the independent with the non-independent Islamic peoples.

Accordingly, if a universal Caliph were appointed for all Muslims, he would not possess the requisite authority and the Caliphate to which he would pretend would not be a Caliphate in accordance with the Islamic Law, in the true sense of the term, but an illusory Caliphate without any authority, small or great.

Considering these difficulties which, in consequence of the actual condition of the Islamic peoples, prevent the creation of a Caliphate according to the Islamic Law, and considering further the very great importance of the Caliphate and the real advantages which would result from its establishment among Muslims, the Commission has expressed, in answer to the fourth question on the program of the Congress, the opinion that

The Caliphate according to the Islamic Law, fulfilling all the conditions laid down for it in the Scriptures, as summarized in the Report of the First Commission which has been approved at the fourth sitting of the Congress — the most important of the said conditions being ability to defend the possessions of the Faith in all Islamic countries and to put into execution the precepts of the Islamic Law — is incapable of realization at the present time, in view of the situation in which Muslims find themselves.

On the other hand, out of regard to the inadmissibility of leaving Muslims in their present state of neglect and lack of leadership, we consider that the only possible solution of this difficulty is that the Islamic peoples should organize in concert, in the several Islamic countries, successive congresses which will give them the opportunity for periodical exchanges of views until they succeed in solving the question of the Caliphate in conformity with Islamic interests.

In order to provide for the contingency that circumstances might not permit these congresses to meet regularly, and in order to guard against the inconveniences which might result from a prolonged interregnum in the office of the Caliphate and from the absence of a higher authority to which Muslims could appeal on religious questions of a general nature, it would be advisable to establish a central committee consisting of distinguished Islamic leaders and dignitaries. This committee would meet annually to examine problems of interest to Islam. It would have in each Islamic country a national executive committee with which it would keep in constant touch and which would be entrusted with the execution, in its own territory, of the central committee's decisions.

It follows from the above that in present circumstances the establishment of the Caliphate is difficult, if not impossible, from the practical point of view, and accordingly that it is advisable for the time being to dismiss the idea of appointing a Caliph. The appointment of a Caliph would not solve the problem of the Caliphate in the present situation of the Islamic peoples. On the contrary, it would involve a risk of complicating the problem still further — not to speak of the fact that, in the first place, there does not yet exist a body of authorized persons legally entitled to make the payment of allegiance, while in the second place several Islamic peoples which were invited to this Congress have abstained from participation.

Consequently, the Commission, in answer to the fifth question on the program of the Congress, considering that

the position of Caliph possesses, in the eyes of Muslims in East and West and in the eyes of the peoples of the whole world, a supreme importance which places it in the category of questions which it is impossible to settle now, for reasons above mentioned; and considering that in solving this question it is necessary to look to a solution which may be approved as expedient by the consensus of Muslims now and hereafter.

has expressed the opinion that

the Administrative Council of the Islamic Caliphate Congress at Cairo ought to be maintained in being, on the understanding that the Council shall establish branches in the several Islamic countries, with which it shall keep in touch with a view to convening in those countries successive congresses, as need arises, to examine the question of the Caliphate and arrive at a decision in consonance with the dignity of the office.

The Islamic peoples need not take it to heart if, so far, they have not been able to solve the question of the Caliphate according to the Islamic Law or to appoint a Caliph. Nor, again, need the present Congress take it to heart if it has not succeeded in finding a definitive solution for the question of the Caliphate and the Caliph. It is sufficient for the Congress to know that it has rendered an immense service to Muslims in diagnosing for them the disease and indicating to them the remedy. It has thus fulfilled its religious duty towards Islam and Muslims.

God has promised to those among you that believe and do righteousness that He will make them to inherit the earth, even as He made them that were before them, and that He will assuredly establish firmly for them this religion which it hath pleased Him to give them, and, after their fear, will give them security in place thereof. Me will they worship, and will have none other gods but Me. They who hear this warning and remain in their unbelief, these are the transgressors.

7. Secularism in the Ideology of the Turkish Revolution

The program of the People's Party, adopted in 1935, summarized the main ideological tenets of the Turkish Revolution. The process of secularization is reflected in all six of the Kemalist principles, which are also stated in Art. 2 of the Turkish Constitution.[7]

▶ ▶

PROGRAM OF THE PEOPLE'S PARTY
OF THE REPUBLIC

INTRODUCTION

The fundamental ideas that constitute the basis of the Program of the Republican Party of the People are evident in the acts and realizations which have taken place from the beginning of our Revolution until today.

On the other hand, the main ideas have been formulated in the general principles of the Statutes of the Party, adopted also by the Grand Congress of the Party in 1927, as well as in the Declaration published on the occasion of the elections to the Grand National Assembly in 1931.

The main lines of our intentions, not only for a few years, but for the future as well, are here put together in a compact form. All of these principles which are the fundamentals of the Party constitute Kemalism.

PART I

PRINCIPLES

1 — THE FATHERLAND. The Fatherland is the sacred country within our present political boundaries, where the Turkish Nation lives with its ancient and illustrious history, and with its past glories still living in the depths of its soil.

---

[7] From Donald E. Webster, *The Turkey of Atatürk* (Philadelphia: American Academy of Political and Social Science, 1939), pp. 307–309. Used by permission.

The Fatherland is a Unity which does not accept separation under any circumstance.

2 — THE NATION. The Nation is the political Unit composed of citizens bound together with the bonds of language, culture and ideal.

3 — CONSTITUTIONAL ORGANIZATION OF THE STATE. Turkey is a nationalist, populist, *étatist*, secular [*laïque*], and revolutionary Republic.

The form of administration of the Turkish nation is based on the principle of the unity of power. There is only one Sovereignty, and it belongs to the nation without restriction or condition.

The Grand National Assembly exercises the right of sovereignty in the name of the nation. . . .

PART II

THE ESSENTIAL CHARACTERISTICS OF THE REPUBLICAN PARTY OF THE PEOPLE

5 — The Republican Party of the People is: (a) Republican (b) Nationalist (c) Populist (d) Étatist (e) Secular (f) Revolutionary.

(a) The Party is convinced that the Republic is the form of government which represents and realizes most safely the ideal of national sovereignty. With this unshakable conviction, the Party defends, with all its means, the Republic against all danger.

(b) The Party considers it essential to preserve the special character and the entirely independent identity of the Turkish social community in the sense explained in Art. 2. The Party follows, in the meantime, a way parallel to and in harmony with all the modern nations in the way of progress and development, and in international contacts and relations.

(c) The source of Will and Sovereignty is the Nation. The Party considers it an important principle that this Will and Sovereignty be used to regulate the proper fulfillment of the mutual duties of the citizen to the State and of the State to the citizen. . . .

(d) Although considering private work and activity a basic idea, it is one of our main principles to interest the State actively in matters where the general and vital interests of the nation are in question, especially in the economic field, in order to lead the nation and the country to prosperity in as short a time as possible. . . .

(e) The Party considers it a principle to have the laws, regulations, and methods in the administration of the State prepared and applied . . . on the basis of the fundamentals and methods provided for modern civilization by Science and Technology.

As the conception of religion is a matter of conscience, the Party considers it to be one of the chief factors of the success of our nation in contemporary progress, to separate ideas of religion from politics, and from the affairs of the world and of the State.

(f) The Party does not consider itself bound by progressive and evolutionary principles in finding measures in the State administration. The Party holds it essential to remain faithful to the principles born of revolutions which our nation has made with great sacrifices, and to defend these principles which have since been elaborated.

III

The Secularization of Law

A secular concept of law is a basic characteristic of a modern political system. In the West, the secularization of law is a process which has been taking place since the fifteenth century. In the West, secularization was facilitated by the existence of an essentially secular Roman law alongside of the church canon law which had extensive jurisdiction in both civil and criminal matters. As we shall see, the church in Latin America has thus far been quite successful in resisting secularist attacks on canon law principles.

Both Hinduism and Islam elaborated comprehensive systems of religious law. Apart from unwritten custom, there was no major source of secular law comparable to the Roman law in Europe. In the Hindu and Muslim worlds, the secularization of law began with the intrusion of Western imperialism. The criminal law was the first to be replaced by the secular law of the colonial rulers. Even in the Ottoman Empire, which escaped the full force of direct imperialist conquest, the influence of Western legal notions began to be felt.

Family law, especially relating to marriage and divorce, remains the last bastion of the religious concept of law in the Third World. And it is interesting that the centers of conflict are so similar in Hindu, Muslim, and Catholic countries. In addition to matters of marriage and divorce, the Hindu and Muslim laws now in force also control succession, inheritance, and adoption. Only in the Theravada Buddhist countries is the religious concept of law nonexistent.

The secularization of law has been motivated by two primary considerations: the sovereignty of the modern state and the requirements of social reform. On one hand, there is the insistence that the legislative function is at the heart of the modern state, and the existence of areas of law beyond the state's jurisdiction is *ipso facto* an admission of backwardness. This approach largely motivated the abolition of the *shari'ah* by the Turkish Republic and other revolutionary regimes. On the other hand, there is deep dissatisfaction with the *content* of traditional religious law. Law which is considered sacred is of necessity unchanging, but if social reform demands the abolition of polygamy among Hindus or Muslims, or the provision of divorce among Catholics, sacred law will have to be either changed, thus undermining its sacred character, or discarded altogether.

Ecclesiastical courts exercised extensive jurisdiction in cases involving the clergy in nineteenth-century Latin America, and separate religious courts have applied the provisions of the *shari'ah* to Muslims in various countries which were formerly part of the Ottoman Empire. The process of secularization has eliminated such religious judicial systems as well as religious law.

SECULARIZATION OF JUDICIAL SYSTEM IN EGYPT

In the Ottoman Empire, of which Egypt was a province, the *shari'ah* was the general law of the land, and *shari'ah* courts applied the Islamic law to Muslims in all cases of marriage, divorce, inheritance, adoption, and so on. There were also many non-Muslim subjects, of course, and Ottoman policy tended to make each socio-religious group into a separate legal and political entity. The religious head of each community became the political spokesman as well and represented his group before the Ottoman authorities. A natural concomitant of this basically tolerant approach to the problem of minorities was the evolution of separate courts which applied the family law of each religion to members of that community. Thus the Jews, Greek Orthodox, Copts, etc. were subject to the jurisdiction of their respective communal courts. The legal system was a mosaic of judicial institutions.

After the dismemberment of the Ottoman Empire following World War I, the religious courts were abolished in some of the former provinces. For various reasons, they were retained in Egypt. After the

Revolution of 1952 the regime took steps to bring all Egyptians under the jurisdiction of a single, secular judicial system.

1. Abolition of the Religious Courts

The following are excerpts from an explanatory memorandum which accompanied the text of the 1955 law abolishing the *shari'ah* and communal courts in Egypt. The basic arguments are that the sovereignty of the state, and the consolidation of the Egyptian people, required the elimination of this anachronistic system of courts. [1]

▶ ▶ The rules of public law require that the sovereignty of the state be complete and absolute internally, and that all those who live in it, without distinction of nationality, be submitted to the laws of the country, to its courts and to a single juridicial jurisdiction, taking into account the diversity of the conflicts *ratione materiae* and of the laws applied to them. But in Egypt the situation contradicts this principle. The jurisdictions to which the Egyptians themselves submit in matters of personal status are numerous. Each jurisdiction applies its own legislation and its own peculiar procedure without any bond uniting them, and without any organism to preside over its judicial activity. This has been the situation despite the fact that the nation has already reassumed its judicial prerogatives with regard to foreigners, so that the national courts have become exclusively competent in all their conflicts, even in those that pertain to their personal status.

Egypt has inherited from the past a multiplicity of judicial organizations in matters of personal status. Thus the shari'ah courts were established, and then, in parallel, the communal courts; then the communal courts multiplied and diversified until each community obtained a particular jurisdiction, with all the particular legislation and procedure that this implies. This led to anarchy, and consequently, to damage to the parties. . . The fundamental source establishing the Hatti Humayun was promulgated in Turkey in 1856, and in other regulations, ordinances and circulars preceding or subsequent to it. All these are vestiges of Ottoman legislation which applied then to Egypt. These legislative vestiges were not inspired in their substance and their explanations by a desire for clarity and precision; they were, in reality, the fruit of premeditated ignorance which was imposed by the political circumstances at the time.

[1] From Nadav Safran, "The Abolition of the Shar'i Courts in Egypt. I," *The Muslim World*, vol. 48, no. 1 (January 1958), pp. 21–23. Used by permission.

From this situation many conflicts arose between the different jurisdictions, giving rise to contradictory sentences on the same issue. . . .
Thus the sentences piled up by the hundreds, seeking in vain a way to
execution. It was natural, therefore, that having suppressed the privileges
which certain citizens of foreign nations enjoyed and having submitted
their subjects to the regular regime of justice before the national courts,
there should not remain in the country any vestige of an exceptional
organization, which would limit the power and the sovereignty of the
state vis-à-vis certain categories of citizens. . . .

That sentences concerning the very status of the person be carried
out by non-responsible jurisdictions, acting without the intervention
of the state, or that these jurisdictions be submitted to foreign organisms,
acting outside the national territory . . . (Rome, for instance) and that
some judges in the communal councils be foreigners and ignorant of the
language of the parties and that they pronounce their sentences regarding
Egyptians in a foreign language, all this is in opposition to national
sovereignty. . . .

From all parts ceaseless complaints have been formulated against the
situation of the jurisdiction of personal status. The parties criticized them
bitterly, pointinq out particularly the absence of the minimum requirements which would facilitate and guarantee the procedure of these
courts. The non-Muslim communities possess fourteen different jurisdictions, some of which sit only at very long intervals and in localities
remote from the homes of the parties. This makes the process of justice
very onerous for some persons and shows signs of tyranny and oppression.
The juridical rules which most of these jurisdictions apply are not
written, and it is not easy for the common party to know them because
they are dispersed in the columns of heavenly books, the explanations
and commentaries of some jurists, members of the clergy, and are written
in Latin, Greek, Syriac, Hebrew, Armenian, or Coptic — all languages
not understood by the majority of the parties. . . . The rules of forming
the courts, of procedure, and of appeal are neither uniform nor stable.
The judiciary fees are not unified; some of these courts do not even have
any regulation in this matter. Most of these courts do not even have a
regular judicial corps to fulfill their obligations. . . . In the face of this
abnormal situation, in the face of this anarchy which has become un-
bearable, many attempts at reform were made in the past. However
fragmentary and limited these attempts were, they did not succeed
because of certain opposition which they encountered at the time. This
situation remained unchanged until our days; its only victims are the
parties and the sovereignty of the nation.

Since the Revolution has set for itself the task of realizing the reforms necessary for the country and of dealing a deadly blow to evil in all its manifestations, the difficulties mentioned above could not stop the government from fulfilling its duties with regard to the judicial organization by facilitating the paths to justice to all its citizens without distinction or partiality. . . . The government cannot suffer the existence on the national territory of judiciary autonomies which impose their will upon it, oppose its policy of reform, or, lastly, choose their own way of reform. . . .

MUSLIM FAMILY LAWS IN PAKISTAN

While revolutionary regimes have been able to secularize law with a minimum of debate and controversy, governments operating under democratic procedures have had to proceed more cautiously. Impelled chiefly by the social-reform motive, the Government of Pakistan in 1955 appointed a Commission on Marriage and Family Laws. The modernist and reformist orientation of the commission may be gauged by the fact that of seven members, three were women, and only one came from the ranks of the *ulama*. As expected, the commission's report the following year recommended severe restrictions on the practices of polygamy and the husband's unilateral right of divorce, and in other ways championed the equal rights of women. The lone Maulana on the commission issued a vigorous note of dissent, written in Urdu (the majority report was in English).

Opposition from the traditionalist sectors of society prevented the government from taking any action on the report. After the military coup of 1958, however, public opinion could be ignored with greater impunity, and the military government promulgated the Muslim Family Laws Ordinance of 1961 which incorporated the basic recommendations made by the commission five years before.

2. The Commission's Modernist Interpretation

In the majority report great stress is laid on the progressive and dynamic nature of Islam, and the principle of *ijtihad* (private judgment) as the key to the reform of Islamic law. The commission's recommendation on polygamy is also found in the following selection.[2]

---

[2] From *The Gazette of Pakistan*, June 20, 1956, pp. 1198–99, 1202–03, 1230.

▶ ▶ *The Origin of the Commission*

We shall state briefly the reasons for the formation of this Commission. It is an indisputable aritcle of Muslim creed professed by every Muslim that so far as the basic principles and fundamental attitudes are concerned Islamic teaching is comprehensive and all-embracing, and Islamic law either actually derives its principles and sanctions from divine authority as revealed in the Holy Qur'an or clear injunctions based on the Sunnah. It is this belief which has been affirmed in the Objectives Resolution and the Constitution of Pakistan. It might be objected that if a well-defined code about Marriage and Family Laws already existed, where was the necessity of appointing a Commission for the purposes of any revision or modification? This question can be easily answered both by reference to the history of Muslim jurisprudence and the present-day circumstances. So far as the Holy Book is concerned the laws and injunctions promulgated therein deal mostly with basic principles and vital problems and consist of answers to the questions that arose while the Book was being revealed. The entire set of injunctions in the Holy Qur'an covers only a few pages. It was the privilege of the Holy Prophet to explain, clarify, amplify and adapt the basic principles to the changing circumstances and the occasions that arose during his lifetime. His precepts, his example and his interpretation or amplification constitute what is called Sunnah. As nobody can comprehend the infinite variety of human relations for all occasions and for all epochs, the Prophet of Islam left a very large sphere free for legislative enactments and judicial decisions even for his contemporaries who had the Holy Qur'an and the Sunnah before their eyes. This is the principle of *Ijtihad* or interpretative intelligence working within the broad framework of the Qur'an and the Sunnah.

Ijtihad

Although there was primitive simplicity in the life of Arabia during the time of the Holy Prophet, his prophetic wisdom was conscious of the fact that there may be situations and problems not clearly envisaged in the Qur'an, and that in such cases the Qur'an could only lay down basic principles which could offer light and guidance even in unpredictable circumstances. He knew that his own explanations and amplifications too could not be expected to cover all details or encompass the novelty of situations and circumstances. He enjoined on his companions, to whom important duties were entrusted, to exercise their own rational judgment with a pure conscience if the Holy Qur'an and the Sunnah did not provide any precise guidance in any particular situation.

The great *Khalifas* [caliphs] and others endowed with wisdom and imbued with the spirit of Islam exercised *Ijtihad* when the Muslim State and Society were developing. This is what Iqbal, the great Philosopher and revivalist of Islam, calls the dynamic principle which according to him is a distinguishing characteristic of Islam. [pp. 1198–99]

Islam, a progressive religion

No Muslim can believe that Islam is an outworn creed incapable of meeting the challenge of evolutionary forces. Its basic principles of justice and equity, its urge for universal knowledge, its acceptance of life in all its aspects, its world-view, its view of human relations and human destiny, and its demand for an all-round and harmonious development, stand firmly like a rock in the tempestuous sea of life.

Islam is not a priest dominated theocracy

Many a nation of the West, after centuries of bitter conflict between the Church and the State resorted to Secularism having despaired of divine guidance in the matter of law. Islam was never theocratic in the sense in which this term is used in the history of Western politics. For Islam life is an indivisible unity in which the spiritual and the mundane are not sundered. Religion, according to Islam, means life in the world lived with a spiritual attitude which sublimates all that it touches. For this very reason Islam never developed a Church with ordained priests as a class separate from the laity. According to the Holy Qur'an, the demands of God and the demands of Caesar are not to be satisfied separately because of mutual contradictions and conflicts as Islam recognizes no Caesars. As it countenances no kings who can do no wrong and who stand above the law, so it recognizes no priests. Some may be more learned in the Muslim law than others, but that does not constitute them as a separate class; they are not vested with any special authority and enjoy no special privileges.

Birth of Pakistan

Pakistan was carved out of the Indian subcontinent by leaders of Muslim thought beginning with Sayyed Ahmad Khan and culminating in the person of Qaid-e-Azam Muhammed Ali Jinnah. Islamic ideology was expounded by Iqbal, with the firm conviction that Islam, properly understood and rationally interpreted, is not only capable of moving along with the progressive and evolutionary forces of life but also of directing them into new and healthy channels in every epoch. The creation of Pakistan was a revolutionary step, and all revolutions demand primary remolding of the educational system and the recasting of laws and the judicial system to fulfill the aspirations of a free and expanding life. But Pakistan, at its very inception was faced with problems of sheer existence and self-preservation. Ugly situations created by the hostility of neighbors and economic chaos, for which Pakistan was not responsible, made the country concentrate its energies on problems of sheer subsistence, leaving little mental or material resources for educational reconstruction and legal and judicial reform. The work of legal and judicial reform requires intensive and extensive efforts over a period of time, and can be undertaken fruitfully only by a team of scholars and legal experts who possess a vast experience in the legal field, are conversant with Muslim law and jurisprudence and are progressive enough to believe that reconstruction and fresh adaptation of the basic injunctions of Islam are urgently needed to remedy the evils and remove the hurdles created by unsalutary traditions and customs masquerading in the garb of religion. The task entrusted to this Commission is of vital importance as legislation relating to human relationships cannot brook any further delay. The entire revision of our Procedural Law is likely to take a considerable time, and it is only right that a beginning should be made in this respect by tackling Family Laws first of all. [pp. 1202–03]

With respect to polygamy which has become a hotly debated issue in every Muslim society, the Commission has adhered to the Qur'anic view. Polygamy is neither enjoined nor permitted unconditionally nor encouraged by the Holy Book, which has considered this permission to be full of risks for social justice and the happiness of the family unit, which is the nucleus of all culture and civilization. It is a sad experience for those who have practiced it and for those who have watched its tragic consequences that in most cases no rational justification exists and the practice of it is prompted by the lower self of men who are devoid of refined sentiments and are unregardful of the demands of even elementary justice. The Qur'anic permission about polygamy was a conditional permission to meet grave social emergencies and heavy responsibilities were attached to it, with the warning that the common man will find it extremely difficult, if not impossible, to fulfill the conditions of equal justice attached to it. The members of the Commission, therefore, are convinced that the practice cannot be left to the sweet will of the individual. It is thoroughly irrational to allow individuals to enter into second marriages whenever they please and then demand *poste facto* that if they are unjust to the first wife and children, the wife and children should seek a remedy in a court of law. This is like allowing a preventible epidemic to devastate human health and existence and offering advice to human beings to resort to the medical profession for attempting a cure. Great evils must be nipped in the bud and prevention is always more rational and more advisable than cure. The Commission is conscious of the fact that in rare cases taking of a second wife may be a justifiable act. Therefore it recommends that it should be enacted that anyone desirous of taking a second wife should not be allowed to do it without first applying to a Matrimonial Court for permission. If the court sees any rational justification in the demand of such a husband he may be allowed only if he is judged to be capable of doing justice in every respect to more than one wife and the children. To ask the first wife and her children to resort to a court for the demands of justice is unjust and impracticable in the present state of our society where women, due to poverty, helplessness, social pressure and suppression are not in a position to seek legal assistance. The function of the court is not merely to remove injustice when it is done. In our opinion a more vital function of the legal and the judicial system is to adopt measures that minimize the practice of injustice. Therefore permission of the Matrimonial Court for a contemplated second marriage, so that the demands of justice are fulfilled and guaranteed, is the fundamental reform proposed by the Commission. [p. 1230]

3. The Maulana's Note of Dissent

In his note of dissent on the report of the Commission on Marriage and Family Laws, Maulana Ihtisham-ul-Haq challenged the modernist majority on virtually every point of both broad principle and minute detail. The commission, as he saw it, was simply attempting to inject Western ideas into Pakistani society in the name of Islam.[3]

But the selection of members of the Commission, made for the purpose of achieving this objective, is most disappointing and surprising. What greater injustice could be done to Islamic *shari'ah* than entrusting the work of bringing the marriage laws into conformity with Islamic *shari'ah* to a Commission the majority of whose members have neither the detailed knowledge of the Islamic teachings and injunctions nor are they versed in the interpretation and application of those laws. In this connection I was told that in constituting the Commission some of the members were included purely for the reason of their possessing legal

[3] From *The Gazette of Pakistan*, August 30, 1956, pp. 1561–62, 1564–65, 1572–73, 1591–92.

and judicial experience, the women members were taken in on the ground that they were conversant with family problems and conditions more than men, and only one member was added to advise on *shari'ah*. There was no apparent harm in utilizing diverse talents but in the meetings of the Commission every member, save myself, assumed the position of an expert authority on *shari'ah* and an absolute *Mujtahid*. Hence they all remained one and united in contravening the Holy Qur'an and the Sunnah and in ridiculing the Muslim jurisprudence, and by calling their action as *Ijma* [Consensus] in the Report, they have debased this technical term of *shari'ah*. [pp. 1561–62]

The members of our Commission, who hasten to declare, so sweetly, the Holy Qur'an and the Sunnah as their source and fount, are neither prepared to perform the feat of codifying a new set of laws of jurisprudence in supersession of the existing one by generalizing from specific provisions, nor are they willing to be guided by the established laws of jurisprudence as their guiding star and beacon light. It is obvious, therefore, that to take personal and individual whims as the basis for the derivation of laws and principles is neither *Fiqh* nor *Ijtihad* but amounts to distorting the religion of God and the worst type of heresy. In spite of their blatant departure from the view of the Muslim commentators and jurists, no member of the Commission could take the place of Fakhruddin Razi or Abu Hanifa. This is the reason that certain recommendations, which reflect subservience to the West of some of the members and their displeasure with Islam, constitute an odious attempt to distort the Holy Qur'an and the Sunnah with a view to giving them a western slant and bias. . . .

In order to seek a justification for the arbitrary *Ijtihad* of the Commission, the Introduction of the Report says this about the Holy Qur'an and the Sunnah:

The Holy Qur'an and the Sunnah depict events and contain answers to the questions as they took place and arose while the Book was being revealed. As nobody can comprehend the infinite variety of human relations and situations for all occasions and for all epochs, the Prophet of Islam left a very large sphere free for legislative enactments and judicial decisions even for his contemporaries who had the Holy Qur'an and the Sunnah before their eyes. This is that principle of *Ijthihad* or interpretative intelligence working within the broad framework of the Qur'an and the Sunnah.

It is a matter of surprise that persons utterly ignorant of elementary propositions concerning God, His Glory, the Prophethood, and the comprehensiveness and universality of religion, should have the temerity to write on such subjects. Perhaps our Introduction–writer does not know that the Qur'an is the sacred Word of God and embodies His Divine Guidance, who has the fullest knowledge and embodies prescience of every minor event of every period and every epoch from the beginning of Time to its end. He knows all the infinite varieties of human relationship which can happen in any period or epoch in all futurity. Hence His revealed Book and His appointed Prophet with prophetic wisdom, all are based on the truth that until doomsday all teachings and injunctions of the Holy Qur'an and the Sunnah shall be the authoritative guidance and final work for all the infinity of events that may take place in this Universe. This is the basic and fundamental article of faith in Islam owing to which Islam is a religion for all times. If the scope of the Qur'an and the Sunnah were limited to the circumstances and events that arose during the Prophet's lifetime or while the Qur'an was being revealed, then it would be meaningless to call the Holy Qur'an and the Sunnah as the revealed Word of God, and Islam as His Revealed Religion. It would then be more correct to dub the Qur'an and the Sunnah as the work and compilation of an individual who could not see beyond the limited horizon of his own time. [pp. 1564–65]

Their sole motive to malign the *ulama* was that Muslims should ignore the *ulama* and these so-called progressives should install themselves in the place of Ghazali and Razi themselves. But in spite of the destructive propaganda Muslims had enough religious consciousness and feeling for faith to turn for religious guidance to the pious *ulama* who possess the knowledge of *shari'ah* and act upon it. It is an obvious fact that in all technical matters only experts and specialists are consulted. This prerogative of the specialist is not based on any racial or tribal ground but is rooted in reason. When people did not take any notice of the nontechnical *Ijtihad* and opinions of these anglicized, West-ridden Sahibs, they started propaganda against the *ulama* that they have created priesthood in Islam, so that their own opinion may have the right to encroach upon their domain. They should know that the *ulama* have not got a special privilege of interpreting and quoting the Holy Qur'an and the Sunnah on the basis of any racial distinction. *Ulama* is not the name of any race or tribe but everyone who has devoted the greater part of his life to the acquisition of knowledge on religious subjects is an *alim*. This right of theirs is based on their erudition and experience in exactly the same way in which the right of explaining and interpreting the provisions of the Pakistan Penal Code vests in lawyers and barristers only. It is obvious that the lawyers are not a tribe but they have studied law. The right of prescription and treatment belongs only to a doctor. As anyone who studies law is a lawyer or barrister, in the same way anyone who studies *shari'ah* and religion is an *alim* no matter to what race or tribe he belongs. [pp. 1572–73]

The main cause of raising this question [of polygamy] is inferiority complex against the West and the desire to copy it blindly. Our young men and women, who happen to visit Europe, often find themselves in situations in which their country is ridiculed for permitting polygamy. Unable to think out for themselves, these young things readily take to the course of condemning polygamy as the greatest evil in society. It is in fact this class of persons who have, on their return from abroad, taken up arms against polygamy permitted by Islam in an attempt to copy the West and to uphold the condemnation to which they have pledged themselves while in foreign lands. In fact polygamy is not a matter for any human society to be ashamed of, nor does its abolition constitute any achievement of Europe that may be worth emulaton by others. Moreover, if we cannot put Europe to shame for permitting free indulgence in adultery, we have no cause to blush at the permission granted by *shari'ah* for lawfully marrying a second wife. The real comparison in this regard is that of contentment with one woman and this contentment is equally absent in Europe as well as in our own society. The difference is that we proceed to take a second wife by entering into a solemn agreement with her and accepting certain bona fide responsibilities in the form of *nikah*, while they choose the unworthy and irresponsible course of playing with the chastity of women in return for a few coins. Thus it is clear that marrying a second wife in the lifetime of the first is nothing discreditable; the sin and the shame of it lies in indulging in adultery while living with a lawfully wedded wife—a practice which has not been declared a penal offense in any European country if it is committed with the consent of the woman involved. It is nothing but a sad demonstration of our own shortsightedness and inferiority complex that we feel shy of a just and reasonable injunction of our religion and do not venture to put others to shame for their glaring fault.

In short, we do not have the slightest excuse for imitating the ways of a people with a social setup and a legal system which tolerates sexual satisfaction by means other than marriage. It is indeed hard to imagine a worse type of blind imitation than the one we find in the present case wherein the women who have kicked up so much dust on the question of polygamy and the Commission which has supported their views have not chosen to utter a word against adultery or recommended it to be declared a penal offense, although this form of vice not only means a flagrant violation of the rights of the lawfully wedded wife but also constitutes a deprecation committed on the chastity of others. The question of adultery in this way becomes purely a question of matrimonial and family life in its bearing. The institutions so vociferously advocating the rights of women and the leaders who dub polygamy as the greatest bane on womanhood, would do well to take the trouble of going round the bazaars in Pakistan and cast a glance on the legions of prostitutes who are daily corrupting unmarried as well as married men in the thousands and breaking up many a happy home by sowing the seeds of hatred in the minds of young men against their innocent wives. In this background the conclusion is inescapable that polygamy is to be penalized while adultery is to be left to flourish free of all legal restrictions and that holy alliance between man and woman, as permitted by *shari'ah*, is to be declared a crime while moral depravity is to be left unscathed. [pp. 1591–92]

HINDU MARRIAGE ACT IN INDIA

In the early years of independence, proposals to change the Hindu law became a major focus of the forces of social reform. In 1949 legislation was enacted which for the first time validated all forms of intercaste marriage, a momentous step in terms of the history of Hindu law. The Hindu Code Bill not only codified the law but introduced major innovations, and in the 1950–51 election campaign Nehru asserted that he would stake his prime ministership on the passage of this bill. After legislative delays, however, it was divided into several parts which were enacted separately. The Hindu Marriage Bill, enacted in 1955, occasioned the fiercest debate, particularly over the provisions for monogamy and divorce.

Although Hindu social reform was the most prominent motive in this legislation, the state is constitutionally committed to the complete secularization of law. Article 44 of the Constitution directs: "The state shall endeavour to secure for the citizens a uniform civil code throughout the territory of India." The major obstacle to the implementation of this directive, however, is the attitude of the Muslim minority, which would regard any attempt to displace the *shari'ah* as a most serious violation of their freedom of religion.

4. Social Change and Man-Made Laws

The Hindu Marriage Act of 1955 introduced radical changes into a corpus of religious law which had two thousand years of history behind it. While this law had evolved slowly over the centuries, it had retained its legitimacy as divine law. In this speech in Parliament, however, Law Minister H. V. Pataskar indicated that the time had come for man-made law, responsive to changing social needs, to replace "immutable" divine law. [4]

▶ ▶   The main questions involved in this Bill are broadly three: (1) the abolition of caste as a necessary requirement of a valid marriage; (2) enforcement of monogamy; and (3) divorce or dissolution of marriage on certain grounds. As regards the first, I may say that Parliament has already passed the Hindu Marriages Validity Act, 1949, and accepted in principle the underlying necessity for a provision of this character. . . . As regards the enforcement of monogamy, I may say that monogamy has all along been a normal feature of the Hindu society. It may be that there was no legal prohibition against allowing polygamy, but as a result of the social and economic changes in society, polygamy is on its last legs. There might have been some cases where there was polygamy, but monogamy has been a normal feature of our society in my view. However, the time has come when there should be express prohibition against polygamy. As regards the third, there is still some opposition in certain quarters to which I shall refer at a later stage. [cols. 6470–6471]

I shall now try to deal with some of the main objections which have been raised with respect to the principles underlying the Bill. Those that object to this law base their objections mainly on the following three grounds: (1) that we are interfering with the ancient law; (2) that we are trying to effect *varna sankar* [the mixing of castes]; and (3) that we are trying to destroy the sacramental character of marriage by permitting divorce.

Now, it would be appropriate to find out what really was the ancient law on the basis of which some of our friends take objection to a measure of this kind. Now, for instance, one of the oldest books on this subject is the code of Manu — *Manava Dharmashastra*. Then there is a commentary written subsequently after about five centuries by Yagnavalkya and [another] a few hundred years later by Narada. Then, there is also Kautilya's *Arthashastra*. As a matter of fact, what was this ancient law? Has ancient law remained immutable? In its very conception was it intended that for all times to come it would remain immutable? I think that was not even the idea of those that laid down these *shastras*. . . .

Even Manu foresaw that *dharma* should be a thing which must be

[4] From *Lok Sabha Debates*, 1955, part 2, vol. 4, cols. 6470–71, 6475–79, 6482, 6485–87, 6500–01.

in the interests of the people and which should be guided by considerations of what was to the benefit and advantage of the soul and person. On that basis I am prepared to look at it. How far should it be made applicable to the present circumstances? This to my mind removes a lot of confusion. Manu did not merely refer to *Vedas* or *Smritis*. He also referred to *sadachara* and *Swasyacha Priyamatmanah* — what is agreeable to one's body and soul or good conscience. I will request the Hon. Members to exercise their good conscience and then find out whether what we are doing is right or not. Many do not want to do that. I know there might be differences of opinion. I am not one of those who want to say that there should not be differences of opinion. But this is not the proper time to consider what Manu said 2,000 years ago divorced from its context with the present time. What Manu then laid down for those times may be right or may be wrong. We have no knowledge of conditions which existed then. Therefore, I am not one of those who say that from the present angle of view or from the present spectacles we wear, or under circumstances by which our minds are influenced at present, we should judge the code of Manu for condemning it or for approving what Manu said. . . .

I have always . . . [regarded Yagnavalkya and Narada] as commentators of Manu explaining these things with some changes that were desirable because that was the machinery by which they could make those changes as the time may require. By their commentaries they have effected changes in the original code in conformity with the changed conditions of society in their own respective days. What is known as Hindu law at present is entirely different from what was laid down by Manu or Yagnavalkya or any of those other sages centuries back. It is too late in the day, therefore, to contend that this is ancient divine law and must not be changed or altered. It has already been altered from time to time to suit the different conditions of society. Methods might have been different as different conditions permitted different methods.

Society is never static and, similarly, law also must not be so. The original laws of Manu dealt with all aspects of social life, not merely with marriage or succession, but they also dealt with administration and what is now known as criminal law and other branches of the present civil law governing society. All these different aspects of law excepting marriage and succession are governed by different enacted laws which have been made applicable to our country during the last 250 years and more by the British administrators. And, I do not find any voice raised against them. They were good enough in so far as they were suitable in the changed conditions of life. To that extent, the divine ancient laws have been changed already.

As early as 1856, the Widow Remarriage Act was passed because in certain so-called regenerated classes of Hindu community remarriage was not allowed. Similar sentimental objections were raised then also. But, what is the present state of affairs? That law was not passed by any elected House like this. It was passed by a few — five or six people — Europeans who formed the Council then. They passed it and it has been found that it has not worked any hardship. On the contrary it has been found to be more and more used by those people many of whom at one stage wanted to object to even that reform taking place. [cols. 6475–6479]

The present Hindu Law which some of my Hon. friends want to stick to, is not the ancient law, is not the law either of Manu or Yagna-valkya. It is the law made by . . . judicial decisions. Who gave the decisions? There were judges who knew law. But they depended on the *pundits* for Sanskrit. If I may say so, their decisions were based on the opinion of Sanskritists who did know law and judges who knew law but had no knowledge of Sanskrit. That is what we now call the Hindu Law. I appeal to the Hon. Members to bear this in mind. I am not one of those who find fault with our ancient law-givers. I have nothing to say against them. We must see what the present state of things is . . . and how we can remedy these matters. [col. 6482]

[Cunningham in 1877] found that judicial decisions in Hindu law took the form of deciding not what the law ought to be, but what it is according to the interpretation of primitive texts or forgotten phases of society unmodified by contemporaneous opinion. That was the opinion given regarding this Law in 1877. Can one contend that judicial decisions of this order are preferable to the deliberate, well-weighed, well-informed action of the legislature grounded solely on consideration of public welfare and guided by the wishes and opinions of those who form that legislature as the representatives of the whole nation?

I hope I have been able to convince some of my critics, even the most sceptical people, that the ancient law, as it prevailed several centuries back, is not in existence, that in no case can it be resurrected, that the present law on this subject is neither logical nor consistent nor uniform. It is also entirely inconsistent with the present state of society. So far as this objection regarding the ancient law is concerned, and the view that it should not be changed, I think I have tried to explain the position as dispassionately as I possibly could.

The next charge is that we are creating *varna snakar*. Now is this really the time when anybody can raise his voice in favor either of perpetuating or trying to create divisions in society? On the one hand, I am being charged, "Why are you bringing forward a Hindu Bill only and not a Bill applicable to all Indians?" On the other hand, the same kind of groups raise the objection, "Well, you are destroying our *varnas*." Well, I do not see the logic of this. . . . It is true that Manu did recognise this classification of men and women on the basis of birth. The women and *shudras* were given a very inferior place. But the course of conduct recommended by Manu more than two thousand years ago cannot be made applicable to the present state of society. . . .

The *varnas* as envisaged in *Bhagavad Gita* on the basis of *guna* and *karma* are not in existence anywhere and the present castes are only a perverted form of that ancient classification. Whatever its merits or demerits some two thousand years back, that system has now degenerated into casteism and must be ended. . . .

The third and the last objection is that we are destroying the sacramental character of the ancient marriage system by introducing divorce. . . .

It is not true that our ancient law givers ever regarded the marriage as indissoluble or as a sacrament. I do not know what basis there is for that view. At the most, it can be said that *Manu Smriti* does not lay down any procedure for divorce. To that extent I am prepared to go. But beyond that, this idea of sacrament is only of recent growth. But in those days when a wife could be sold or deserted, how can we find a procedure for divorcing her? You have to look at what Manu laid down in terms of the conditions which existed then. There you find a provision that a wife could be deserted or even sold. [cols. 6485–6487]

I know that the idea of divorce is to some people as good as a matter of religious faith or sentiment. I would say that I have respect for such people. I have nothing to say against them, because everybody is free to have his own faith in these matters. But I am convinced that by this measure I am not doing anything which would in any way prevent them from adhering to their faith, beliefs and sentiments. Even after the passage of this Bill, it is not as if it is compulsory that people should divorce. If there are people who think that they should preserve their faith and sentiments and try to avoid divorce, then that is in fact consistent with the spirit in which this Bill has been framed. In fact we are also going to put in a provision that as far as possible even if the parties go to a court, the court should make attempts to keep them together rather than separate them. Nobody wants that there should be any such separation.

Therefore, I say that I have the highest and fullest sympathy for such sentiment. But I would say that let them not also try to impose it on
another. . . .

Individual matters of faith and religion and sentiment have to be
respected; and they are respected; but that does not mean that they can
hold up the progress of society or that they can be allowed to impose
their will on others. [cols. 6500–6501]

5. A Conservative Hindu Attack

President of the All-India Hindu Mahasabha and a prominent
Opposition leader in Parliament, N. C. Chatterjee led the conservative
attack on the bill. Although basically opposed to any changes in the
law, he challenged the government to produce a uniform civil code for
all citizens, instead of singling out the Hindu community for "social
reform" dominated by ideas from the West. [5]

▶ ▶   The Hindu Marriage and Divorce Bill is sought to be rushed through
the Parliament. The leaders of the Congress who are Members of the
Government continually harp on secularism and condemn communalism
in any shape or form. It is amazing that they are introducing a "communal" measure simply for one community. Is this Bill not wholly
inconsistent with the concept of secular democracy?

The Constitution of India sets before the State and the Parliament the
ideal of equality of laws for all citizens. Under Article 44 of the Constitution the Republic of India solemnly declares its clear objective
"to secure for all the citizens a uniform Civil Code throughout the
territory of India." Is not a "communal" code for only one community
repugnant to Article 44 of the Constitution and destructive of the
objective solemnly enjoined by the makers of the Constitution?

We are quite sure that if any plebiscite is taken or a referendum
is ordered a large majority of our citizens will turn down any proposal
of introducing divorce among members of the Hindu community. Every
nation adheres to certain principles which it cherishes and which it
holds dear. For centuries marriage has been looked upon by the Hindus
as a sacrament, and the marital bond has been held to be sacred and
indissoluble. According to the Hindu concept, marriage is more than a
charter or licence for sexual intercourse. The Hindu ideal of marriage

---

[5] From N. C. Chatterjee, *Whither India?* (New Delhi: All-India Hindu Mahasabha
[n.d.]), pp. 1–3. Used by permission.

has always been a fellowship between a man and a woman who seek to live creatively in a partnership for the pursuit of the four great objects of life, namely, *dharma, artha, kama* and *moksha*. Its main aim is the enrichment of human personality and the sanctity of the household with the wife as the dominant partner, [and this] has always been the essential element in the social fabric for the uplift of society at large.

The important provisions of the new Marriage and Divorce Bill are the enforcement of monogamy and granting the right of divorce on very easy terms. If monogamy is good for Hindus, why is it not good for Muslims? If Hindu women are to be rescued from the curse of polygamy, why deny that blessing to millions of Muslim women who are in greater need of such protection? Polygamy has practically died out amongst the Hindus, and monogamy has become the rule of Hindu society. Divorce is not unknown amongst the lower classes of Hindu society. Hindu society has always been a progressive organism, and it has steadily absorbed non-Aryan tribes and creeds. But Hinduism did not imitate the arrogance of Western imperialism but tolerated and respected non-Aryan customs and beliefs.

But a very strong and dominant section of Hindu society still believes that the marriage tie is sacrosanct and cannot be dissolved. Now that the Special Marriage Act recently enacted gives right to persons who have contracted marriages according to Hindu rites to get their marriages registered under that Act and also to apply for divorce, it is not at all necessary to enact a law for divorce for Hindus and to tamper with the marriage laws of those who believe in the sanctity and indissolubility of marriage. Those who take delight in calling themselves "progressive" can easily take recourse to the Special Marriage Act and disrupt the marital tie, if they deem it necessary or desirable.

Cheap imitation of western countries and the introduction of laws making divorce easy and convenient would disrupt Hindu society and would destroy the very basic foundation of [the] Hindu social organism. As a matter of fact even among certain castes or tribes where divorce is permissible according to their special custom this will compel them to go to courts of law and will subject them to all the costs and hardships and uncertainties of legal proceedings. People's courts ruled by tribal elders have always been more effective and have given verdicts in tune with the norms and standards of the people concerned. They are far more efficient, expeditious and cheap compared to the courts functioning under the complicated procedures with costly paraphernalia and legal trappings.

If there is to be any real effort to improve the laws on this important subject there should not be any Hindu Marriage Law or Muslim Marriage Law. But the State should enact a uniform marriage law for the citizens of India as a whole. We feel that the leaders of the party in power have neither the courage nor the wisdom to act up to their professions or the spirit of the Constitution. We maintain that this Hindu Marriage and Divorce Bill is discriminatory in character. It will discriminate against a community on the ground of religion or accident of birth. It is, therefore, contrary to the clear injunction which is embodied in Article 15 of the Constitution and which is a fundamental right guaranteed by the Constitution.

We also maintain that unless there is an undue anxiety to pander to the wishes or whims of the so-called forward, unorthodox or fashionable people this Hindu Marriage and Divorce Bill is wholly unnecessary after the enactment of the Special Marriage Act. To destroy the fabric of society is very easy. But to build up and to keep society to its moorings is both desirable and necessary. If India really wants to keep herself immune from the menace of Communism or atheism, then the nation should pass its verdict unhesitatingly against such un-Hindu and un-Aryan measures destructive of the cardinal principles of Hindu civilization. Provision for easy divorce has led to the disintegration of family life in western countries and they are now attempting to tighten up their marriage and divorce laws. Hindu society has never been static. Hindu society has always progressed. Now that we are relieved of the incubus of British imperialism the progress of social conscience will lead to the development of our social laws.

DIVORCE LAW IN LATIN AMERICA

The Roman Catholic Code of Canon Law states in very clear terms the divine law relating to marriage and divorce. Since matrimony is one of the sacraments, its regulation by the church was an ecclesiastical monopoly preserved over centuries of Spanish rule. After independence, the civil code of Peru and other countries prescribed that "marriages in the Republic shall be celebrated with the formalities established by the Church in the Council of Trent." Marriages outside of the church were prohibited, and in Peru it was not until 1897 that the civil marriage of non-Catholics was legalized.

Throughout the nineteenth century, anticlerical Liberals agitated for the secularization of marriage and divorce law. In the early years of the Mexican Revolution of 1910, attention was given to the need for laws which could respond to changing social conditions. In his explanation of the divorce law decreed in 1914, Carranza carefully examined the situation of the different strata of Mexican society and decided that the social consequences of the decree would be both moral and desirable.

6. Code of Canon Law

The following canons of the 1917 Code of Canon Law lay down the basic principles of divine law regarding marriage and divorce. The principles, of course, go back to the early years of the Christian church. The 1917 Code is still in force, although a revision is now being prepared.[6]

CAN. 1012. 1. Our Lord raised to the dignity of a sacrament the contract of marriage between baptized persons.

2. Hence between baptized persons there can be no valid contract of marriage without there being a sacrament.

CAN. 1013. 2. The essential properties of marriage contract are unity and indissolubility, to which the sacrament gives a special firmness in Christian marriage.

CAN. 1016. The marriage of baptized persons is regulated not only by divine but also by canonical law, the civil power remaining competent in regard to the civil effects of marriage.

CAN. 1038. 1. It belongs to the supreme ecclesiastical authority alone to declare authentically when the divine law renders a marriage illicit or invalid.

2. To the same supreme authority belongs exclusively the right to establish, for persons baptized, other impediments, prohibitive or diriment, by way of universal or particular law.

CAN. 1118. Valid marriage ratified and consummated can be dissolved by no human power and by no other cause than death.

7. Divorce in Latin America

As shown in the following recent article, over half of the population of Latin America still lives under laws fashioned in accordance with the Roman Catholic Code of Canon Law.[7]

---

[6] From H. A. Ayrinhac, *Marriage Legislation in the New Code of Canon Law* (New York: Benziger Brothers, 1918), pp. 21, 24, 28, 76, 284.

[7] From "El Divorcio en América Latina," *Visión* (Mexico City), vol. 37, no. 11 (November 21, 1969), front cover and p. 50. Used by permission. Translated by the editor.

▶ ▶ "I . . . take thee . . . for my lawful wedded wife, to have and to hold from this day forward, for better or for worse, for richer or for poorer, in sickness and in health, until death us do part." Husband and wife forever? Fifteen of the American republics permit absolute divorce [i.e., with the right to remarry] but in five republics it is not allowed. In these latter countries, Argentina, Brazil, Colombia, Chile and Paraguay, with more than half of the population of Latin America, many persons, separated legally from their spouses, and without being able to contract matrimony again, practice concubinage.

In Argentina, Brazil, Chile, and perhaps in Colombia also, the consensus of progressive opinion favors a law of divorce. In the past, this question has been a burning political problem, fiercely debated in parliaments, where influential minorities have been able, until now, to stop the approval of divorce bills which have frequently been presented. In reality, those four countries lack divorce laws because of the vehement opposition of the powerful and conservative Catholic Hierarchy. Nevertheless, broad sectors of Catholic opinion, including elements of the clergy, show themselves less opposed now than previously. Monsignior Arauda Cámara, the principal opponent to the divorce law in the Congress of Brazil, admits in private that his group will not be able to resist much longer.

The hypocrisy of pretending that the problem of divorce does not exist is responsible for the growing practice of concubinage, of "living together" — surprising as it might seem in other countries — in middle-class social circles of Argentina and Brazil, where it is assuming a certain respectability.

Concubinage is accepted socially in those places, although within certain limits: it is not tolerated, for example, in the case of men and women in certain prominent positions. It is said that in Brazil an outstanding general was quickly eliminated from the group of those considered to be "presidential material" because he was legally separated from his wife and living with another. But with respect to persons of less elevated station in life, concubinage elicits no raising of eyebrows or murmurs of disapproval in Sao Paulo, Rio de Janeiro, or Buenos Aires.

It exists because there is no other alternative. And although the laws in force do not permit divorce, society in practice accepts it.

In Argentina, Judge Federico Peltzer, a Catholic lawyer and writer, says: "In the last twenty years the social stigma inherent in divorce and remarriage has totally vanished. Two decades ago I was opposed to changes which would have permitted divorce. Now, like the majority of the Argentines, I understand that it is a lamentable necessity. If the question of permitting divorce were submitted to a vote today, it would win overwhelmingly."

And an outstanding journalist of Buenos Aires, who asked that his name not be mentioned, commented: "The Argentine ruling class believes in adultery, but not in divorce. Public clamor for a divorce law cannot build up because the government does not dare to stimulate it. . . . It already has enough problems without starting a fight with the archbishops. Furthermore, President Juan Carlos Onganía is a fervent Catholic and is opposed, of course, to divorce. And the press, in general, is conservative and anti-divorce."

8. The Mexican Law of Divorce, 1914

Like the sacred canon law, the man-made laws of the Mexican Revolution claimed to be based on universal moral principles. In the following message Carranza analyzed the social, psychological, and moral consequences of the prevailing law in Mexican society, and then decreed a new law providing for divorce with the right to remarry.[8]

▶ ▶ Venustiano Carranza, First Chief of the Constitutionalist Army, In Charge of the Executive Power of the United Mexican States and Chief of the Revolution, by virtue of the authority invested in me, and CONSIDERING:

That the institution of marriage has as its essential objects the procreation of the species, the education of the children, and the mutual help of the contracting parties to bear the burdens of life; that it is therefore always contracted as a definitive union, for by becoming united the parties intend to achieve by this means the fulfillment of their highest ideals; but, unfortunately, the ends for which matrimony was contracted are not always attained, and although these cases may be exceptions, the law must justly seek to remedy them, relieving the parties of the obligation to remain together throughout their lives in an irregular state contrary to nature and to human needs;

That what has until now been called divorce in our legislation, the simple separation of the parties without dissolving the legal tie, the only form which the law of December 14, 1874 permitted, far from satisfying the social need to reduce to a minimum the consequences of unfortunate unions, only creates an irregular situation worse than that

---

[8] From Isidro Fabela, ed., *Documentos Históricos de la Revolución Mexicana* (Mexico: Fondo de Cultura Económica, 1963), pp. 119–122. Translated by the editor.

which it seeks to remedy, for it foments discord among families, deeply hurting the affection between parents and children and extending demoralization in society;

That the simple separation of the parties creates, furthermore, an anomalous situation of indefinite duration, which is contrary to nature and to the right which every human being has to seek his well-being and the satisfaction of his needs, for it condemns the separated parties to a perpetual inability to seek the highest ends of life;

That the experience and example of civilized nations show that the divorce which dissolves the legal tie is the only rational means to correct, to whatever extent possible, the errors of unions which cannot or should not continue;

That admitting the principle established by our Laws of the Reform, that marriage is a civil contract, formed principally by the spontaneous and free will of the contracting parties, it is absurd that it should continue when that will is completely lacking, or when causes exist which make definitely irreparable the disunion already brought about by circumstances;

That concerning unions which, through complete incompatibility of personalities, might have to be severed by the will of the parties, it is necessary only to certify the definitive will of the parties to be divorced and of the absolute impossibility of remedying their disagreements or resolving their crises, which can be proved by the passage of a reasonable period of time from the celebration of the marriage until its dissolution is permitted, to be convinced thus that the moral disunion of the parties is irreparable;

That, in addition, divorce by mutual consent is a discreet means of covering up the grave faults of one of the parties by the will of both to be divorced, without the necessity of leaving on the respective families, or on the children, the stigma of dishonor;

That, furthermore, it is well known that among the disinherited classes of this country marriage is the exception, the majority of unions being by arrangements which are hardly ever legalized, either because of the poverty of the parties or their instinctive fear of contracting a tie of irreparable consequences, and in these circumstances it is evident that the institution of divorce which dissolves the legal tie is the most direct and powerful means to reduce to a minimum the number of illegitimate unions among the masses which form the immense majority of the Mexican Nation, thereby reducing the number of children whose status is at present outside the law;

That, furthermore, it is a fact beyond all doubt that in the Mexican middle class the woman, owing to the special conditions of education and custom of that class, is incapacitated for the economic struggle for life, and consequently the woman whose marriage becomes a failure is converted into a victim of her husband and finds herself in a condition of slavery from which it is impossible to escape if the law does not emancipate her by unchaining her from the husband;

That, in fact, in the middle class separation is almost always provoked by the fault of the husband and it is ordinarily the woman who needs it, without having obtained anything more until now than temporarily separating her from the husband, but without remedying in any way her economic and social conditions for which the establishment of divorce would doubtless tend, principally in our middle class, to raise up the woman and give her possibilities of emancipation from the condition of slavery which is her present lot;

That, in addition, the institution of divorce would not encounter any serious obstacle in the upper educated classes, since the demonstration of other countries where it is established has accustomed them to look upon divorce which dissolves the legal tie as perfectly natural;

That the experience of such advanced countries as England, France, and the United States of America has already demonstrated by evidence that divorce which dissolves the legal tie is a powerful factor of morality because, facilitating the formation of new legitimate unions, it avoids the multiplicity of cases of concubinage and therefore the pernicious influence that they necessarily exercise in public customs, gives greater stability to conjugal affection and relations, assures the happiness of a greater number of families and does not have the serious drawback of obliging those who have married in error or haste to pay for their fault with slavery for the rest of their lives. . . .

Religion and Political Behavior

IV

Religion and Nationalist Movements

The relationships between religion and nationalist movements in the Third World have been many, varied, and important. In this complex pattern, we can identify four elements which have recurred with great regularity. First, religion has provided an important part of the leadership of Asian and North African nationalist movements. In the early twentieth century, the *ulama*, scholars of Islamic law, played a major role in Indonesian, Persian, Egyptian, and Algerian nationalist struggles against imperialism. The Buddhist monks played a similar role, especially in Burma, and while M. K. Gandhi was an England-trained lawyer, much of his political effectiveness in the Indian nationalist movement derived from his reputation as a Hindu saint (*Mahatma* or "Great Soul").

Second, religion has provided powerful emotional symbols of group identity which have bound people together in opposition to foreign rulers. The first major nationalist issue in Burma arose from the Europeans' insistence on walking on Buddhist pagoda platforms with their shoes on. Insults to the national religion, real or imagined, have unified colonial peoples instantaneously when secular nationalist appeals have failed. Third, religion has provided legitimation for resistance to established rule. The weight of Islamic tradition has strongly favored obedience to the ruler, whatever his moral or administrative failings might be, for bad government is better than anarchy. However, the *ulama's* formal proclamation of *jihad* (holy war) against a *kaffir* (infidel) foreign government proved to be a powerful legitimizer of revolt.

Finally, religion has provided techniques of political resistance, or at least the raw materials out of which they have been fashioned. In India, the Extremist leader Tilak transformed the religious Ganapati festival into a potent vehicle for nationalist propaganda. Gandhi drew from the resources of Hindu religious thought his technique of *satyagraha* ("truth force," or nonviolent resistance) which was directed at the British rulers.

Religion has played an unequivocal role in support of nationalist movements which sought to displace colonial regimes. Nationalism when anti-imperialist in motivation, created no particular problems. However, in going beyond this to posit the nation as the individual's highest loyalty, the conflict soon became clear in the case of Islam. Nationalism as supreme loyalty was not acceptable. The whole concept of the *ummah* (Islamic community), ruled over by a caliph, expressed the strong universalism of Islam which clashed with nationalism in the second sense. There was little of this tension in Hinduism, an ethnic religion, or Buddhism, despite its international character.

HINDUISM AND INDIAN NATIONALISM

The renascence of Hinduism in the nineteenth century was the prelude to Indian nationalism. The religious reform movements, from Rammohan Roy onward, proclaimed the essential greatness of India's spiritual heritage, which only had to be liberated from the illiberal accretions of the centuries. The reformers, by reawakening pride in India in the face of a confident and frequently arrogant West, prepared the way for the secularly oriented Indian National Congress founded in 1885.

By the turn of the century strongly Hindu elements, the so-called Extremists, challenged the secular leadership of the Congress itself. On the far left, terrorists in Bengal committed ritual political assassinations as offerings to the goddess Kali. The Extremists never gained control of the Congress, and the Moderates, steeped in the principles of British parliamentarism, were also committed to keeping the Muslims within the nationalist movement.

After 1916, Gandhi assumed a major leadership role. While he constantly emphasized Hindu-Muslim unity and read from the Qur'an and New Testament as well as the Gita in his daily prayer meetings,

Gandhi's political style was undeniably religious. And his basic technique of *satyagraha* drew heavily on Hindu sources. Throughout its long history the Congress was predominantly secular, but the influence of Hinduism was significant enough to give credence to some of the charges of communal bias made by the Muslim League.

1. Hindu Nationalism and Universalism

The Bengali Extremist, Aurobindo Ghose, emphasized both the close connection between Hindu religious revival and Indian nationalism, and the potentially universal nature of Hinduism. The success of the religious nationalist movement would enable India to stand forth as a "light unto the nations" in the proclamation of its universal religious message. In an address given in 1908 he spoke of messages which had come to him mystically while in jail. [1]

▶ ▶ The second message came and it said: "Something has been shown to you in this year of seclusion, something about which you had your doubts and it is the truth of the Hindu religion. It is this religion that I am raising up before the world, it is this that I have perfected and developed through the rishis, saints, and avatars, and now it is going forth to do my work among the nations. I am raising up this nation to send forth my word. This is the Sanatan Dharma, this is the eternal religion which you did not really know before, but which I have now revealed to you. The agnostic and the sceptic in you have been answered, for I have given you proofs within and without you, physical and subjective, which have satisfied you. When you go forth, speak to your nation always this word, that it is for the Sanatan Dharma that they rise, it is for the world and not for themselves that they arise. I am giving them freedom for the service of the world. When therefore it is said that India shall rise, it is the Sanatan Dharma that shall rise. When it is said that India shall be great, it is the Sanatan Dharma that shall be great. When it is said that India shall expand and extend itself, it is the Sanatan Dharma that shall expand and extend itself over the world. It is for the Dharma and by the Dharma that India exists. To magnify the religious means to magnify the country. I have shown you that I am everywhere and in all men and in all things, that I am in this movement and I am not only working in those who are striving for the country but I am working

---

[1] From Aurobindo Ghose, *Speeches* (Calcutta: Arya Publishing House, 1948), pp. 76–80. Used by permission of Sri Aurobindo Ashram Trust, Pondicherry, India.

also in those who oppose them and stand in their paths. I am working in everybody and whatever men may think or do they can do nothing but help on my purpose. They also are doing my work, they are not my enemies but my instruments. In all your actions you are moving forward without knowing the way you move. You mean to do one thing and you do another. You aim at a result and your efforts subserve one that is different or contrary. It is Shakti [divine power] that has gone forth and entered into the people. Since long ago I have been preparing this uprising and now the time has come and it is I who will lead it to its fulfillment."

This then is what I have to say to you. The name of your society is "Society for the Protection of Religion." Well, the protection of the religion, the protection and upraising before the world of the Hindu religion, that is the work before us. But what is the Hindu religion. What is this religion which we call Sanatan, eternal? It is the Hindu religion only because the Hindu nation has kept it, because in this Peninsula it grew up in the seclusion of the sea and the Himalayas, because in this sacred and ancient land it was given as a charge to the Aryan race to preserve through the ages. But it is not circumscribed by the confines of a single country, it does not belong peculiarly and forever to a bounded part of the world. That which we call the Hindu religion is really the eternal religion, because it is the universal religion which embraces all others. If a religion is not universal, it cannot be eternal. A narrow religion, a sectarian religion, an exclusive religion can live only for a limited time and a limited purpose. This is the one religion that can triumph over materialism by including and anticipating the discoveries of science and the speculations of philosophy. It is the one religion which impresses on mankind the closeness of God to us and embraces in its compass all the possible means by which man can approach God. It is the one religion which insists every moment on the truth which all religions acknowledge that He is in all men and all things and that in Him we move and have our being. It is the one religion which enables us not only to understand and believe this truth but to realize it with every part of our being. It is the one religion which shows the world what the world is, that it is the Lila of Vasudeva [the play or sport of God]. It is the one religion which shows us how we can best play our part in the Lila, its subtlest laws and its noblest rules. It is the one religion which does not separate life in any smallest detail from religion, which knows what immortality is and has utterly removed from us the reality of death.

This is the word that has been put into my mouth to speak to you today. What I intended to speak has been put away from me, and beyond what is given to me I have nothing to say. It is only the word that is put into me that I can speak to you. That word is now finished. I spoke once before with this force in me and I said then that this movement is not a political movement and that nationalism is not politics but a religion, a creed, a faith. I say it again today, but I put it in another way. I say no longer that nationalism is a creed, a religion, a faith; I say that it is the Sanatan Dharma which for us is nationalism. This Hindu nation was born with the Sanatan Dharma, with it it moves and with it it grows. When the Sanatan Dharma declines, then the nation declines, and if the Sanatan Dharma were capable of perishing, with the Sanatan Dharma it would perish. The Sanatan Dharma, that is nationalism. This is the message that I have to speak to you.

2. Gandhi and Nonviolent Resistance

In *satyagraha* ("truth force"), Gandhi fashioned a political technique of compelling emotional power, and succeeded in training many thousands of his followers in its use during the freedom struggle. In the following passages, Gandhi discusses the Hindu religious sources and implications of *satyagraha*. [2]

I have admitted in my introduction to the Gita known as *Anasakti Yoga* that it is not a treatise on nonviolence, nor was it written to condemn war. Hinduism, as it is practiced today or has even been known to have ever been practiced, has certainly not condemned war as I do. What, however, I have done is to put a new but natural and logical interpretation upon the whole teaching of the Gita and the spirit of Hinduism. Hinduism, not to speak of other religions, is ever evolving. It has no one scripture like the Qur'an or the Bible. Its scriptures are also evolving and suffering addition. The Gita itself is an instance in point. It has given a new meaning to *Karma, sannyasa, yajna*, etc. It has breathed new life into Hinduism. It has given an original rule of conduct. Not that what the Gita has given was not implied in the previous writings, but the Gita put these implications in a concrete shape. I have endeavored, in the light of a prayerful study of the other faiths of the world, and what is more, in the light of my own experiences in trying to live the teaching of Hinduism as interpreted in the Gita, to give an extended but in no way strained meaning to Hinduism, not as buried in its ample scriptures, but as a living faith speaking like a mother to her aching child. What I have

---

[2] From *Harijan*, October 3, 1936; *Young India*, August 11, 1920; *Harijan*, September 1, 1940; *Harijan*, July 26, 1942.

done is perfectly historical. I have followed in the footsteps of our fore-fathers. At one time they sacrificed animals to propitiate angry gods. Their descendants, but our less remote ancestors, read a different meaning into the word "sacrifice," and they taught that sacrifice was meant to be of our baser self, to please not angry gods but the one living God within. I hold that the logical outcome of the teaching of the Gita is decidedly for peace at the price of life itself. It is the highest aspiration of the human species. [*Harijan*, October 3, 1936]

Let me not be misunderstood. Strength does not come from physical capacity. It comes from an indomitable will. . . . We in India may in a moment realize that one hundred thousand Englishmen need not frighten three hundred million human beings. . . . I am not a visionary. I claim to be a practical idealist. The religion of nonviolence is not meant merely for the *rishis* and saints. It is meant for the common people as well. Non-violence is the law of our species as violence is the law of the brute. The spirit lies dormant in the brute, and he knows no law but that of physical might. The dignity of man requires obedience to a higher law — to the strength of the spirit.

I have therefore ventured to place before India the ancient law of self-sacrifice. For *satyagraha* and its offshoots, noncooperation and civil resistance, are nothing but new names for the law of suffering. The *rishis*, who discovered the law of nonviolence in the midst of violence, were greater geniuses than Newton. They were greater warriors than Wellington. Having themselves known the use of arms, they realized their uselessness, and taught a weary world that its salvation lay not through violence but through nonviolence.

Nonviolence in its dynamic condition means conscious suffering. It does not mean meek submission to the will of the evildoer, but it means the pitting of one's whole soul against the will of the tyrant. Working under this law of our being, it is possible for a single individual to defy the whole might of an unjust empire to save his honor, his religion, his soul, and lay the foundation for that empire's fall or its regeneration. [*Young India*, August 11, 1920]

Just as one must learn the art of killing in the training for violence, so one must learn the art of dying in the training for nonviolence. Violence does not mean emancipation from fear, but discovering the means of combating the cause for fear. Nonviolence, on the other hand, has no cause for fear. The votary of nonviolence has to cultivate the capacity for sacrifice of the highest type in order to be free from fear. He recks not if he should lose his land, his wealth, his life. He who has not overcome all fear cannot practice *ahimsa* [nonviolence] to perfection.

The votary of *ahisma* has only one fear, that is of God. He who seeks refuge in God ought to have a glimpse of the *Atman* [soul] that transcends the body; and the moment one has a glimpse of the Imperishable *Atman* one sheds the love of the perishable body. Training in nonviolence is thus diametrically opposed to training in violence. Violence is needed for the protection of things external, nonviolence is needed for the protection of the *Atman*, for the protection of one's honor.

This nonviolence cannot be learned by staying at home. It needs enterprise. In order to test ourselves we should learn to dare danger and death, mortify the flesh, and acquire the capacity to endure all manner of hardships. He who trembles or takes to his heels the moment he sees two people fighting is not nonviolent, but a coward. A nonviolent person will lay down his life in preventing such quarrels. The bravery of the nonviolent is vastly superior to that of the violent. The badge of the violent is his weapon — spear, or sword, or rifle. God is the shield of the nonviolent. [*Harijan*, September 1, 1940]

If the struggle which we are seeking to avoid with all our might has to come, and if it is to remain nonviolent as it must in order to succeed, fasting is likely to play an important part in it. It has its place in the tussle with authority and with our own people in the event of wanton acts of violence and obstinate riots, for instance.

There is a natural prejudice against it as part of a political struggle. It has a recognized place in religious practice. But it is considered a vulgar interpolation in politics by the ordinary politician though it has always been resorted to by prisoners in a haphazard way with more or less success. By fasting, however, they have always succeeded in drawing public attention and disturbing the peace of jail authorities.

My own fasts have always, as I hold, been strictly according to the law of *satyagraha*. Fellow satyagrahis too in South Africa fasted partially or wholly. My fasts have been varied. There was the Hindu–Muslim unity fast of twenty-one days in 1924, started under the late Maulana Mohamed Ali's roof in Delhi. The indeterminate fast against the Mac-Donald Award was taken in the Yeravda prison in 1932. The twenty-one day's purificatory fast was begun in the Yeravda prison and was finished at Lady Thakersey's, as the Government would not take the burden of my being in the prison in that condition. Then followed another fast in the Yeravda prison in 1933 against the Government refusal to let me carry on anti-untouchability work through *Harijan* (issued from prison) on the same basis as facilities had been allowed me four months before. They would not yield, but they discharged me when their medical advisers thought I could not live many days if the fast was not given up.

Then followed the ill-fated Rajkot fast in 1939. A false step taken by me thoughtlessly during that fast thwarted the brilliant result that would otherwise certainly have been achieved. In spite of all these fasts, fasting has not been accepted as a recognized part of *satyagraha*. It has only been tolerated by the politicians. I have, however, been driven to the conclusion that fasting unto death is an integral part of [the] *satyagraha* program, and it is the greatest and most effective weapon in its armory under given circumstances. Not every one is qualified for undertaking it without a proper course of training.

I may not burden this note with an examination of the circumstances under which fasting may be resorted to and the training required for it. Nonviolence in its positive aspect as benevolence (I do not use the word love as it has fallen into disrepute) is the greatest force because of the limitless scope it affords for self-suffering without causing or intending any physical or material injury to the wrongdoer. The object always is to evoke the best in him. Self-suffering is an appeal to his better nature, as retaliation is to his baser. Fasting under proper circumstances is such an appeal par excellence. If the politician does not perceive its propriety in political matters, it is because it is a novel use of this very fine weapon. To practice nonviolence in mundane matters is to know its true value. It is to bring heaven upon earth. There is no such thing as the other world. All worlds are one. There is no "here" and no "there." As Jeans has demonstrated, the whole universe including the most distant stars, invisible even through the most powerful telescope in the world, is compressed in an atom. I hold it therefore to be wrong to limit the use of nonviolence to cave dwellers and for acquiring merit for a favored position in the other world. All virtue ceases to have use if it serves no purpose in every walk of life. I would therefore plead with the purely political-minded people to study nonviolence and fasting as its extreme manifestation with sympathy and understanding. [*Harijan*, July 26, 1942]

BUDDHIST NATIONALISM IN CEYLON AND BURMA

Among the Asian religions, Buddhism was peculiarly amenable to religious nationalism. Hinduism was divided into innumerable castes and sects far smaller than potential national units, and had little inherent unifying power. Islam, at the other extreme, was universal in its scope, and its history emphasized the development of supranational loyalties. Buddhism, however, had a long history of association with traditional kingdoms in Burma, Ceylon, and other Theravada countries. Buddhism could provide the Burmese with a powerful sense of group identity, for this religion had molded the culture and legitimized the political institutions of the Burmese people since the conversion of King Anawratha in the eleventh century. And in Ceylon Buddhism had played this role since the third century B.C.

Ceylon's independence was achieved in 1948 without a major struggle, largely as a by-product of Indian independence. The real rise of Sinhalese Buddhist nationalism came after independence, reaching its height in the 1956 election campaign (see VI. 1 and 2). In Burma, however, Buddhist monks and Buddhist issues played a major rule in the decade after World War I, and sporadically thereafter. Burmese independence, also in 1948, came under secular and even Marxist-inclined leadership, but here again it was followed by a resurgence of Buddhist political activity.

3. Buddhism and Sinhalese National Identity

The following passages from an influential book published in 1953 reveal the crucial role of Buddhism in the development of a sense of national identity. The unifying role of Buddhism among the majority, however, led to the corresponding alienation of the minorities, especially the Hindu Tamils and the Christians.[3]

▶ ▶

The purpose of this work is to commemorate a great and unique event of modern times, namely, the completion of 2,500 years of a threefold history. This history is that of the Buddhist Faith, of the Sinhalese Race, and of the Land of Ceylon.

According to the Mahavamsa and the ancient Pali Commentaries, the passing away of the Buddha, and the landing in Lanka of Vijaya, the founder of the Sinhalese race, took place on one and the same day. The Mahavamsa relates that the Buddha, on the day of His passing away, addressed Sakra, the king of the gods, thus: "My doctrine, O Sakra, will eventually be established in the Island of Lanka; and on this day, Vijaya, eldest son of Sinha Bahu, King of Sinhapura in the Lata Country, lands there with seven hundred followers, and will assume the sovereignty there. Do thou, therefore, guard well the King and his train and the Island of Lanka."

On receiving the Buddha's command, Sakra summoned Vishnu: "Do thou, O lotus-hued One, protect with zeal Prince Vijaya and his

[3] From D. C. Vijayavardhana, *The Revolt in the Temple: Composed to Commemorate 2,500 Years of the Land, the Race, and the Faith* (Colombo: Sinha Publications, 1953), pp. 3–4, 438. Used by permission.

followers, and the Doctrine that is to endure in Lanka for full five thousand years."

Thus the Mahavamsa synchronizes the death of the Buddha with the founding of the Sinhalese race; and, therefore in 1956 will occur the unique threefold event — the completion of 2,500 years of Buddhism, of the life of the Sinhalese race, and of Ceylon's history.

This Mahavamsa tradition has been ingrained in the Sinhalese mind for centuries, and out of it had arisen certain beliefs among them. For more than two thousand years the Sinhalese have been inspired by the ideal that they were a nation brought into being for the definite purpose of carrying the Torch lit by the Buddha. It was through the same tradition that Vishnu was made the patron deity of Ceylon. In almost every Buddhist temple there is an image to the deity who is venerated as the protector of the Land, the Race and the Faith.

Another tradition that is current amongst the Sinhalese is that, when Buddhism shall have completed 2,500 years, a prince named Diyasena will establish a Buddhist Kingdom in Ceylon. Then, it is said, the faith will shine forth in glory and be a beacon to the whole world, and Lanka itself will be prosperous and joyous. This prediction, which originated from a verse in a poetical work, written during the reign of Parakrama Bahu VI of Kotte — the last period of brilliant achievement of the Sinhalese — has been a source of hope and consolation for the Sinhalese during the vicissitudes of the past five hundred years.

The Buddha's blessing of Vijaya and his band of followers and the land which they "went forth to possess," foreshadowed the intimate connection of the Land, the Race and the Buddhist Faith. Vijaya himself was a Brahmin in faith, and the best authorities' opinion is that Buddhism was not actually established in Ceylon, and not adopted by the Sinhalese people, until the coming of the missionary, Mahinda Thero, nearly three hundred years later than Vijaya's landing in the Island. Nevertheless the blessing of the Buddha was there: the prophecy was in due course fulfilled: the land and the race flourished, and the arts of civilization were fostered; and through all the vicissitudes of their fortunes from that day to this, the Sinhalese race as a whole (and therefore the vast majority of Ceylon's inhabitants), have remained faithful to the Buddha and the Buddhist precepts, on which their ancient kings founded their legislation and social organization.

Buddhism has been throughout a humanizing influence in Ceylon history. There have been times of retrogression when the sacred precepts were forgotten or ignored; times when alien conquerors imposed on portions of the country their faith and their manners. But again and again these alien kings are to be found adopting the Buddhist faith and ethics, and identifying themselves with the Sinhalese people. And through all these vicissitudes, the teaching of the Doctrine and the practice of the faith went on in the temples, the monasteries and the schools. All the materials for the history of Ceylon are to be found in Buddhist chronicles and Buddhist monumental inscriptions.

Thus it is clear that the unifying, healing, progressive principle in the entity called Ceylon was the Buddhist faith. This is said with no intention of denying or belittling the contributions of other races and other faiths — each in their own way, each in their own degree. But, when all has been taken into account, the outstanding fact is the unbroken continuity, for 2,500 years, of interaction of the land and the people and the faith on each other, and their resultant contribution to civilization. [pp. 3-4]

As with man, so with a nation or a race. Its life-span has a beginning, a middle and an end. When the Sinhalese nation came into being, with the blessings of the Buddha, twenty-five centuries ago, it was a destined event of high import and purpose. The chosen race was allotted a life-span of fifty centuries to fulfill its great destiny. It will thus be noted that we are today on the threshold of a glorious era in the history of our race.

When the Sinhalese, united by bonds of blood and religion, and inspired by the burning desire to live a free life and develop their own culture, formed a new element in the political arena of Ceylon, the Britisher made a mistake for which he at least has the excuse that some minorities who should have known better shared it. They thought that the essence of the whole movement was merely a desire for power and domination, whereas it was the love of creation, the innate ineradicable desire to build up something in one's own image. Just as in the springtime of life the same message bursts from the unconscious to the conscious self and becomes objective so to the Sinhalese there had come a reawakening, a desire to create a State which should be Sinhalese, reared up by Sinhalese hands, and breathing a Sinhalese atmosphere in the land of Sinhalese tradition.

A liberating nationalism is without doubt the highest form of patriotism — the only patriotism worthy of the name, worth fighting for or dying for. And some of the finest men and women who have ever lived have fought for it and died for it, and so long as tyranny and injustice exist in the world, it will continue to command the religious fervor and self-sacrifice of such men and women. The last wish (*prarthana*), of Keppetipola Disava, uttered in the temple of the Sacred Tooth where he was taken for worship, before being led to be beheaded for his part in the Uva Rebellion [1818], speaks the voice of that patriotism which is the pure flame of an impassioned and selfless idealism. He said: "May I be reborn in Lanka to continue the struggle for freedom!" [p. 438]

4. Footwear on Pagodas and the Nationalist Struggle

In 1916, a nationalist agitation was launched in Burma to protest the practice of European visitors of keeping their shoes on while walking around the Buddhist pagodas, contrary to Burmese custom. The following excerpts from the reply of the Government of Burma provide interesting insights into the nature of both Buddhist nationalism and British colonial administration.[4]

▶ ▶   This memorial raises a very important question and one of great public interest to all classes in Burma. Hitherto Europeans have enjoyed the privilege of visiting pagodas and other Buddhist religious buildings in Burma without the obligation having been imposed upon them of removing their shoes. The memorialists represent that this privilege is obnoxious to the feelings of Burman Buddhists and should no longer be continued, and they desire that the Government shall in deference to the feelings of the Buddhist community recognize that discontinuance, and make a pronouncement to that effect for the guidance of all concerned. The memorialists themselves recognize that neither the Government nor the European community have ever had any desire to wound the religious susceptibilities of their Buddhist fellow subjects, and the Lieutenant Governor would like to lay great emphasis on the very sympathetic relations that have always obtained between the Government and the Buddhist religious authorities. It is nothing but the truth to say that Buddhism is a religion which has attracted many admirers and not a few adherents from the West, and it has gained the respect of all Englishmen on account of the purity and selflessness of its tenets and the toleration and kindness which its followers extend to those who profess different religions. Christians of all degree recognize and admire in the founder of the Buddhist religion one of the greatest Teachers of humanity that the world has produced. It stands to reason therefore that if both Government officers, high and low, and the European community have visited pagodas without removing their shoes, they have done so in complete ignorance that they were thereby offending the sentiments of

---

[4] From *Rangoon Gazette Weekly Budget* (Rangoon), November 3, 1919.

their Buddhist friends. It is now nearly a century since Arakan and Tenasserim came under British rule. It is two-thirds of a century since the Pegu Province was annexed to the British Crown, and it is a third of a century since the annexation of Upper Burma, and it is therefore inconceivable that if such offense was being caused, the fact would not have come to the knowledge of Government and of the numerous Europeans who have lived for years in all parts of Burma in perfect amity with their Burmese fellow-subjects and with Buddhist religious authorities. Several experienced officers have informed the Lieutenant Governor that on occasions when they themselves have in ignorance or unwittingly done anything in pagodas or *pongyi kyaungs* [monasteries] to which exception on religious grounds could be taken, the monks or other religious authorities concerned have pointed out to them politely wherein they offended, accepting their apologies and assurances that they would not similarly offend again. It is the universal experience that trustees of pagodas have readily invited Europeans to come in and view them, and have never made the request that shoes should be removed, though some of them have asked that the visitor should take off his hat in accordance with his own method of showing respect. Similarly the persons in charge of *pongyi kyaungs* have repeatedly given hospitality and shelter to European officers and travelers touring in the interior without requiring them to walk about barefooted.

It is very necessary that the public should understand the subject in all its bearings in order that no misapprehension may arise as to the attitude of the Government in regard to it. Up till 1875 there is no official record of any reference to this matter of the removal of shoes. In that year certain elders of the Town of Rangoon represented to the Chief Commissioner that the feelings of the people were being hurt at seeing persons, whose own creed required that they should put off their shoes when about to kneel at prayers, ascending the great Shwe Dagon Pagoda platform with their shoes on. The position of Europeans, whose creed prescribed other methods of respect, was appreciated by the elders in their representation, and the substance of the representation was that permission should be granted to prohibit persons other than Europeans (the actual term used was "English people") from ascending the pagoda platform with their shoes on. The petitioners were informed that their request was considered reasonable, and for the past forty-four years the accepted practice regulating the visits of non-Buddhists to pagodas, adopted at the instance of the Buddhist elders of the Town of Rangoon, has been that those persons, whose creed required them to show respect by taking off their shoes, should take off their shoes on visiting a pagoda.

During this period some attempts have been made to agitate the question, but it is significant that prior to 1916 none of them was made by Burmese. . . .

The present agitation for the removal of foot-coverings by Europeans on visiting pagodas, which is the only movement that is Burmese in its origin, dates from the year 1916. It was initiated at Prome by the first memorialist himself, but it did not attract much notice until 1918 when correspondence in the press which tended to become acrimonious was followed by a meeting styled an "All-Burma Conference of Buddhists" held at the Jubilee Hall, Rangoon, on Sunday the 19th of May, 1918. Eleven resolutions on the subject of the use of footwear by visitors to pagodas were passed at the meeting. No steps were taken by the organizers of the meeting to bring the resolutions to the notice of the Local Government, but the intervention of the Local Government was rendered necessary by the fact that attempts had been made to intimidate pagoda trustees into acting upon the resolutions of that meeting against their own wishes, and also by the possibility that the methods of agitation adopted were likely to arouse ill-feeling between the Burmese and European communities. The meeting was held during one of the most critical phases of the war, and while disclaiming any intention of intervening in matters of religious controversy, the local Government in the interest of public tranquility called a truce to all public discussion on the subject. . . . The memorialists refer to these orders in paragraph 15 to 18 of the memorial and contend that the action then taken by the Local Government was unnecessary. . . . It is sufficient comment on these contentions that on the 4th of October, or only nineteen days after the submission of the memorial, a sudden and savage attack was made at Mandalay, by persons in the garb of Buddhist *pongyis* [monks], on a party including four ladies, the members of which were wearing shoes on the platform of the Eindawya Pagoda. They had not been asked to remove their shoes, and at the time of the attack were on the point of leaving the pagoda after a brief visit to the festival which was being held there. This attack was made nine days after a provocative article had been published in the vernacular press, an article which was in all probability intended to be an incitement to the use of violence against persons wearing shoes when visiting pagodas, and it has been followed by articles which were calculated to convey to the mind of the average reader an extenuation of the crime. . . .

It is of course impossible for the Government to enter into any discussion as to how far the wearing of shoes is permitted or prohibited by Buddhist scriptures, or as to whether the founder of the

Buddhist religion would or would not, if he had lived in modern times, have instructed his followers how to meet changed circumstances. . . . The memorial opens with the statement "That the universal custom of the Burmese people and the teaching of Buddha as accepted by all sects of Buddhism in Burma prohibit the use of footwear within their sacred precincts." No change in material, and no superimposition of other coverings, would therefore meet the case. "Footwear" must include even socks or stockings. On their own showing the demand of the memorialists would mean that Europeans should only enter pagoda precincts barefooted. . . .

Nevertheless, it is not for the Government to lay down what observances should be followed by persons entering the religious edifices of others, but neither can any public meeting held in any particular place pass an authoritative decree which is binding on everybody throughout the land. Throughout the whole of India there is no common rule for all religious buildings, there exists no single body which can lay down rules applicable to all. The degree of strictness or indulgence is decided not by any central authority, nor by any meetings of citizens, but by the managers, trustees or priests in charge of the particular religious edifice concerned. Following this precedent, the Local Government will therefore leave it to the trustees and managers of every pagoda or religious edifice in Burma to lay down the rule in this matter which they desire to be observed. If such managers desire to exclude Europeans from such buildings, except on the impossible condition that they should walk barefooted up long flights of steps and about pagoda platforms, wet or dry, clean or dirty, the matter lies within their own authority.

ISLAMIC RESURGENCE AND NATIONALISM

Across the vast area stretching from Morocco to Indonesia, "Islam in danger!" was the common battle cry of early opposition to Western imperialism. In Algeria the children in Qur'anic schools began each day by chanting in unison: "Islam is my religion, Arabic is my language, Algeria is my country." And in Indonesia the leader of Sarekat Islam, H. O. S. Tjokroaminoto, proclaimed Islam as a "binding social factor and national symbol." There was a strong presumption under Islamic law that the Europeans, as *kaffirs* (infidels), had no rightful claim to rule over Muslim peoples.

However, once nationalism moved beyond anti–imperialism to become an ideology positing the nation as the supreme loyalty, conflict with Islam became inevitable. Even the movement for the creation of

Pakistan received scant support from the *ulama* until just before the partition of India was effected, for the orthodox divines saw the movement as essentially one of secular nationalism in the guise of Islam. And in the Arab world to the west, the ideological question whether Islam and Arab nationalism are opposed is still being debated.

5. Holy War Against British Imperialism

A nineteenth-century British administrator discussed the significance of the formal decisions (*fatwas*) of the *ulama* regarding the status of British-ruled India. If India was considered to be *Dar-ul-Harb* ("country of the enemy"), Muslims would be morally bound to revolt.[5]

▶ ▶   While the more fanatical of the Musalmans have thus engaged in overt sedition, the whole Muhammadan Community has been openly deliberating on their obligation to rebel. During the past nine months, the leading newspapers in Bengal have filled their columns with discussions as to the duty of the Muhammadans to wage war against the Queen. The collective wisdom of the Musalman Law Doctors of Northern India was first promulgated in a formal Decision (Fatwa). Next the Bengal Muhammadans put forth a pamphlet on the question; and even the Shiah sect, a comparatively small body in India, have not been able to restrain themselves from print. For some months the Anglo-Indian Press was inclined to smile at the pains which the loyal sort of Musalmans were taking to ascertain whether they could abstain from rebellion without perdition to their souls. But the universal promulgation of formal Legal Decisions by the Muhammadan Law Doctors, soon convinced our countrymen that the subject might have a serious as well as a ludicrous aspect. The cumulative papers now published — papers drawn up and issued by the Muhammadans themselves — leave not a shadow of doubt as to the danger through which the Indian Empire is passing. They will convince every reasonable mind, that while the more reckless among the Musalmans have for years been engaged in overt treason, the whole community has been agitated by the greatest State Question that ever occupied the thoughts of a people. The duty of rebellion has been formally and publicly reduced to a nice point of Muhammadan Law. Somehow or other, every Musalman seems to have found himself called on to declare his faith; to state, in the face of his

[5] From W. W. Hunter, *The Indian Musalmans* (London: Trübner and Co., 2nd ed., 1872), pp. 10–11, 141–44, 218–19.

coreligionists, whether he will or will not contribute to the Traitors' Camp on our Frontier; and to elect, once and for all, whether he shall play the part of a devoted follower of Islam, or of a peaceable subject of the Queen. In order to enable the Muhammadans to decide these points, they have consulted not only the leading Doctors of their Law in India, but they have gone as far as Mecca itself. The obligation of the Indian Muslamans to rebel or not rebel, hung for some months on the deliberations of three priests in the Holy City of Arabia. [pp. 10–11]

The Wahabis to a man, and a large proportion of the devout Musalmans, believe India to be now a Country of the Enemy. But the more sensible majority of them, while sorrowfully lamenting its lapsed state, are willing to accept the duties belonging to that condition. . . .

The more acute among the Law Doctors long ago detected the coming change in the status of the Musalmans of India, the change which has now become an accomplished fact. From time to time Decisions have appeared, which show that, in spite of the cautious timidity of the East India Company, the revolution did not go on unperceived. One of these Decisions declared that India would remain a Country of Islam only so long as the Muhammadan Judges, whom we have abolished, continued to administer the Law. But perhaps the two most important were those of Shah Abd-ul-Aziz, the Sun of India, and of his nephew Maulavi Abd-ul-Hai. As we gradually transferred the administration to our own hands, pious Musulmans were greatly agitated touching the relation which they should hold to us. They accordingly consulted the highest Indian authorities on the point, and both the celebrated men above-mentioned gave forth responses. Here are their decisions word for word:

"When Infidels get hold of a Muhammadan country," Abd-ul-Aziz declared, "and it becomes impossible for the Musulmans of the country, and of the people of the neighboring districts, to drive them away, or to retain reasonable hope of ever doing so; and the power of the Infidels increases to such an extent, that they can abolish or retain the ordinances of Islam according to their pleasure; and no one is strong enough to seize on the revenues of the country without the permission of the Infidels; and the (Musalman) inhabitants do no longer live so secure as before; such a country is politically a Country of the Enemy (*Dar-ul-Harb*)."

When we consolidated our power, the decisions of the Doctors became more and more distinct as to India being *Dar-ul-Harb*. Maulavi Abd-ul-Hai, who belongs to the generation after Abd-ul-Aziz, distinctly ruled as follows: "The Empire of the Christians from Calcutta to Delhi, and other countries adjacent to Hindustan proper (i.e. the North-West

Provinces), are all the Country of the Enemy (*Dar-ul-Harb*), for idolatry (*Kufr* and *Shirk*) is everywhere current, and no recourse is made to our holy law. Whenever such circumstances exist in a country, the country is a *Dar-ul-Harb*. It is too long here to specify all conditions; but the opinions of all lawyers agree in this, that Calcutta and its dependencies are the Country of the Enemy (*Dar-ul-Harb*)."

These Decisions have borne practical fruit. The Wahabis, whose zeal is greater than their knowledge, deduce from the fact of India being technically a Country of the Enemy, the obligation to wage war upon its rulers. The more enlightened Musalmans, while sorrowfully accepting the fact, regard it not as ground of rebellion, but as a curtailment of their spiritual privileges. . . .

A still greater number would break their connection with the Wahabi party if they could see their way to doing so without peril to their souls. The Formal Decisions lately issued by the Law Doctors of Northern India, with the historical amplification now set forth, will give peace to thousands of devout men. [pp. 141–44]

THE DECISION OF THE LAW DOCTORS OF NORTHERN INDIA, TRANSLATION OF THE ISTIFTA OR QUESTION, PUT BY SAYYID AMIR HUSAIN, PERSONAL ASSISTANT TO THE COMMISSIONER OF BHAGALPUR

What is your Decision, O men of learning and expounders of the law of Islam, in the following? —

Whether a *Jihad* is lawful in India, a country formerly held by a Muhammadan ruler, and now held under the sway of a Christian Government, where the said Christian Ruler does in no way interfere with his Muhammadan subjects in the Rites prescribed by their Religion, such as Praying, Fasting, Pilgrimage, Zakat, Friday Prayer, and Jama'at, and gives them fullest protection and liberty in the above respects in the same way as a Muhammadan Ruler would do, and where the Muhammadan subjects have no strength and means to fight with their rulers; on the contrary, there is every chance of the war, if waged, ending with a defeat, and thereby causing an indignity to Islam.

Please answer, quoting your authority.

Fatwa dated the 17th Rabi-us-sani, or Rabi II., 1287 H., corresponding with the 17th of July, 1870.

The Musulmans here are protected by Christians, and there is no *Jihad* in a country where protection is afforded, as the absence of protection and liberty between Musalmans and Infidels is essential in a religious war, and that condition does not exist here. Besides, it is necessary that there should be a probability of victory to Musalmans and glory to the Indians. If there be no such probability, the *Jihad* is unlawful. [pp. 218–19]

6. Nationalism Is Opposed to Islam

In this booklet Maulana Maudoodi, then leader of the Jama'at-i-Islami in India, condemned all forms of ideological nationalism. Both the *nationalist Muslims*, who followed the Congress line of secular nationalism, and the *Muslim nationalists*, who believed in a Muslim nation and a separate Muslim state, were denounced for their infidelity to the one supreme ideology of Islam.[6]

▶ ▶   The most important philosophy of life that is today governing not only India but the entire world is the philosophy of nationalism. This unfortunate passion of nations has made the life of man miserable on this planet. The strangest thing is that even Muslims, who by the very nature of their creed ought to have been free of this bias, have succumbed to it. . . .

In this matter Muslims should display at least that amount of steadfastness which was shown by the followers of Marx at the outbreak of the Great War of 1914–18. When the war had started a great difference arose among the members of the Second International on this very issue of nationalism. Many socialists who had gathered on the Socialist International Front, seeing that their respective nations had plunged into the war, were swayed over by nationalistic sentiments and wished to join their national armies. But the Marxists said that they were pledged to fight for an ideology according to which the capitalists of all nations stood as their enemies and the laborers of all nations stood as their friends; therefore they could not support that nationalism which creates dissensions and divisions among laborers and brings them to opposite fronts in the company of capitalists. On this ground the Marxists separated from their comrades with whom they had relations of long standing. They could bear the break-up of the Second International but could not bear giving up their cherished principles. Nay, they proceeded further. Those who were true communists broke the idol of nationalism with their own hands. To defend their principles the German communists fought against Germany, the Russian communists against Russia, and similarly the

[6] From Sayyed Abulala Maudoodi, *Nationalism and India* (Malihabad, U.P., India: Maktaba-E-Jama'at-E-Islami [Hind], 1948), pp. 5–11, 42. Used by permission.

communists of other countries fought against the governments of their own respective nations.

Exactly like a communist, a Muslim also possesses an ideology of his own. Then why should he degrade himself so much that in order to gain something or to save his head from injury he may have to shift his position? And if he shifts at all, he must have the consciousness as from what position he is shifting and what other position he means to occupy. Because to shift one's position for nothing is sheer weakness, but having shifted to a new position to think that one is at one's old position carries with it weakness and stupidity both. I am a Muslim only so long as I uphold the Islamic viewpoint in every concern of life. If I have shifted to another viewpoint it would be simply absurd on my part to think that I still retain the state of being a Muslim. To be a Muslim and to adopt a non-Islamic viewpoint is only meaningless. "Muslim Nationalist" and "Muslim Communist" are as contradictory terms as "Communist Fascist," "Socialist Capitalist," "Chaste Prostitute!"

Even a cursory glance at the meaning and essence of nationalism would convince a person that in their spirit and in their aims Islam and nationalism are diametrically opposed to each other. Islam deals with man as man. It presents to all mankind a social system of justice and piety based on creed and morality and invites all towards it. And then it admits him in its circle, with equal rights, whosoever accepts this system. Be it in the sphere of economics or politics or civics or legal rights and duties or anything else, those who accept the principles of Islam are not divided by any distinction of nationality or race or class or country. The ultimate goal of Islam is a world-state in which the chains of racial and national prejudices would be dismantled and all mankind incorporated in a cultural and political system with equal rights and equal opportunities for all, and in which hostile competition would give way to friendly cooperation between peoples so that they might mutually assist and contribute to the material and moral good of one another. Whatever the principle of human good Islam defines and whatever the scheme of life it prescribes, it would appeal to mankind in general only when they would free themselves of all ignorant prejudices and dissociate themselves altogether from their national traditions, with their sentiments of racial pride, and with their love of sanguinary and material affinities, and be prepared, as mere human beings to enquire what is truth, where lies righteousness, justice and honesty, and what is the path that leads to the well-being of, not a class or a nation or a country, but of humanity as a whole.

As opposed to this, nationalism divides man from man on the

basis of nationality. Nationalism simply means that the nationalist should give preference to his nationality over all other nationalities. Even if he were not an aggressive nationalist, nationalism, at least, demands that culturally, economically, politically and legally he should differentiate between national and non-national; secure the maximum of advantages for his nation; build up barriers of economic preferences for national profit; protect with tenacity the historical traditions and the traditional prejudices which have come down to make his nationality, and breed in him the sentiments of national pride. ...

This is a mere outline of the principles, aims and spirits of the two creeds, a little reflection on which would amply evidence that these two creeds are the reverse of each other. Islam cannot flourish in the lap of nationalism, and nationalism too cannot find a place in the fold of Islam. The progress of nationalism would starve Islam to death and the progress of Islam would sound the death-knell of nationalism. Now it is obvious, a person can give support to the progress of only one creed at a time. [pp. 5–11]

Among the Indian Muslims today we find two kinds of nationalist: the "Nationalist Muslims," namely, those who in spite of their being Muslims believe in "Indian Nationalism" and worship it; and the "Muslim Nationalists," namely, those people who are little concerned with Islam and its principles and aims, but are concerned with the individuality and the political and economic interests of that nation which has come to exist by the name of "Muslim," and they are so concerned only because of their accidence of birth in that nation. From the Islamic viewpoint both these types of nationalists are equally misled, for Islam enjoins faith in truth only; it does not permit any kind of nation-worshipping at all. But unfortunately both these types of nationalists are ignorant of their un-Islamic position. Particularly the second type of people are today vaunting loudly that they are the champions of Islam in India, although their position is hardly different from that of the Hindu nationalists. A Hindu Nationalist, because he is born in the Hindu nation, endeavors to enhance the cause of those who are Hindus; and those Muslim Nationalists, because they are born in a nation which is called "Muslim," want to exalt those who are connected with this nation. Neither of the two comes forward with a moral end or with a creed that is supported by universal principles. As the Hindu would be satisfied in his own case, so these people would be fully satisfied if Muslims were to rule supreme — they would little mind if they had established their government on un-Islamic foundations, and if their behavior and procedure did not differ, in the least, from those of non-Muslims. [p. 42]

7. Islam and Arab Nationalism Are Not Opposed

In this article, which refutes the line of reasoning taken in the preceding selection, it is also argued that there is no conflict between Arab nationalism and Islam because of the Arabic origin of the Prophet and the Holy Book. The conflict exists, however, for other Muslim peoples.[7]

▶ ▶   The question is: Is it possible for one of us to be a loyal nationalist and a sincere Muslim, at one and the same time? Is there a fundamental contradiction between Arab nationalism, in its precise scientific sense, and true Muslim feeling? And does the acceptance of the one entail the rejection of the other? . . . Allow me to simplify the question a little and to say: Does a contradiction or opposition lie in our saying, "This man is a nationalist Muslim," or "This man is a Muslim nationalist," as when we say "This man is an atheist believer," or "He is a religious atheist," or when we join opposites, as "This man is a communist fascist," or "He is a democratic dictator? . . ."

I think the apparent contradiction between Islam and Arab nationalism which is still present in the minds of many people is, in the first place, due to misunderstanding, misrepresentation, and misinterpretation, involving both Islam and Arab nationalism.

The misunderstanding of Islam is due to the wrong significance attributed to the word "religion." We are influenced here — as a result of the intellectual imperialism under which a group of us still labor — by the Western concepts which restrict religion within narrow limits not extending beyond worship, ritual and the spiritual beliefs, which govern a man in his behavior, in relation to his God and to his brother man, in his capacity of an individual independent of society. Islam does not admit this narrow view of religion, but opposes it and the purpose it serves to the utmost. Many people still believe that Islam is similar to Christianity or Buddhism, and consists in devotional beliefs and exercises, ethical rules and no more. But, in fact, Islam in its precise sense, is a social order, a philosophy of life, a system of economic principles, a rule of government, in addition to its being a religious creed in the narrow Western sense. . . .

---

[7] From Sylvia G. Haim, ed., *Arab Nationalism: An Anthology* (Berkeley: University of California Press, 1964), pp. 172–78, 181–82, 185–86. Used by permission. Originally published by the University of California Press; reprinted by permission of the Regents of the University of California.

Just as Islam has been misunderstood, so has Arab nationalism. The reason for this may be that some think that nationalism can be built only upon racial appeal or racial chauvinism, and that it would therefore be contrary to the universal nature of Islam. The exaggeration of some nationalists has undoubtedly been one of the important reasons for this misunderstanding; and no doubt what some Umayyad governors, princes, and walis have done in their enthusiastic tribal chauvinism and their racial propaganda was contrary to the nature of Islam. But the Arab nationalism in which we believe, and for which we call, is based, as our national pact stipulates, not on racial appeal but on linguistic, historical, cultural, and spiritual ties, and on fundamental vital interests. In this respect, too, there is no contradiction between Arab nationalism and Islam. Many young people have greatly misunderstood Arab nationalism. They know something of the history of the West, of its national revivals, and have found there obvious signs of contradiction between Christianity and these national movements; this is, of course, natural in Western societies. The Church, which used to claim great spiritual power over all the Christians, looked askance on all political movements which aimed at shaking off ecclesiastical authority. In other words, European society gave allegiance to two fundamental authorities, the spiritual authority of the Pope and the temporal authority of the Emperor.

This dualism, although it has come to us in some stages of our slow social evolution, is not known in true Islam, where it is not admitted. On the contrary, the unity of creed has led to the unity of life, and the unity of life has made the caliph of the Muslims the leader in prayer, the leader of the army, and the political head at the same time. The opposition of German or Italian nationalism to Christianity, for instance, does not therefore necessarily mean that Arab nationalism should be opposed to Islam. It befits us to remember here the great difference between the relation of Christianity to the West, and the relation of Islam to the Arabs. Christianity is a religion introduced to the West. It arose out of the spirituality of the East, and is in complete opposition to the nature of the Teutonic tribes in Germany and the Celtic in France; that is why the German or the French nationalist finds great difficulty in reconciling it with the elements of the nationality which he cherishes, and realizes that Christianity has not found it possible to penetrate to the roots of Germanic and Celtic life. The opposite is true of Islam and its influence over Arab society and the Arab nation, as we shall explain in some measure. . . .

By misinterpretation I mean, in the first place, the misinterpretation of some Qur'anic verses relating to the preaching of Islam. Islam, although it is a universal religion suitable for all peoples and has in fact been disseminated among many nations and races, is undoubtedly a religion revealed first to the Arabs themselves. In this sense, it is their own special religion. The Prophet is from them, the Qur'an is in their language; Islam retained many of their previous customs, adopting and polishing the best of them. In expressing this opinion, we are not speaking out of an uncontrollable national feeling, nor from emotion, nor do we speak heedlessly; we base ourselves on the wisdom of the Qur'an itself, on the true laws of the Prophet, and on the actions of the early caliphs of Islam who represent it best. It is these which represent true Islam, not the false and obscure concepts which have gradually become common in the Islamic world, and which the Muslims have followed as the power of the foreigners grew and they became the leaders in both the political and the intellectual sphere.

The Qur'anic verses which support this view are many, but I select the following from them:

In surat *Ibrahim* (XIV) verse 4, the Qur'an says: "We have never sent a messenger save with the language of his people." The Arab messenger, then, has been sent to his people in their own Arabic tongue. . . .

These gracious verses and many others, both Meccan and Medinese, confirm that Islam is the religion of the Arabs before being a universal religion. This does not contradict other verses, such as verse 107 of surat *al-Anbiya'* (XXI): "We have sent thee only in mercy for mankind," because it is proved historically that the sending of the Prophet to the Arabs revived the Arab nation in its entirety and resurrected it. This resurrection was, at the time, beneficial to all the inhabited universe. The Arabs were the propagators of Islam and the saviors of the world from the reigning oppression and from the absolute ignorance which was then supreme; they were, as Gustave Lebon said, the most merciful conquerors that the world has known.

There is more to support this view in the Tradition. Al-Bukhari and Muslim report Ibn Umar's saying about the Prophet: "Power will remain in Quaraish so long as two of them still exist." There is also the Tradition, "The Imams are from Quaraish," and the Tradition attributed to Salman al-Farisi, who said, "The Prophet said to me: 'O Salman, do not hate me and part with your religion'; I said: 'O Prophet of God, how can I hate you, seeing that it is through you that God directed us?' He said: 'If you hate the Arabs, you hate me.'" The actions of the Muslims of the early period confirm indeed the Arab nature of Islam. . . .
[pp. 172–78]

Nationalism is a political and social idea which aims, in the first place, to unify each group of mankind and to make it obey one political order. The factors and the assumptions of nationalism are varied, and we do not intend to analyze them in this lecture. But we can assert that modern nationalism is based on language, history, literature, customs, and qualities. On the whole, the ties that bind individuals together and make them into a nation are both intellectual and material. If we examine these assumptions carefully and inquire into the position of Islam toward each of them, we find a great similarity, and sometimes complete agreement, between what Arab nationalism teaches and what is affirmed by Islam. Language, then is the primary tenet of our national creed; it is the soul of our Arab nation and the primary aspect of its life. The nation that loses its language is destined to disappear and perish. It is the good fortune of the Arabs that their language is not only a national duty but also a religious one, and the influence of Islam on its propagation and preservation is very great. The German Orientalist Johan Fück says in his book *Arabiya*: "No event in the history of the Arabs was more important for their future destiny than the rise of Islam. In that age, more than thirteen hundred years ago, when Muhammad recited the Qur'an to his compatriots in a pure Arabic tongue, a strong connection was established between his language and the new religion, and it boded great results for the future of this language." Moreover, as we have explained above, the Arabs had a glorious history before Islam, and their history is even more glorious and of greater moment after Islam; the Muslim Arab, when he exalts his heroes, partakes of two emotions, that of the pious Muslim and that of the proud nationalist. [pp. 181–82]

The conclusion is that no fundamental contradiction or clear opposition exists between Arab nationalism and Islam. The nearest analogy for the relation between them is that of the general to the particular. If we wanted to represent that relationship geometrically, we can imagine Islam and Arabism as two circles overlapping in the greater part of their surface, and in what remains outside the area that is common to the two circles, the two are not in fundamental opposition to each other. This is a truth which we must realize, and it befits the Arabs to rejoice in this great good fortune, that their nationalism does not contradict their religion; the Muslim Turk, for instance, who wants to glory in his nationalism, finds an insoluble difficulty in reconciling this sentiment with his sincere religious feeling. His national feeling requires him to be proud of his language and to purify it of other foreign languages; this may drive him to belittle Arabic, which is the flowing source from which Turkish language and literature drew from the earliest days. And if he wants to exalt the glorious actions and the heroes of the past, this will drive him, in most cases, to feel that the Muslim Arabs were strangers to him and that they were, in spite of external appearances, his real colonizers, mentally, spiritually, and culturally; the nationalist Muslim Arab will not often encounter this kind of difficulty. . . .

It also befits us to make it clear that there is nothing in this national call of ours which need exercise the non-Muslims among the Arabs or diminish their rights as good compatriots. Chauvinism, in all its aspects and forms, is incompatible with the nature of the Arabs; the non-Muslim Arabs used to enjoy all their rights under the shadow of the Arab state, from the earliest times, and the scope open to them was wide. The loyal nationalists among the Arab Christians realize this and know that Islam and the civilization which accompanied it are an indivisible part of our national heritage, and they must, as nationalists, cherish it as their brother Muslims cherish it. [pp. 185–86]

V

Religion and Internal Revolt

Religion has played a significant role not only in anti-colonial nationalist movements, but also in internal revolts seeking to overthrow national governments. In this chapter we are concerned with such attempts made through extraparliamentary agitations and violence; in the following chapter we shall examine some major transfers of power through political-party competition and the electoral process.

Religion has contributed to movements of internal revolt some of the same elements noted in Chapter IV: leadership, a sense of group identity, legitimacy, symbols, and techniques. In all three of the major cases we shall examine, most of these elements were present. Each of these cases, however, had unique features of great importance, and the patterns are not the regularly recurring ones found in the study of nationalist movements.

The Buddhist agitation which led to the 1963 overthrow of the Diem regime in South Vietnam succeeded because the Buddhists mobilized the masses with unprecedented effectiveness, and the top military leadership remained united and carried out the coup. A unique feature of the South Vietnam situation, and one which became extremely important in mobilizing the anti-Diem forces, was the religious difference between the Catholic oligarchy led by Diem and his family and the majority of the people, who practiced an ill-defined amalgam of Buddhism, Confucianism, and Taoism. The Buddhist group identity which emerged was more an effect than a cause of the political struggle. The monks provided the essential leadership in starting the agitation, and the most powerful symbol and technique was the self-immolation carried out by seven monks and one nun in antigovernment protests.

Father Camilo Torres, the young priest and sociologist, sought vainly for several years to form a stable United Front composed of all groups and parties, from Marxists to Catholics, who wanted a fundamental change of socio-economic-political structures in Colombian society. While considerably influenced by Marxist social thought, Torres developed his own radical Christian notion of revolution and in the early stages received support from the small Christian Democratic movement. Frustrated in his efforts to forge an effective leftist unity, Torres joined the guerrilla group known as the Army of National Liberation and was killed in the mountains by government forces in 1966.

In Egypt, the Muslim Brotherhood built up an impressive following in the decade preceding the revolution of 1952. Preaching an ideology of Islamic fundamentalism, the Brotherhood at first made common cause with the revolutionaries, but was too powerful and too ideologically distinct for partnership with Nasser, and was soon outlawed. The group was charged several times thereafter with attempts on Nasser's life and plots to overthrow the government. The leadership of the Brotherhood has continued its work of subversion from exile in Europe, and is still far from being a spent political force.

In these very different situations, in South Vietnam, Colombia, and the U. A. R., the significance of religion as both the inspirer and the instrumentality of revolutionary politics has been amply demonstrated.

BUDDHIST REVOLT IN SOUTH VIETNAM

The Buddhist crisis developed in May, 1963, over the government's refusal to permit the public display of the Buddhist flag, but there were many long-standing grievances against the Catholic Diem regime. With extreme obduracy, the dictatorship refused to make concessions until too late, and the delays served to convince the Buddhists that organized opposition to the regime was the only reasonable strategy. Led by the monks, fourteen Mahayana sects came together to form the United Buddhist Church. The pagodas became the centers of agitation, and thousands of laymen crowded into the pagoda compounds to hear the monks' fiery speeches denouncing the regime.

On June 11, 1963, the Venerable Thich Quang Duc, a 73-year-old monk, burned himself to death on a crowded Saigon street in a dramatic protest against the government. Seven other ritual suicides followed over the next several months. While criticized by some as contrary to Buddhism, self-immolation has scriptural approval in the Mahayana tradition and was practiced by Chinese monks centuries ago.

The regime's massive attack on the pagodas in August was a last desperate attempt to crush the Buddhist opposition. However, this led to the almost complete withdrawal of American support for Diem, and the military coup took place on November 1, 1963.

1. Diem Regime's Persecution of Buddhism

The following letter, which lists Buddhist grievances against the Catholic-dominated government, was written by the Action Committee of the Buddhists of Vietnam and published in *World Buddhism*.[1]

The world has just come so know what happened to the Buddhists in Vietnam on May 8, 1963, on the occasion of Lord Buddha's Birthday. The main reason is the order from Vietnam's President Diem forbidding the Buddhists to show their flag. The order was issued two days before the Birthday of the Buddha. But that is only the "drop that broke the dam."

The truth is that since the last five years, many things have happened and the Buddhist religion has been systematically suppressed and persecuted and the Roman Catholic religion has been encouraged and sponsored by the Diem regime. Eighty percent of the people of Vietnam are Buddhists, and these have been subjugated and terrorized by Diem who was foisted upon us by foreign powers who have created his police state.

Phu-Yen, Quang-Ngai and Binh-Dinh were the strongholds of Buddhism and the points of greatest persecution by Diem. Many followers and dignitaries of the Faith have been falsely accused, arrested, imprisoned and beaten, and many of them killed or buried alive. Thousands have been forced to pay money to the authorities for the privilege of worshiping in their pagodas. Thousands more have been uprooted from their homes in accordance with Diem's policy of dis-

---

[1] From "Buddhists Persecuted in Vietnam," *World Buddhism*, vol. 11, no. 11 (June, 1963), p. 13. Used by permission.

seminating Buddhist religious communities and destroying Buddhist communal life.

The cry of the victims and their complaints have remained unheard while the Government continues to give all privileges to the Roman Catholics, such as government land for church buildings, permitting their priests to exploit thousands of acres of forests tax free and hundreds of square miles of farm land.

The Army Engineers Corps has been constantly used by the Roman Catholic Church for constructing platforms and arches for their religious ceremonies. Military transportation has been utilized for constructing Roman Catholic churches and the town halls for celebrating Christmas while the Catholic flags are freely allowed to fly from public buildings. At the same time, Buddhists have been denied such privileges and instead systematically repressed. The separation of State and Church has been eliminated as is often the case where the Roman Catholic Church obtains power one way or another. . . .

The most recent massacre of faithful Buddhist innocents by the orders of Ngo-dinh-Canh, the brother of Diem and the virtual Dictator of Central Vietnam, was perpetrated by armed soldiers, in armored cars on the Buddhist followers who were innocently gathered at the Hue Radio station and its public address system to hear the devotional broadcast of Lord Buddha's Birthday Celebrations, when, to their amazement, the broadcast was cancelled and the Vietnamese troops under Major Dang-Si were told to shoot and the innocent tragically heard another kind of broadcast — the chatter of machine guns and the howling of the dying and wounded.

The latest report is that 12 were killed and 50 wounded. Whatever fabrication Diem's gagged press may put out about this heinous crime is false. The town of Hue is under martial law and helicopters are in the sky. Many hundreds of followers have been arrested and are even now silently being tortured and killed.

We, the miserable Buddhists of Vietnam, send this SOS to the Buddhists of the world and the great humanitarian leaders. We are paralyzed and are being falsely accused. Please help us and uphold the principle of religious freedom in this dark land.

We don't want Diem to use foreign-aid weapons and ammunition to kill us. We don't want to have Buddhist flags torn down in Vietnam. We don't want to have Buddhists, who are 80 percent of the country's population, subjugated and terrorized by a tyrant foisted upon us by foreign money and arms. The time of reckoning must come soon. Let those who have blindly helped the tyrant arise to clear themselves in the eyes of humanity or become permanently associated with him.

We thank all the governments of all the countries and humanitarian organizations who help us in this cause of religious freedom for the salvation of Buddhism in Vietnam.

2. Self-Immolation in the Buddhist Scriptures

Chapter 22 of the Sanskrit work, *The Lotus of the True Law*, records the self-sacrifice by burning of a Bodhisattva to honor the Lord and Tathagata (the Buddha). Note the glowing terms in which this act is praised.[2]

▶ ▶   After a while, the Bodhisattva rose from that meditation with memory and full consciousness, and reflected thus: "This display of magic power is not likely to honor the Lord and Tathagata so much as the sacrifice of my own body will do." Then the Bodhisattva instantly began to eat Agallochum, Olibanum, and the resin of Boswellia Thurifera, and to drink oil of Kampaka. So the Bodhisattva passed twelve years in always and constantly eating those fragrant substances and drinking oil of Kampaka. After the expiration of those twelve years the Bodhisattva wrapped his body in divine garments, bathed it in oil, made his (last) vow, and thereafter burnt his own body with the object to pay worship to the Tathagata and this Dharmaparyaya of the Lotus of the True Law. Then eighty worlds equal to the sands of the river Ganges were brightened by the glare of the flames from the blazing body of the Bodhisattva, and the eighty Lords Buddhas equal to the sands of the Ganges in those worlds all shouted their applause and exclaimed: "Well done, well done, young man of good family, that is the real heroism which the Boddhisattvas Mahasattvas should develop; that is the real worship of the Tathagata, the real worship of the law. No worshiping with flowers, incense, fragrant wreaths, ointment, powder, cloth, umbrellas, flags, banners; no worshipping with material gifts or with Uragasara sandal equals it. This, young man of good family, is the sublimest gift, higher than the abandoning of royalty, the abandoning of beloved children and wife. Sacrificing one's own body, young man of good family, is the most distinguished, the chiefest, the best, the very best, the most sublime worship of the law."

3. The Last Will of Ven. Thich Quang Duc

The first monk to make the supreme sacrifice on behalf of Vietnamese Buddhism gave the following will to his companions. He then sat

[2] From *The Saddharma-Pundarika or The Lotus of the True Law*, trans. by H. Kern (Delhi: Motilal Banarsidass, 1963), pp. 378–80.

down in the middle of a crowded Saigon street, poured gasoline over his body, and set fire to himself.[3]

▶ ▶   On seeing that Vietnamese Buddhism is being subjected to the most dangerous upheaval, I being an elder son of the Tathagatha, cannot remain a silent spectator of the destruction of the Buddha Dharma, willingly make the vow to burn this impermanent body of mine, as an offering to the Buddhas and as a dedication to the consolidation and protection of Buddhism.

May the Buddhas of ten quarters, may all ven. bhikkus [monks] and bhikkunis [nuns] be witness to my vow and help to fulfill my following wishes:

May the blessings of Lord Buddha give light to President Ngo Dinh Diem to grant the five minimum demands of the Buddhists as mentioned in their manifesto!

May Vietnamese Buddhism be lasting forever through the compassion of Lord Buddha!

May Lord Buddha protect all ven. bhikkhus, bhikkunis and all Vietnamese Buddhist followers from persecution, arrest and imprisonment by wicked people!

May peace and happiness be with the country, and people of Vietnam!

Before closing my eyes and returning to Buddha Land I have the honor of requesting President Ngo Dinh Diem to be compassionate and charitable to his people and enforce a policy of equality of religions so that our land be consolidated forever.

I earnestly appeal to all ven. bhikkus and bhikkunis and lay Buddhists to stand united and be ready for any sacrifice for the protection of Buddhism.

Homage to the ever victorious Buddha!

4. Troops Raid Pagodas, Centers of Opposition

The regime's massive attacks on the pagodas, August 20–21, 1963, marked a desperate attempt to silence the Buddhist opposition. This action, however, cost the regime whatever support it still had, both internally and externally. Rumors of a military *coup d'êtat*, referred to in the following report, materialized a little over two months later.[4]

---

[3] From *World Buddhism*, vol. 12, no. 2 (September, 1963), p. 27. Used by permission.

[4] From "Troops and Police Raid Pagodas," *World Buddhism*, vol. 12, no. 2 (September, 1963), pp. 16–18. Used by permission.

▶ ▶   Troops in camouflage uniforms and steel-helmeted riot police stormed Buddhist pagodas in Saigon and took over the post office and other key points as martial law was declared in South Vietnam. As the troops fanned out over the city, the official Vietnam Press Agency said the Roman Catholic President, Ngo Dinh Diem, had signed a decree declaring a state of seige throughout the territory of South Vietnam. The Government threw out a complete communications blackout after Government troops cleaned out the five main pagodas in Saigon. Foreign correspondents were not allowed to get any information out of the country. . . .

Hundreds of heavily-armed troops and police, firing pistol shots and using tear gas bombs and hand grenades, swarmed into the main Xa Loi Pagoda and arrested the monks. Troops also raided three other pagodas in Saigon in the most serious flare-up of violence in the fifteen-week dispute between the Government and the Buddhist majority. The sudden crackdown on Buddhist headquarters led Western observers to believe that the crisis might have reached a climax.

Diem's brother Ngo Dinh Nhu's wife, the beautiful and politically powerful Madame Nhu, has been the most outspoken critic of the Buddhist protests. A Catholic convert from Buddhism, she has said she had no sympathy with Buddhists who "barbecue" themselves in fiery immolations.

Violence was also centered in the ancient capital of Hue, site of the country's biggest University. Professors at the University resigned and said they would stay off their jobs until the Government settled the crisis. The Catholic authorities in Saigon deemed it necessary to issue a Pastoral letter declaring that the Catholic Church is not involved in the dispute. . . .

There were strong signs of dissension in the armed forces and some diplomatic observers forecast a possible coup d'état soon. Police were believed searching for Ven. Thich Tri Quang, Chief Monk, regarded as the Buddhists' underground leader, who apparently escaped the dragnet.

Saigon police carried out mass arrests of Opposition leaders, Buddhist sympathizers and intellectuals, and raided several of the city's smaller pagodas. Throughout the city many Buddhists and other important Vietnamese were reported in hiding, staying in friends' homes. It was unknown what the authorities had done with many hundreds of Buddhist monks and nuns seized during raids. But eye witnesses reported seeing a number in a Saigon hospital with wound apparently inflicted with shot-guns during the raids.

In Hue 500 laymen had been arrested in a bitter riot in which some 6,000 people fought with the police. The riots followed the sacking of the Tu Dam Pagoda, which was later gutted. Government forces also seized the bodies of monks who had committed suicide. Government forces seized pagodas throughout the country at about the same time as the action in Hue. In several cities there were similar riots. . . .

Hundreds of heavily armed government troops and police also carried out mass arrests of students at checkpoints in Cholon and the Saigon University campus area. Eyewitnesses estimate that the number had reached more than a thousand. The mass arrests appeared to be an all-out action by President Diem's regime to crush agitating Saigon University students who had become the latest spearhead in the opposition to the Government now that the Buddhist leadership had been smashed.

Warnings of more protest suicides and demonstrations against the government were given by Buddhist leaders at Hue. Thirteen Buddhist students in that northern city volunteered to commit suicide in protest against the Government's religious discrimination. The latest warning came in a letter to the Provincial Governor from Buddhist leaders demanding the return of the body of a novice monk who burned himself to death. Government troops forcibly seized the 17-year-old novice's body after he killed himself at a pagoda outside Hue.

South Vietnam's Foreign Minister, Mr. Vu Van Mau, shaved his head like a Buddhist monk and tendered his resignation to protest against the policy of the Catholic-led Government which has swooped on Buddhists and declared martial law. He wanted to go to India and become a Buddhist monk.

Asked why he had shaved his head, Mau replied that he had handed in his resignation "to protest against the Government" and had shaved his head to express his sympathy with other Buddhists in the country. Mr. Mau, a quiet, reserved man who has served President Ngo Dinh Diem faithfully for years is a devout Buddhist and was shocked by the crackdown. A disclosure that Mr. Mau was arrested threatened to trigger more anti-Government demonstrations by students.

Mr. Tran Van Chuong, South Vietnamese Ambassador to the United States, also resigned. He said in a statement: "I cannot go on representing a Government which ignores my advice and of which I disapprove." Ambassador Chuong disavowed anti-Buddhist statements made by his daughter [Madame Nhu] and accused her of "lack of respect" for Vietnam's Buddhist majority.

Many foreign observers regard this as one of the first open signs of crumbling within the ruling circle.

FATHER TORRES AND GUERRILLA WARFARE IN COLOMBIA

Camilo Torres, born into an influential aristocratic family, entered the priesthood, studied sociology at the University of Louvain in Belgium, and returned to Colombia committed to radical social change. Starting with the idea that "love thy neighbor" is the very center of Christian ethics, Torres examined the reality of the hierarchical Colombian society, with its impoverished and powerless masses, and decided that any serious application of the Christian ethic could only mean revolution. Excerpts from his writings on these subjects are found in readings IX.8 and X.3.

Since Colombia's socio-economic structures were so oppressive and dehumanizing, they had to be overthrown. And since Marxists and other revolutionaries had come to similar conclusions, there was, Torres thought, a solid basis for cooperation. However, he met with bitter disappointments in attempting to bring together the disparate ideological elements in a United Front. The decision to opt for the role of guerrilla fighter drastically shortened his career, for he was killed a few months later. But Camilo Torres has become a powerful symbol of revolutionary change throughout Latin America.

5. Early Support from the Social Christian Democrats

Camilo received early support for his leftist platform from various groups in the small Christian Democratic movement in Colombia. Much of the support was soon lost, however, as the United Front came increasingly under Marxist control.[5]

▶ ▶   The Social Christian Democratic Party of Manizales, considering:

1. That the socio-economic theses expressed by Father Camilo Torres have wakened an unusual reaction of alarm within the oligarchy represented in the companies, the press, and the high ecclesiastical hierarchy.

2. That these theses are a faithful interpretation of the Christian thought expressed in the Encyclicals.

3. That the myth of Communism has stopped being an effective weapon of the oligarchy for combating those nonconformists who are simply claiming justice.

---

[5] From *Camilo Torres* by German Guzman. Sheed and Ward, Inc., 1969, pp. 168–69. Used by permission.

4. That the vindication of the people demands the integration of all groups and all progressive and revolutionary persons in only one front; and declares:

1. That the Social Christian Democratic party of Manizales identifies itself with the socio-economic Platform of this illustrious priest; and at the same time that it offers its spiritual and material endorsement, it condemns the ill-intentioned reaction of those who retain power and exploit the Colombian people in an inhuman and anti-Christian way.

2. That the attitude of certain people who call themselves Christians and deliberately refuse to recognize everything from the works of mercy to the pontifical documents is irresponsible.

3. That the people no longer fear the oligarchy nor the epithet of Communist, and they have decided to fight for their rights, call them what you wish.

4. Lastly, the Christian Social Democratic Party of Manizales feels itself obliged to issue a call to all the peasant worker organizations and to all conscientious men, so that, forgetting differences, we might constitute one front in the fight for a system which guarantees the dignity of the human person and the social, economic, cultural, and political progress of the country.

6. Camilo Torres' Call to Arms

In January 1966, Camilo Torres announced that he had joined the Army of National Liberation fighting in the mountains. He issued this call for a revolutionary uprising against the oligarchy on all fronts.[6]

Colombians:

For many years the poor of our country have awaited the battlecry to hurl themselves against the oligarchy.

In those moments when the desperation of the people became extreme, the ruling class has always found some way to deceive the people, to distract them, to pacify them with new slogans which always come to the same: suffering for the people and well-being for the privileged caste.

When the people asked for a leader and found him in Jorge Eliécer Gaitán, the oligarchy killed him. When the people asked for peace, the oligarchy sowed violence in the countryside. When the people no longer

---

[6] From *Camilo Torres, Por el Padre Camilo Torres Restrepo (1956–1966)* (Cuernavaca, Mexico: Centro Intercultural de Documentación, 1966), pp. 42, 375–77. Used by permission. Translated by the editor.

resisted violence and organized guerrilla warfare in order to seize power, the oligarchy attempted the military coup so that the guerrilla fighters, deceived, would surrender. When the people asked for democracy they were again deceived with a plebiscite and a National Front which imposed on them the dictatorship of the oligarchy.

Now the people will not believe any more. The people do not believe in elections. The people know that the legal ways are exhausted. The people know that only the armed way remains. The people are desperate and determined to risk their lives so that the next generation of Colombians not be one of slaves. So that the sons of those who now want to give their lives may have education, housing, food, clothing and, above all, dignity. So that future Colombians may have their own country, independent of the North American empire.

Every sincere revolutionary has to recognize the armed way as the only one which remains. Nevertheless, the people expect the leaders, by their example and presence, to raise the battlecry.

I want to say to the Colombian people that the moment has come. I have not betrayed them. I have traversed the public squares of the towns and cities on behalf of the unity and the organization of the masses for the seizure of power. I have asked that we dedicate ourselves to these objectives unto death.

All is now prepared. The oligarchy wants to organize another comedy of elections; with candidates who withdraw and then run again; with bipartisan committees; with movements of renewal based on ideas and persons that are not only old but have betrayed the people. What more are we waiting for, Colombians?

I have joined the armed struggle. From the Colombian mountains I plan to continue the struggle with weapons in hand, until power is won for the people. I have joined the Army of National Liberation because in it I found the same ideals of the United Front. I found the desire and the fulfillment of a unity at the base, the peasant base, without religious differences or differences of traditionalist parties. Without any desire to fight the revolutionary elements of any sector, movement or party which without bosses seeks to liberate the people from exploitation, the oligarchies and imperialism. [Revolutionary elements] will not lay down their weapons until power is entirely in the hands of the people. . . .

For the seizure of power for the masses, to the death!

To the death, because we are determined to go to the end.

To victory, for once a people commits itself unto the death it always achieves victory.

To final victory, with the watchword of the Army of National Liberation.

Not one step back . . . liberation or death!

7. Eulogy for a Fallen Fighter-Priest

Reactions to Camilo's death ranged from the severest denunciations of him as a Marxist in religious habit who had received the fate he deserved, to extravagant eulogies. Father Carlos Pérez Herrera, press secretary of the Archdiocesan Curia of Panama, issued the following statement. [7]

▶ ▶ Free men of America have the right to lament the death of Father Camilo Torres Restrepo which occurred, according to the dispatches of the UPI, in a battle with the regular army in the mountains of Santander. Father Torres believed in insurrection as the only way to redeem a people hungry for bread and thirsty for justice; and like the Mexican clerics, precursors of emancipation, Camilo has paid for his rebellion with his life in a sacrifice which will be appreciated in its just dimensions for generations to come.

To be silent before the death of the recently sacrificed Colombian priest would seem to be the most prudent thing in order to avoid nasty epithets and bitter criticism. But silence would be hypocritical and lacking in courage.

In history we frequently have the case of soldiers who change the uniform of the soldier for the religious habit. To exchange the habit of the cleric for the uniform of the guerrilla is less frequent. Father Camilo sought from the ecclesiastical authority the release from his ministry in order to launch the fight against misery from an angle which until now is reserved for political revolutionaries.

Then he abandoned the city in order to fight in the mountains next to the guerrillas. If it had been possible for us, we would have reminded Father Torres that clerics are not military men nor do we know military strategy.

Mistaken or not, Father Camilo embraced as an idealist the warlike projection of his social apostolate in the uneven fight between the public forces at the service of the oligarchy and a handful of idealists who raised the standard of justice for the people. Mistaken or not, Father Torres

[7] From *Camilo Torres* by German Guzman,   Sheed and Ward, Inc., 1969, pp. 270–71. Used by permission.

left the newspaper conflicts and his university conferences in order to try to obtain in the mountains that which he could not obtain from the pages of his periodical or in the academic halls. Mistaken or not, Father Torres preferred to be called a Communist rather than remain silent before the lack of social sensibility of a society which is resisting the Christian message of justice and charity. Mistaken or not, Father Torres has opened up a high road on which many idealists who seek justice will walk. Therefore, before the remains of the visionary who dreamed of a free people, healthy and productive, we are reverent, humbly asking God for eternal rest for the priest, the guerrilla, the patriot who has fallen wrapped in a blood-stained banner on Colombian soil.

MUSLIM BROTHERHOOD AND COUP ATTEMPTS IN U.A.R.

The Muslim Brotherhood was founded in 1928 by an Egyptian schoolteacher, Hasan al-Banna. Originally a nonpolitical organization striving by indoctrination of its followers to restructure Muslim society along fundamentalist Islamic lines, toward the end of World War II the Brotherhood shifted its emphasis to direct political action and began to function as a political party. While its ideology was neotraditionalist, it was severely critical of the *ulama* for their lethargy, and utilized modern organizational means to pursue its objectives. Like Maulana Maudoodi in India, who was influenced by it, the Brotherhood has reserved its fiercest attacks for the secular nationalists. (See reading IV.6.)

The Brotherhood developed a mass following in Egypt, Sudan, and Syria. It has been characterized at times by unyielding fanaticism and the use of terrorism and political assassination. Its ideology and rhetoric has made much of the symbol of an Islamic Revolution, which must first destroy existing regimes, whether traditionalist, modernist, or secularist, in order to build on their ashes a truly Islamic state and society.

8. The Muslim Brotherhood and the Egyptian Revolution

The Ikhwan-ul-Muslimun, or Muslim Brotherhood, a movement of radical Islamic ideology, played a major role in political events leading to the Egyptian Revolution of 1952. This pro-Brotherhood account traces its relations with the revolutionary regime from an initial tacit alliance to protracted hostility and conflict.[8]

---

[8] From Khalil Hamidi, "The Movement of Al-Ikhwan-ul-Muslimun," *Muslimnews International*, vol. 5, no. 4 (October, 1966), pp. 18, 40. Used by permission.

▶ ▶   [In] July 1952 . . . the Egyptian army gave the tottering [Farouk] regime its *coup de grace*. The relations between the army and the Ikhwan [Brotherhood] were of sufficient standing. Anwar-us-Saadat, now a Vice President in the present government, writes: "The party most anxious to fight a *Jihad* in Palestine was the Ikhwan. . . . On the eve of the troops' departure for Palestine Hasan Al-Banna and Sheikh Farghali addressed the volunteers as a result of which the latter's enthusiasm knew no bounds. . . . During the guerrilla operations in Suez the army officers and the Ikhwan came into close contact and this cemented their relations. . . . A group in the Egyptian army regarded the Ikhwan as the only hope for the liberation of Egypt." (Anwar-us-Saadat's Diary, pp. 177, 180, 156)

    The Ikhwan actively supported the army in staging the Revolution. The success of the Revolution depended largely also on the dislike and hate that the teachings and struggle of the Ikhwan had implanted in the hearts of the people. . . . During this period the Ikhwan also helped the Revolutionary government keep the law and order situation well in hand and this was duly acknowledged by the revolutionaries.

    For a considerable period after the Revolution the two movements cooperated with each other.

    But it was not possible for long to reconcile the objectives of a dynamic, comprehensive, essentially Islamic movement with those of the hot-headed, impatient and materialistic young revolutionaries who, as it appeared later, considered Islam not as a doctrine to be practised but as a cover to make their own appeal acceptable to the people of Egypt. Differences arose, firstly, when the Ikhwan refused to accept three posts in the Cabinet which were offered to them. Hasan al-Hodeiby was not prepared to merge his movement with the Revolution. He said that he wanted to be left free to support the Government as a well wisher but also to criticize it when it did not follow the right course. The second point of difference was one of principle. The Ikhwan demanded that the whole nation and specially the youth should be educated and trained on Islamic lines so that they may be relied on to promulgate a truly Islamic order in the country. They also demanded an end to the gambling dens and imposition of prohibition. The government was not prepared to accept any but a few minor demands of the Ikhwan. The third point of fundamental importance related to the question of giving the country a new constitution. When Hasan al-Hodeiby realized that the Committee formed to frame one was loaded in favor of the secularists he demanded a referendum to ascertain whether the people preferred the promulgation of an Islamic Constitution and laws or whether they would follow the revolution blindly. This was the parting of ways between the parties.

On December 10, 1952, the old Constitution was abrogated and on January 16, 1953, all political parties in the country were dissolved. Resisting the demands of hot heads in his own party Hasan Al-Hodeiby wrote to the government that he protested against regarding the Ikhwan merely as a political party for they had a more comprehensive program than simply fighting the elections and forming governments. He intimated the Ikhwan would not take part in the elections. Then on January 23, 1953, the government formed its own party as the single political party in the country and invited the leaders and workers of other parties to join it. Hasan Al-Hodeiby refused to merge his party in the government's.

The relations had become so strained by now that the government seemed to be seeking an opportunity to settle accounts. This they got when the Ikhwan opposed mere talk with the British Government to settle the problem of the evacuation of British troops. They were, they said, not prepared to accept any condition that may provide a loophole for the British to re-station their troops in Egypt. They said that evacuation must be complete and unconditional. In the course of these public exchanges one Mr. Evans of the British embassy met Hasan al-Hodeiby to discuss matters with him. The latter, as Evans also corroborates, fully supported the government's stand. To be extra careful he called Major Salah Salem and gave him a full report of what had transpired between him and Evans. But the government made great propaganda out of the meeting labeling it as a conference of conspiracy between the Ikhwan and the British.

The crisis now was fast approaching. On January 12, 1954, some Ikhwan students were fired upon from a jeep belonging to the government party and the Ikhwan returned the fire. The Government outlawed the Ikhwan, arrested its leaders, and General Naguib who had led the Revolution was dismissed by the Revolutionary Council. But there were immediate repercussions. There were riots all over the country and even the army was divided. Naguib had to be reinstated again and withdrew the decree banning political parties. But three days later the government party engineered extensive riots and the political situation deteriorated. Gamal Abdul Nasser was hankering after such an opportunity and he with a military Junta to back him overthrew Naguib and assumed full powers himself.

It was this Junta which on September 1, 1954 reached an agreement with Britain for the evacuation of the Canal Zone but also providing its reoccupation by the British army in certain contingencies. The Ikhwan denounced and totally rejected the agreement as substracting from full Egyptian sovereignty. In these conditions the struggle between the Junta and the Ikhwan entered a crucial stage. On October 24, 1954, there was an attempt to assassinate Nasser and the Ikhwan were chosen as the scapegoat, charged with conspiracy to murder Nasser. Thousands of innocent persons were arrested, tortured and victimized. The Ikhwan leaders were tried and six of them including the great Muslim jurist and judge Abdul Qader Audah were sentenced to death and executed. The drama of persecution of the Ikhwan has been since repeated from time to time and has very recently concluded in another bloodstained last act. [A reference to the execution of Sayyid Qutb in 1966.]

9. U.A.R. Report on the Muslim Brotherhood

In December 1965, the Legislative Committee of the United Arab Republic National Assembly issued a lengthy report on the activities of the Brotherhood and recommended passage of a bill giving the President powers to enforce special penalties against its members with no right of appeal. The report attempted to prove the Republics' loyalty to Islam, and the Brotherhood's distortion of it and rejection of Arab nationalism, culminating in crimes of conspiracy against the state.[9]

▶ ▶   The Committee noted that most of these cases of conspiracy were perpetrated by a group known as the "Muslim Brotherhood." Before examining this law and expressing its opinion, the Committee felt that its first duty was to analyze this group which has done so much harm to religion, turning it into a slogan and a facade to mask their real motives and aims. Its precepts were misinterpreted and distorted and its sublime and divine wisdom perverted. Their aim was to arrest development and progress and to deprive the people of their hard-won gains, acting as agents of imperialism and reaction.

Reaction, in its various forms and at various stages, has attempted to depict religion as a purely spiritual force, divorced from life and its problems. It has gone even further and attempted to make religion seem to contradict science, knowledge and progress. The policy of the Muslim Brotherhood was one such reactionary attempt which challenged an accepted fact, namely, that the core of divine revelation does not contradict the facts of life. Rather, such conflict only arises when reaction

---

[9] From "Report by the Legislative Committee of the U.A.R. National Assembly on the Republican Law Regarding the Muslim Brotherhood," in Walid Khalid and Yusuf Ibish, eds., *Arab Political Documents, 1965* (Beirut: Political Studies and Public Administration Department, American University of Beirut, 1966), pp. 453–56. Used by permission.

attempts to misuse the nature and spirit of religion to impede progress, by concocting interpretations of religion which conflict with divine wisdom.

The Charter of the U.A.R. brought out the importance of religion, believing it to be an essential part of the popular struggle, to guarantee the Arab people of Egypt a total revolution for the freedom of our homeland and our citizens, and to build a society based on self-sufficiency and justice. The Charter lays down that one of the essential factors of this revolution is "an unshakeable faith in God, His Prophets and their sacred revelations sent to humanity for their true guidance in every time and place. . . ."

The principles of the Brotherhood stem from a series of epistles and books which they have adopted as their ideology and as their manual of conspiratorial action. Their hatred of society and their call to sever all contacts with it, their desire to throw society back into a state of regression, poverty and underdevelopment, their plots against the state — this has been the inspiration for their actions. In these epistles and books they strive to interpret religion and the Holy Qur'an in a contradictory and deceptive manner, and try to misrepresent the true call of Islam and its genuinely progressive nature by inventing antireligious interpretations. To sum up, their teachings point to the following:

1. Denial of Arab Nationalism. In one of their books they state that "the Prophet Muhammad could have turned his mission into an Arab nationalist one, seeking to unify the tribes of Arabia and to raise high the banner of Arabism in order to establish a national unity throughout the Peninsula. But God Almighty did not so direct His Messenger because He knew that this was not the way, and that men should not merely pass from Byzantine or Persian tyranny into Arab tyranny." In their view, the Arab nationalist call is one that is not sanctioned by God because it represents Arab tyranny, on an equal footing with Byzantine or Persian tyranny.

2. Their defence of class divisions and exploitation. They state that, "God sent forth His Messenger with this religion when Arab society was at its worst and when a handful owned all the wealth and commerce and the vast majority were poor and hungry. It may be said that the Prophet could have made his call a social one and advocated a reform of conditions and the handing over to the poor of the wealth of the rich. But God Almighty in His wisdom did not direct His Prophet in this path for He knew that this was not the true path." This in effect implies that God shuns social justice and does not want His Prophet to espouse it. It also means that in their view, Islam believes in the division of classes. . . .

3. Rejection of patriotism, the family and relatives. The Brotherhood holds patriotism, the family and relatives as of no account. In their view: "The homeland of the Muslim for which he longs and which he defends is not a plot of land; the nationality of the Muslim is not a juridical one, the tribe of the Muslim is not one of blood relationship; the flag that the Muslim fight for and for which he lays down his life is not a national flag; the victory of the Muslim to which he aspires, and for which he thanks God, is not the victory of an army." For "the ties of clan, tribe, nation, race, colour and land are small, divergent and ignorant."

4. The destruction of society. In one of their books they state that "the rebirth of Islam begins from a small group which detaches itself from ignorant society (i.e., any society which does not owe them allegiance) and fights against it. It recognizes neither homeland, nor family, nor law, nor custom, and knows only one thing: a violent destruction which shatters everything in its path. All the apparatus of governments must be totally destroyed for they are ignorant, even those which claim to be Islamic in their charters and constitutions, and even those whose members believe in God but accept what they term political or collective leadership. . . ."

The Brotherhood strives to gain power by bloodshed, destruction and ruin. For this they employ their secret apparatus and turn to treason by cooperating with imperialism and reaction. The Brotherhood has adopted terror as their norm of action and their philosophy. They misrepresent Qur'anic verses concerning "Jihad" (Holy War). Their terror was not directed against the soldiers of foreign occupation but against innocent citizens. The Brotherhood tried to impose their mandate upon the Revolution, but the Revolution, which arose with no other backing than the expression of the needs and will of the masses to remove the yoke of imperialism and reaction, could not accept the patronage of the Brotherhood. When the Brotherhood realized that the Revolution was serious in its intention to carry out its six principles, especially in the destruction of imperialism and its Egyptian agents, feudalism, monopolies and capitalism, it plotted against the Revolution in a criminal alliance with reaction and imperialism. Then the Government was forced to face the situation with firmness, for it was convinced that there must be no new reactionary tragedy perpetrated in the name of religion, that no one could be allowed to trifle with this country's destiny because of a private whim, and that religion must not be pressed into service for private ends. Therefore, the Council for the Revolutionary Command issued a decree on January 14, 1954, dissolving the Brotherhood.

Meanwhile their secret apparatus was planning to incite civil war and spread panic, to assassinate the leader of the Revolution and gain power, in order to prevent the Revolution from following its natural course. God protected the Revolution and its leader from their plots and the Brotherhood suffered the consequences of their criminal acts. When the Brotherhood was dissolved and their secret agents were put on trial, the country went on from one triumph to the next. . . .

Our people were forgiving. Many of those convicted of terrorism and sabotage were pardoned. The Government even went so far as to restore their jobs to them, as decreed in Law No. 176 in 1960. But it appears that this group were not really willing to mend their ways. . . . President Nasser declared the suspension of martial law in March, 1964, and the release of all detainees, so that all citizens, even those who had consciously harmed their country's interests, could join in the building up of our new society, based on social justice and equality of opportunity — principles which stem from Islam. Despite all this, a conspiracy was uncovered in August, planned by the outlawed Muslim Brotherhood. Secret organizations were unveiled, weapons and explosives were discovered. Their money was supplied by Sa'id Ramadan, a member of the Brotherhood who had fled the country and was plotting against the people's Revolution in collusion with imperialism and reaction. The confessions made by members of the Brotherhood indicated that they were plotting to blow up buildings and installations built through our people's hard work, such as at Qanater al Khairiyya, the Electric Power Station for north Cairo, the main Telephone Exchange, Cairo International Airport and the TV and radio stations. They also planned to assassinate the ambassadors of the Soviet Union, the U.S.A., the U.K. and France in order to incite a series of crises with these states. The signal to begin was to have been the assassination of President Nasser. But God Almighty protected Egypt, its Revolution and its leader.

VI

Religion
and
Party
Politics

There are two major kinds of phenomena involving religion and party politics in the Third World: the religious political party and the religious issue in elections contested by secular parties.

The widespread tendency for religions to find political expression through parties attests to the continued vitality of comprehensive religious values for many in the Third World, and the refusal to relegate religion solely to the sphere of private faith and practice. There are Hindu, Islamic, and Catholic political parties, and if we were to move beyond the scope of this book, we would include Orthodox religious parties in Israel and a vigorous Mahayana Buddhist party in Japan.

We must distinguish at least three kinds of religious political parties. *Communal parties*, such as the Hindu Mahasabha or the Jana Sangh in India, spring up in the context of religious pluralism. They do not offer a formulated ideology, for their basic *raison d'ètre* derives from conflict with other religious communities; their primary function is to protect and promote the largely secular economic and political interests of their respective communal groups. Both the Hindu Mahasabha and the Muslim League in prepartition India were communal parties in this sense. (On communal conflict, see Chapter VII.)

The *sect-based party*, such as the Ummah in Sudan, is somewhat similar, but represents one segment of the larger religious community. While the entire northern part of the Sudan is solidly Muslim, the Ummah became the political expression of the Ansar sect, founded by the Mahdi in the nineteenth century.

Finally, there are *ideological religious parties*, traditionalist or modernizing, generally functioning in societies in which the religious minorities are politically unimportant. These parties are not oriented to communal group conflict, but to the ideological assumptions which shape society. Among the traditionalist parties are the Latin American Conservative parties, especially of thirty or more years ago; among the modernizing parties of religious ideology are the Christian Democrats in Chile and the Masjumi in Indonesia.

Even where religious political parties are nonexistent, and this has been the case most notably in the Theravada Buddhist countries of Burma and Ceylon, religious issues can become so important as to decide major elections. In such cases, the basically secular parties must choose sides. In Burma, U Nu's faction of the secular Anti-Fascist People's Freedom League (AFPFL) gradually responded to the premier's emphasis on religious revival and successfully waged the 1960 election campaign on the pledge to make Buddhism the state religion. In Ceylon the Sri Lanka Freedom Party (SLFP), which had no formal Buddhist identity, became strongly committed to the Buddhist cause in the 1956 and 1960 election campaigns.

In many cases, of course, including some we shall examine here, *both* religious political parties and religious issues have been crucial factors in important elections.

BUDDHISM AND POLITICAL PARTIES IN CEYLON

The interrelated issues of religion and language dominated the 1956 general elections. The SLFP led by S. W. R. D. Bandaranaike, and the electoral coalition he put together, pledged themselves to restore Buddhism to its "rightful place" in national life. A major catalyst in bringing the religious issue to the forefront was the publication of a report entitled *The Betrayal of Buddhism*. Prepared by a committee of the All-Ceylon Buddhist Congress, a vigorous pressure group, the report set forth in systematic and forceful fashion the grievances and demands of the Buddhists. In the campaign, Bandaranaike's coalition, the MEP, was ably aided by a well-organized association of Buddhist monks, the United Monks Front. Various segments of the lower middle class were strongly attracted by Bandaranaike's emphasis on language and religion.

Bandaranaike's promises to the Buddhists were largely fulfilled under his administration (1956–1959) and, after his assassination, the administration of his wife, Mrs. Sirimao Bandaranaike (1960–1965). The continuing influence of religion on party politics, however, was revealed by the consequences of her decision in 1964 to bring three Marxist cabinet ministers into a government pledged to the promotion of Buddhism. This decision produced a chain of events which led to her defeat in the elections of 1965.

1. The Betrayal of Buddhism

The major thesis of this report was that great damage had been inflicted on Buddhism over four hundred years of foreign rule and that Christianity, and particularly the Roman Catholic church, had been strongly favored by government policy. Eight years after independence the situation remained unchanged. The ruling United National Party (UNP), although not named in the report, was held responsible. The UNP was generally supported by the westernized upper-middle class and by the Catholics (7 percent of the population). [1]

Of all religious bodies, the Roman Catholic Church is the wealthiest and has the largest sources of wealth, and yet receives most State aid. In addition to the estates it owns, it also engages in certain types of trade, and in business ventures. . . . Annually the Church adds a large acreage to its possessions and acquires shares in the business organizations of the country. Commercial and agricultural activities are an important part of church activity, and thus the Roman Catholic Church is the largest commercial organization in the country. [p. 20]

Democracy in Ceylon is faced today with the gravest danger it can know from religious bodies corrupted with wealth and power. The Colonial Government in 1846 saw a Central Buddhist Committee even under Government supervision, capable of "mischievous influence." How much greater is the danger of centralized religious organizations, incorporated by law with no checks on their power in a democratic state yet in its infancy? A powerful political party controlled by a few leaders may control parliament through members whose nominations are decided by a few party bosses, who hold the party funds. An election is

---

[1] From *The Betrayal of Buddhism: An Abridged Version of the Report of the Buddhist Committee of Inquiry* (Colombo: All-Ceylon Buddhist Congress, 1956), pp. 20, 24, 31, 35, 123–24. Used by permission.

usually won today not on the merits of individual candidates nor on the merits of a party program but on the amount of propaganda, the organization and the expenditure that a party can command. A party without funds is generally helpless at an election, however good its policy may be. This gives a corporation, unrestricted in its powers, the chance of interfering. If it has the money to use for the purpose, it can control the press and thereby control opinion. It can finance the ruling party and thereby control the elections. It can influence Ministers and through them control the Government machine. It can influence public officers and bend the administration to its will. The danger is all the greater in a country like Ceylon where a large section of the voters do not understand the working of a democracy. . . . [p. 24] Over Ceylon, Christianity sits enthroned, and Ceylon bound hand and foot has been delivered at the foot of the Cross. [p. 31]

The manner in which the State provides money to the Christian religious bodies from the Government funds makes the professed religious neutrality of the Government a pure fiction. Schools, orphanages, crêches, have to conform to standards that are beyond the means of any but the organized religio-political commercial corporations. Today the Buddhists lack the capital and the organization to establish the educational and other social service institutions necessary for their needs and the reasons have been to a great extent beyond the control of the Buddhists. [p. 35]

It has become almost an occupational disease among our politicians and other public personages today to exhort the Buddhist public on every conceivable occasion to be tolerant. In their ignorance, whether wilful or unwitting, of our island's past history these gentlemen are deserving of our sympathy, indeed, of our tolerance.

For what is the history of Ceylon during the last four hundred years but a long and poignant chronicle of Buddhist tolerance in the face of oppression and injustice? Who but the Buddhists tolerated harassment by the Roman Catholic Portuguese to give shelter and employment to Muslims? Or endured similar treatment from the Dutch to shelter Roman Catholics? Who but the Buddhists tolerated the rank injustice of the foreign rulers who used the revenue from one of the most sacred places of Buddhist worship, the Dalada Maligawa [Temple of the Tooth], to pay for the construction of St. Paul's Cathedral? Or the like injustice of destroying a Buddhist Vihara in Kotte to erect in its stead a Christian school? Who but the Buddhists tolerated the extortion from them of four hundred pounds a year for the building of Christian churches?

In 1884 all the Government schools, which were the only schools to which the Buddhists could send their children for higher education, were handed over to the Christian missionaries. Up till 1886 Buddhists paid by far the largest amount for the maintenance of the Ecclesiastical Department.

The undertaking to maintain the Buddhist religion given in 1815 has been and is being grossly betrayed.

In the face of all this high-handedness, this riding roughshod by foreign rulers and native henchmen alike of even their most elementary human rights, when their religion was being denounced as a heathen myth, their educational institutions ruined by neglect or deliberate discrimination and their Sangha subjected to insult and humiliation, what did the Buddhists show except tolerance towards the tyrants and their helpers?

Almost every page of this Report bears witness to the extent and duration of Buddhist tolerance.

And yet, fully eight years after this country is alleged to have gained her independence, when the Buddhists ask for some of that justice which has been denied to them for centuries, they are characterized as a truculent majority and asked to show tolerance. By a flagrant disregard of historical fact and contemporary reality, the Buddhists are made to appear in the light of domineering tyrants. . . .

In its travels in various parts of the island, the Committee had ample opportunities to observe at first hand the harassment and obstruction placed in the way of Buddhists in all spheres of life, education, social services, hospitals and so on. The time has emphatically arrived when the Buddhists need to be strong, united and steadfast for the struggle.

But we wish to state with all the authority at our command that this struggle which the Buddhists must make is not a struggle to obtain a favored position at the expense of other religious groups, however much we may have suffered at their hands in former times. We ask for no favors and we expect none. But we do ask for and expect the right to a decent education for our children, the right to save our country from becoming an Eastern outpost of the Vatican, the right to be allowed to profess and practice our religion without let or hindrance, material or spiritual, secular or religious in a free and democratic Ceylon. [pp. 123–24]

2. An Interpretation of the 1956 Elections

The 1956 elections resulted in an overwhelming victory for S. W. R. D. Bandaranaike's coalition, the MEP, which was pledged to the promotion of Sinhalese as the official language and to the restoration of Buddhism to its "rightful place." Shortly after the election, a Ceylonese historian, Dr. G. C. Mendis, analyzed the social, psychological, and religious base of the new political forces.[2]

▶ ▶ Many will agree that there has been a revolutionary change this year in the sphere of politics. A government which had some continuity for over twenty-five years has been wholly overthrown, and a new government with a new outlook and new ideas has come into power. The English-educated class, with its doctors, lawyers, schoolmasters, planters and businessmen, have lost their leadership over the country, and their place in the villages has been taken by the Buddhist monk, the Sinhalese schoolmaster, and the ayurvedic physician. . . .

But what is most remarkable is that the results of the General Election took by surprise not only the defeated but even the victorious, and the ordinary people who could not account for the change thought it was the work of the gods. This shows that we have to search deeper for the causes of this rejection of one section of the middle class and the enthronement of another. What is the significance of this change? [pp. 117–118]

[Under British rule, far-reaching reforms undermined the traditional political, economic, and social system of Ceylon.] But the river of life as a whole stirred little. The current moved mainly on the surface and did not penetrate very much deeper than the English-educated middle class with its new ideas, new economic interests and new forms of life. The section of the people, once they realized their power, began to oppose foreign rule and demand self-government. But the British were not prepared to hand over to them the governmental system they developed unless it was representative of the people as a whole. They granted adult franchise [in 1931] and placed the ultimate responsibility for the government of the country on the entire community. The English-educated class was not deterred by this step. The grant of the adult franchise did not lead to a sudden awakening of the masses as the privilege did not come to them as a result of an agitation on their part. The English-educated class thought out the grounds on which they could solicit the support of the people and put forward their programs. They extended their organizations and did much, with the

---

[2] From G. C. Mendis, "The Revolution of 1956," *The Times of Ceylon*, October 20, 1956. Reprinted in G. C. Mendis, *Ceylon Today and Yesterday* (Colombo: Associated Newspapers of Ceylon, Ltd., 1957), pp. 117–18, 120–23. Used by permission of Lake House Investments Limited, Colombo.

revenues at their disposal, for the betterment of the people in the spheres of education and health as well as in improving labor and economic conditions.

What then was the cause of the political change that took place this year? Was it due to independence as some think? If so, why did the change not take place earlier? Was it due to an awakening of the masses? If so, why was the change in the first budget of the new Government mainly in the interest of the lower middle class? The landslide in the last General Election was due mainly to the fact that there was yet another class who made some progress under British rule, but who felt at the same time that they were doomed to suffer, if not meet with extinction, as a result of recent developments. This is a class between the upper middle class and the masses in general, consisting of the Buddhist monks, the ayurvedic physicians, the Sinhalese schoolmasters and the unemployed persons educated by them.

What were the grievances of the Buddhist monks? Before British rule, they were the leaders of thought in the country, and most of the literary works were their productions. They exercised a great influence over the people who in turn treated them with reverence. When English became the language of the country they came to be excluded from the main currents of life and their influence came to be limited mainly to the stagnant parts of the country. In recent years many of them began to feel even insecure (though they would hardly admit this fear even to themselves) as they thought Buddhism too was declining. Buddhism in the past had adjusted itself to the village community system and the Sinhalese form of feudalism and in more recent times to the caste system. With the development of new economic forces all these institutions began to decline, and as these were the traditional supports of Buddhism it seemed that to some extent its very hold on its adherents was being undermined.

The ayurvedic physicians too exercised great influence in the villages in which they lived. With the advance of Western medicine the position of most of them deteriorated. . . .

The Sinhalese schoolmaster is a more modern product. He came into existence under Dutch rule. . . . With the expansion of English education his status deteriorated further. Though education in Sinhalese was advanced to the Senior School Certificate level the pupils in the Sinhalese schools had no future except as schoolmasters and unemployment began to face those who passed the Sinhales S.S.C. Examination. . . .

The Government Service provides the largest employment to the people of Ceylon. Taking no notice of the fact that it is trained intelligence that mattered and not the medium of instruction, they demanded that the language of government should be made Sinhalese. They expected that those educated in Sinhalese would be able to capture the government posts and those who carried on their activities in Sinhalese would at least get an equal status with those who conducted their affairs in English. . . .

This new class, unlike those in the saddle, thus had definite grievances. They had suffered as a result of British rule or had found that under the old system, which was being continued by the U.N.P. without any radical change, their progress was limited. They found that after independence was attained their conditions did not improve, and in fact their very security was at stake. They were thus not merely concerned with redress of grievances but were fighting for their very existence. They knew how the upper middle class had organized themselves and had got rid of British rule. The Buddhist monks realized what great power a highly organized institution like the Roman Catholic Church exercised in the country and over their adherents. Therefore they too began to organize themselves to gain due place in Ceylon society. When they found their agitation did not lead them very far, they planned political action and decided to influence the General Election. They realized fully that the only way they could get power was by getting the people to vote for the candidates who supported their claims. The ordinary people, except in the towns and perhaps the coastal districts, were still passive and did not take any initiative in politics. This new class was in close touch with the people in the rural areas and had common interests up to a point. Hence they were in a better position than the U.N.P. stalwarts to persuade the masses to act in accordance with their instructions. In short, these currents which had hitherto little force and were being gradually pushed into the backwaters by the main current of active politics rose suddenly and instead of losing themselves in marshes and stagnant pools, flooded the main current itself. [pp. 120–123]

3. Buddhist-Marxist Coalition Government

As head of the Sri Lanka Freedom Party (SLFP) founded by her late husband and as prime minister from 1960, Mrs. Sirimao Bandaranaike continued the strong emphasis on the restoration of Buddhism to a central place in national life. Political necessity compelled her to bring three Marxists into a coalition government in the middle of 1964. The following article from *World Buddhism* describes the controversy which ensued. She was defeated in the general elections of 1965.[3]

[3] From "Coalition Government Will Safeguard Buddhism," *World Buddhism*, vol. 12, no. 12 (July, 1964), p. 13. Used by permission.

The government of the Sri Lanka Freedom Party in Ceylon formed a coalition with the Marxists last month. Three Marxists were given portfolios, the key portfolio of Finance being given to Dr. N. M. Perera, leader of the Lanka Sama Samaj Party, a Marxist party.

When the coalition was mooted, certain sections of Buddhists opposed it on the ground that such a coalition would be inimical to the interests of Buddhism and Buddhists. But the Prime Minister, Mrs. Sirimao Bandaranaike, assured the country that it would not be so. In her first public speech after the formation of the Coalition Government, she said that "despite the forecast of reactionaries that religion would suffer as a result of the coalition, the people have nothing to fear. Nothing will happen." In fact one of the terms under which the Leftists were taken into the Government is that "Buddhism be given its due place as the religion of the majority in Ceylon with adequate safeguards for all other religions, as well as freedom of worship being ensured."

One of the organizations which protested earlier against the formation of a Coalition Government was the Lanka Bauddha Jatika Balavegaya. Its president, Mr. L. H. Mettananda, in an open letter to the Prime Minister, referred to an interview he had with her and said that she had given him the impression that any impending change she would make in the Government would be done [with] due regard to the interests of the Buddhists. "Now, however," he said, "I have reason to believe that far from reconstituting the Government so as to safeguard the interests of the Buddhists, your contemplated action as reported in the Press, will endanger not only those very interests but also our national aspirations." He concluded: "If the contemplated and much publicized change to the Government as reported in the Press is given effect to, under whatever pressure, there can be no doubt that you will forfeit the confidence that the Buddhists of this country have hitherto reposed on you. If, on the other hand, you would at this juncture take the correct step to safeguard the rights of the Buddhists and their aspirations, then there is no doubt they will rally round you."

The Ven. Talpawila Seelawansa Thera addressing a meeting of the Three Nikayas or sects, said that the union of the SLFP and the LSSP was a great surprise to him. The meeting was organized by the All-Ceylon Bhikkhu Congress, the Sri Lanka Mahendra Bhikkhu Sangamaya, and the All-Ceylon Organization of Bhikkhus.

The Ven. Malewana Gnanissara Thera said that Marxism was a destructive philosophy which when entrenched in a country would never provide a place for any other philosophy, not to mention religion and the freedoms which flow from democracies. A committee comprising monks from the three Nikayas was formed to safeguard the country from attacks against democracy and religion by the Marxists.

The Ven. Meddagoda Dhammajoti Nayaka Thera, at another meeting, said that Buddhist monks would come out in protest against coalition with Marxists. He said that the Marxists opposed the granting of funds to the Buddha Jayanti celebrations, and they opposed the national and the Buddhist flags.

But Mr. P. B. G. Kalugalla, Minister for Education, said that Dr. N. M. Perera is a good Buddhist and so are the others who have joined the new Coalition Government. He said there was a mass campaign trying to make the people believe that the Coalition would spell the doom of religion. This was absolutely incorrect, he stressed.

After they were sworn in, the three new Marxist Ministers, along with the others, offered flowers at a Buddhist temple.

Mr. D. S. Goonesekera, the new Minister of Cultural Affairs, said that the Lanka Sama Samaj Party had embraced Buddhism after three of its leaders had joined the Coalition Government. "Now the LSSP leaders and their party are there to work for the development of Buddhism even in our absence. I have no doubt that they will carry forward the banner of Buddhism. All of us should be happy about their embracing Buddhism," said Mr. Goonesekera. He added that if any anti-Buddhist activities were to occur he would be the first to oppose and work against it.

A vote of confidence and felicitations in the Coalition Government was passed unanimously at a mass meeting of Buddhist monks and the laity held in Colombo. The meeting, held under the auspices of the All-Ceylon Bhikkhu Mandalaya, also resolved to request the new Government to coalesce with the other progressive forces to help solve the economic problems of the country. The meeting, attended by over one thousand monks, was presided over by the Ven. Mottune Indrasara Thera. A resolution requesting the Government to take over the remaining schools and implement a national education scheme was also passed.

The Ven. Kadihimgala Soratha Thera said that it was the duty of the Sangha to give a "big hand" to the Coalition Government. "Leftists could not destroy the Sasana nor will they attempt to do it. The danger to the Sasana was from a few capitalist lamas in the country and not from the Leftists," he said. The Ven. Gnanaseeha Thera said that reactionaries were trailing the bogey of Marxist infiltration. Ceylon was literate enough not to be guided by those spent-up forces who failed to realize that Marxism was over one hundred years old and that not a single Marxist country had destroyed religion.

The Ven. Panditha Parawahera Pannananda Thera said that Marxism was nothing new to this country. The Buddha was the greatest Marxist in the world. He taught equality for all and as such there was no danger to the country as a result of Leftists joining the Government.

ISLAM IN THE 1955 INDONESIAN ELECTIONS

The first, and last, general elections in Indonesia, held in 1955, reflected the strong influence of Islam in public life. The Masjumi, an Islamic party closely allied with the reformist Muhammadiyah organization, was the largest party in the country and the principal opponent of the secular PNI (Indonesian Nationalist Party) founded by Sukarno. The Nahdatul Ulama was a much smaller Islamic party led by the more traditionalist *ulama*. The PKI (Communist Party) was the other main contender. As a result of the elections the Masjumi and the PNI each won 21.9 percent of the parliamentary seats, the Nahdatul Ulama 17.3 percent, and the Communists 15 percent. Thus the two Islamic parties, although not allied, together won 39.2 percent of the total seats in Parliament.

The major ideological question which divided the Masjumi and the Nationalists (PNI) was whether the Indonesian state could be based on *Pantja Sila* (see II.4), interpreted in such a way as to accommodate even the Marxist forces. Sukarno had argued, as early as 1926, that nationalism, Islam, and Marxism could peacefully coexist. While Mohammed Natsir, the principal Masjumi spokesman, declared that the principle of *Pantja Sila* was compatible with Islam, other members of his party, such as the right-wing leader Isa Anshary, interpreted this as a sell-out to secularism and argued in particular that Marxism could never be reconciled with Islam.

4. Sukarno on Muslim-Marxist Cooperation

In an article first published in 1926, Sukarno examined the three major ideological movements in Indonesian politics — Nationalist, Islamic, and Marxist — and called for unity in the common struggle against Dutch imperialism. In the following passage, he suggested the basis for an ideological reconciliation between the Islamic and the Marxist movements. [4]

---

[4] From Sukarno, "Nationalism, Islamism and Marxism," *Pantjasila: A Monthly Magazine on Indonesian Politics and Culture* (Department of Information, Republic of Indonesia, Jakarta), vol. 3, no. 18 (January, 1966), pp. 53–54.

▶ ▶   In the same way, too, I am convinced that we can close the ranks of the Muslims with the Marxists, even though basically there is a very great difference of principle between these two groups. I am truly grieved to recall the dark clouds overhanging the Indonesian skies when some years ago we were witnesses to a conflict between brothers, witnesses to the outbreak of enmity between Marxist and Muslim, when we witnessed how the body of our movement was split into parts warring with each other. This conflict fills the darkest pages in our history! It was this conflict between brothers that wasted all the powers of our movement which should have been growing stronger and stronger; it was this conflict that set our movement back for decades!

What a pity! How powerful would our movement now have been had this conflict between brothers not occurred! Without any doubt we would never have been organizationally broken as is the case today; without any doubt our movement would have advanced, no matter what the obstructions might have been!

I am absolutely convinced that there is no important barrier to this Muslim–Marxist friendship. I have already explained above that true Islamism contains socialistic features. Although socialistic does not necessarily mean Marxist, although we know that this socialism of Islam is not the same thing as Marxist principles, since the socialism of Islam is founded upon spiritual principles and the socialism of Marxism is founded upon the principles of materialism; even so, for our purposes it appears to be sufficient if we prove that true Islam is socialistic.

Muslims should not forget that it is the Marxist view of history based on materialist principles which frequently points the way for them regarding difficult and complex economic problems and world politics; nor should they forget that the method of Historical Materialism, in explaining events that have already occurred on the face of this earth, is a method of forecasting events to come, and is extremely useful to them!

Muslims should not forget that capitalism, the enemy of Marxism, is also the enemy of Islam! Because surplus value as understood by the concept of Marxism is essentially no different from profit as understood by the concept of Islam. Surplus value, namely the theory that consuming the proceeds of another's labor, without giving the due part of the profit which should accrue to the worker who worked to make that profit — this theory of surplus value was formulated by Karl Marx and Friedrich Engels in order to explain the origins of capitalism. It is this surplus value that is the very breath of all systems that are capitalistic; it is by waging war on surplus value that the followers of Marxism are waging war on capitalism down to its very roots!

For a follower of true Islam it quickly becomes evident that it is not proper for him to be at enmity with the concept of Marxism which opposed surplus value, because he does not forget that true Islam also wages war on that system, he does not forget that true Islam strictly prohibits the consumption of profit and the imposition of interest. He understands that this profit is in essence none other than the surplus value of the Marxist concept!

"O ye who believe! Devour not usury, doubling and quadrupling (the sum lent), observe your duty to Allah, that ye may be successful." This is what is written in the Qur'an, Surah Al-Imran, verse 129!

The Muslim with a broad outlook, the Muslim who understands the needs of our fight, will certainly agree to friendship with the Marxists, because he will realize that consuming profits and imposing interest are acts prohibited by his religion, that they are forbidden things; he will realize that it is in this way that Islam wages war on capitalism down to its roots and right to its seeds, because, as I have already explained above, profit is the same thing as surplus value which is the very breath of capitalism. He realizes that, like Marxism, so Islam too, "with faith in Allah, acknowledging the Kingdom of God, is a protest against the wickedness of capitalism."

Muslims who are "fanatic" and who attack the Marxist movement are Muslims who are not familiar with the prohibitions of their own religion. Such Muslims do not know that, like Marxism, true Islamism forbids the capitalist accumulation of money, forbids the hoarding of wealth for one's own requirements. He does not remember the verse in the Qur'an which reads: "The ones who hoard up gold and silver and spend it not in the way of Allah, unto them give tidings of a painful doom." He does not know that, like the Marxism which he opposes, so Islam by such means wages war in the clearest possible way on capitalism's coming into being.

And there are still many other duties and stipulations in the religion of Islam that are the same as the objectives and purposes of Marxism! For is it not the case that the duty of *zakat* in Islam is the duty of the rich to distribute their wealth to the poor, a distribution of wealth that Marxism also seeks — though naturally according to Marxism's own methods? Do not Islam's ideas of "liberty, equality and fraternity" match those of Marxism to which many Muslims are antagonistic? Does not true Islam bear "every humanitarian equality on the basis of liberty, equality and fraternity?" Did not the Prophet of Islam himself preach this equality in the following words: "I am only a human being like you;

it has been born within me that your God is the one God?" Was not this fraternity also commanded in the thirteenth verse of Surah Al-Hudjarat which runs: "O mankind! We have created you male and female, and have made you nations and tribes that ye may know one another." Is it not the case that fraternity "does not remain fraternity in theory only" and is it not acknowledged also by those who are not Muslims? Is it not a pity that some Muslims are antagonistic to a movement the essentials of which also run: "liberty, equality and fraternity?"

The people of Islam who do not want to close ranks with the Marxists should remember that this movement, as a Marxist movement, is a growl or the echo of the cries and laments of the Indonesian people whose lives become more and more confined, whose conditions at home become more and more bitter. That group should remember that their own movement has many ideals that accord with those of the Marxist movement, many demands that are the same. Those people should take as their example the envoy of the Islamic Kingdom of Afghanistan who, when questioned by a Marxist newspaper, said that although he was not a Marxist he acknowledged that he was a "real friend" of the Marxists because he was an inveterate enemy of European capitalism in Asia!

What a pity, what a great pity it will be if the Islamic movement in Our Indonesia is at enmity with the Marxist movement! There has never been in Our Indonesia before, a movement that is really and truly a people's movement, like the Islamic movement and the Marxist movement! Never before in our country has there been a movement which has shaken up the people so profoundly as these two movements! How stupendous would it be if two movements, with which the people sleep and with which the people wake, were to become a single mighty flood of the utmost power!

Happy are those of the Islamic movement who comprehend and who want to unite! Happy are they because it is they who are really and truly carrying out the commands of their religion!

Muslims who do not want unity and who think that this attitude of theirs is the correct attitude — well, may they be able to account for that attitude of theirs before their God!

5. Masjumi Ulama's Attack on Marxist Ideology

On the eve of the 1955 elections, the *ulama* of the Masjumi Party issued a *fatwa* on the relationship of communist ideology to Islam. A *fatwa* is a formal interpretation or directive on a question of Islamic law which is binding on those who accept the authority of the issuing scholars.[5]

▶ ▶ ## DECLARATION OF THE ULAMA OF THE MASJUMI PARTY OF WEST JAVA

HAVING STUDIED and analyzed in the deepest manner the nature of the communist-Marxist ideology, both from the point of view of religious faith and theology — from which we see clearly the atheistic and antireligious nature of communism — and from the point of view of politics and economics — from which we see clearly that communism is antidemocratic, proposes the abolition of private property, and advocates class struggle and war between social groups,

MINDFUL that communist-Marxist ideology and teachings are not only in total conflict with the teachings and law of Islam, but that they also constitute a dire threat to religion in general and threaten the security of the Republic of Indonesia which is based on a Belief in One God,

DELIBERATING the necessity for all Muslims, especially the *ulama* and *zu'ama*, to take a firm stand against communist ideology, in keeping with the teachings of Islam (the Qur'an and Hadith), and the responsibility of the Indonesian Islam Community to protect the State and nation from the danger of communism,

HAVING HEARD the views and discussions of the representatives, based on their interpretation of the Qur'an and Hadith,
WE CONCLUDE:

1. The communist ideology is in complete conflict with Islamic law and teachings and constitutes a danger to religion and the State of Indonesia.

2. Muslims who accept the communist faith are hereby excommunicated (*murtad*) from the Islamic faith.

3. It is forbidden (*haram*) for Muslims to become members of the Indonesian Communist Party or bodies and organizations whose clear aim it is to establish the communist ideology and law in Indonesia.

4. We command the establishment of the ANTI-COMMUNIST FRONT by the Masjumi leaders of West Java and urge all

[5] From Boyd R. Compton, *Muslim Radicalism: The Anticommunist Front,* Newsletter Indonesia BRC–27 (New York: American Universities Field Staff, 1955), pp. 7–8. Used by permission.

Muslims in Indonesia to form branches of the ANTI-COM-MUNIST FRONT in their localities, as evidence of a clear stand in opposition to the communist ideology.

5. To adopt an attitude of silence toward the communist ideology sponsored by the Indonesian Communist Party signifies a willingness to tolerate the propagation and victory of an ideology which incurs the wrath of Allah.

6. We call on all Muslim *ulama* and *zu'ama* to implement the teachings of Islam by forming a powerful united Islamic front to prevent the spread of the dangerous ideology of communism.

7. We call on all groups and political parties which are anti-communist to cease their cooperation with the Indonesian Communist Party.

MAHDISM AND THE UMMAH PARTY IN SUDAN

In 1820, Muhammad Ali Pasha, the Ottoman viceroy in Egypt, began the conquest of the Sudan. By the last quarter of the century, European officials were increasingly placed in high administrative posts, and in 1877, the Khedive appointed the British officer C. G. Gordon as governor-general of the Sudan. The Turko-Egyptian administration was directly challenged by a remarkable religio-political leader who in 1881 proclaimed himself the Mahdi, the expected messianic deliverer and restorer of true Islam. The Mahdi's final defeat of Gordon's forces at Khartoum marked the beginning of a period of Sudanese independence which lasted until 1898.

After fifty-eight years of British rule, independence was again achieved by the Sudan in 1956. But the legacy of the Mahdi has continued to find potent expression in Sudanese politics to this day. The descendants of the Mahdi have continued to lead the Ansar religious order which he founded, and the Ummah Party, formed in 1945, has been nothing but its political arm. In fact, the Imam (leader) of the Ansar was also the head of the Ummah Party until these functions were divided between two members of the Mahdi family. However, as we shall see, this division of spiritual and temporal power led to serious conflicts which resulted in the fall of a Mahdi prime minister in 1967.

6. Proclamation of the Mahdi, 1883

In this political proclamation Muhamad Ahmad called on the people of the Eastern Sudan to accept him as the expected Mahdi and to follow him into battle in the *jihad* (Holy War) to restore true Islam. Note the nature of the messianic credentials he presents.[6]

▶ ▶   FROM MUHAMMAD EL MAHDI TO ALL HIS BELOVED, THE BELIEVERS IN GOD AND HIS BOOK. Beloved, bear in mind that real wealth consists in obeying God, and following in the footsteps of those whom God has guided into the right path. The happy man is he who is guided by others, and the foolish man is he who follows after his own ideas. God has distinguished this holy faith by holy war. Any man who takes part in this holy war will be considered a true believer; but any man who refuses to join will be considered as one of those at enmity with the Prophet. . . . Why, therefore, do you disobey the Almighty God? Have you not seen how I have gained victories over the Turks and infidels, whose bodies have been burnt wherever they have been pierced with spears?

Do you seek a greater miracle than this? It is just as the miracles of the Prophet. They (the Turks) are well armed with rifles and held strong positions, but not only were they defeated, they were utterly destroyed. The cause of their destruction is, that I am a light from God, and the Prophet has confirmed me as Mahdi, and has made me sit several times on his own seat in the presence of all the khalifas and prophets, and Elias was present too with all the angels, and every believer from Adam up to the present time. In battle, the Prophet and those above mentioned are with me; he has given me the sword of victory, and has promised that not even the Thakalain (i.e., half-man, half-jinn) can defeat me. The Prophet also informed me that God has placed a mole on my right cheek, as a mark that I am the Mahdi. He has also given me another sign, which is a banner of light carried by Izrail (the angel of death), who walks before me in time of battle. In this manner I have been enabled to capture Kordofan and all the surrounding countries, and God will also open your country for me, and by His will the whole world will submit to me, accepting me as the true Mahdi. Woe, therefore, to those who do not believe in me, for they will all be destroyed. Why did you not set forth as soon as you heard of me, in order to help in the holy war? . . .

Remember that I have come by order of the Prophet. He has set me to be your savior, and you should therefore believe in me. The Prophet has told me that anyone who disbelieves in me disbelieves in

---

[6] From F. R. Wingate, *Mahdism and the Egyptian Sudan* (London: Frank Cass and Co. Ltd., 2nd ed., 1968), pp. 92–93. Used by permission.

God and in His Prophet. I have quoted his own words, and he repeated them three times to me. You are aware that I am descended from the family of the Prophet. I am begotten of the forehead of his father and mother, and the father and mother of my mother are descended from the Abbassides. I am lineally descended from El Hussein (the Prophet's grandson).

I made my *hejira* (flight) to Masat, in the mountain of Gedir, by order of the Prophet, and by his order I came into Kordofan. From there I sent my several proclamations, and I now send this one to you. On receiving it, leave the Turks at once; do not hesitate to leave your property behind you; leave them, and come even to the nearest village, and fight against the Turks with all your strength. . . .

I send you Sheikh Osman Digna, of Suakin, as your emir, in order to revive the true religion. On his arrival, join him and obey his orders, advance against the Turks, and drive them out of your country. All God's people before you have quitted their country and children, in order to conquer the land of the infidels. They did not mind death nor fatigue. The present time will now prove whether you are truly God's people. This you will be if you obey the orders of the Mahdi; but if you disobey, then you must expect nothing but the sword, and your fate will be that of all those who have disobeyed us.

7. Mahdist Politics, 1964–1969

In this article on politics in the Sudan, we see the central influence of the Mahdist legacy: the Mahdi family, the Ansar sect, and the Ummah party.[7]

Sudan, the biggest country on the African continent, can now boast of having the youngest head of government in the world today. The 30-year-old new man of destiny in Khartoum is Sayyid Sadiq El-Mahdi, the great-grandson of Imam Muhammad Ahmad El-Mahdi who was not only the father of Sudan's independence but also the greatest exponent and defender of the country's Islamic identity.

Sayyid Sadiq El-Mahdi was swept into power at the climax of a crisis within the Ummah Party — the majority bloc in Sudan's coalition government — which has been simmering since Mr. Mohammad

[7] From Hassan Kaleemi, "Sayyid Sadiq El-Mahdi: The Dynamic Premier of Sudan," *Muslimnews International*, vol. 5, no. 3 (September, 1966), pp. 12–13. Used by permission.

Ahmad Mahgoub, himself an Ummah man, was appointed to lead the cabinet in June last year. Mahgoub's resignation came on July 25 when an historic censure motion was rammed through the Sudanese Constituent Assembly resulting in his defeat by 126 votes to 30. The party shake-up followed a decision by the parliamentary group of the Ummah Party asking Sadiq El-Mahdi to assume full responsibilities as party leader. The step was taken in strict conformity with the parliamentary practice that the leader of the majority party should become the prime minister.

Differences are known to have cropped up between the religious head of the Ansar — the followers of the Mahdi — Imam Hadi Abdur Rahman El-Mahdi and the political boss of the Ummah Party, Sayyid Sadiq El-Mahdi. The bifurcation of the monolithic Mahdist power took place when during the Abboud regime the then Imam Sayyid Siddiq Abdur Rahman El-Mahdi willed on his death-bed that the Imamate should go to his brother and the political leadership to his son who was quite young at that time. Sayyid Siddiq was, in fact, the last Imam to hold the dual power of religion and politics. Such was the magnetism of his personality and his influence over the people in general that he alone stood as the tower of strength to defy the military dictatorship and became the focus of popular and democratic resurgence in the Sudan. It may be futile to challenge the wisdom of Sayyid Siddiq's decision because as a great patriot and a conscientious holder of the Mahdist traditions, he was [best] qualified to look after the interests of his family and the country.

Be that as it may, the division of power did spark off a controversy which to some observers indicated an ever-widening gulf between the conservative and the progressive forces in the Mahdist family itself.

But Sayyid Sadiq clarified the point by saying that the parliamentary issue had nothing to do with either the so-called differences in the House of the Mahdi or among the Ansar. He reiterated that the Mahdi family and the Ansar were of one opinion as far as obedience to the Imam was concerned according to the terms of the *bai'at* [oath of allegiance]. However, regarding purely political matters, Sadiq insisted that the majority should have its way. To this logic the Imam seems to have given in rather gracefully. He closed the issue by saying that he respected the normal procedures of democracy and that differences should be solved democratically. The Imam also agreed to keep himself above politics.

Thus, the patch-up seems to be enduring and it is obvious that in the greater interest of the country and the party both the uncle and nephew have found a permanent modus operandi. For, it is imperative that the Mahdist image must remain unsullied in the eyes of the Sudanese and the world at large.

And with Sadiq El-Mahdi in the forefront of politics that image stands the chance of a timely refurbishing. Dr. Sadiq, a tall (6 ft 3 in.) bearded economist who took honors at Oxford, is the essence of the new generation in the Sudan. Dignified, gentle, courteous, good looking and a strict Muslim, he is enlightened enough to appreciate that the family unit — a great force in Sudanese life — is fast becoming an anachronism in the latter half of the twentieth century.

No doubt, the Mahdist Revolution was the greatest progressive force the Sudan has ever seen. The Mahdi was a *Mujaddid* (renovator of the faith) who not only preached a return to pristine Islam but also succeeded in establishing an Islamic state on the ruins of the Turko-Egyptian empire. It is the prestige of the great revolutionary which has been serving as the source of power for the Mahdists in the Sudan so much so that today they are considered one of the most powerful families in the Middle East.

It was indeed a miraculous escape by one of the Mahdi's children from the ruthless British reprisals after the battle of Karari (1898) that saved the Mahdists from complete extinction. Having grown up, Abdur Rahman El-Mahdi proved to be shrewd enough to weather the storm of British antagonism by adopting a seemingly compromising posture vis-à-vis the destroyers of his father's state. In his conciliatory efforts he even went to the extent of offering the famous sword of the Mahdi to the British sovereign.

Meanwhile, he also laid the foundations of his family's prosperity by pioneering cotton plantations in the Sudan. Thus, when Imam Abdur Rahman died, he left the Mahdist family as nearly the sole monopolist of the religious, economic and political power in the Sudan. He also bequeathed the political apparatus of the Ummah (the People's Party). Founded in 1945 the Ummah grew from strength to strength with its slogan: "Sudan for the Sudanese." In contradistinction to Azhari's Ashiqqa and the later National Unionist Party (NUP), the Ummah disfavored the idea of the unity of the Nile Valley. There were historical reasons for this stand as it was against the Cairo-based and British-supported progeny of Muhammad Ali Pasha that the Mahdi had waged his *Jihad*.

The strength of the Ummah is mainly derived from the well disciplined Ansar of the Mahdi who comprise nearly two-thirds of the population of the country. The armed bands of the Ansar are still a power to be reckoned with. Their affiliation provides the Ummah with a ready-made militia. The power of the Ansar has on many occasion influenced the course of events in the country. In March, 1954, on the occasion of the second ceremonial sessions of the Sudanese Parliament, the Ansar showed their strength. Among the foreign invitees were President Naguib and Colonel Nasser of Egypt. The Ummah and other opponents of union with Egypt planned and held such a great demonstration at the Khartoum airport that the Egyptian delegation had to be taken to the governor-general's palace by a roundabout route. Another show of strength took place when strongman Abboud tried to stop the Ansar from staging their armed parade on the anniversary of the Prophet's birthday. The Ansar held their parade as usual, clashed with the government, were killed but took an equal toll from the police force also.

It is this formidable apparatus which is now held by Sadiq El-Mahdi. But he is aware of the loopholes in the organization and knows how to turn the archaic Ummah into a fast-moving dynamic political party. He believes it is a disadvantage that the leadership of the Ummah comes largely from his own family. During the last few years he has tried to broaden at least the base of the party. Now he claims that "the Ummah party is a modern political force and not a Mahdi family party." In his manifesto, Sadiq El-Mahdi said that all Ansar were in the Ummah party but every member of the party was not necessarily from the Ansar sect. He also says that as a Mahdist party "the Ummah would be certain to fall" but "as the Ummah party it would succeed."

8. Fall of the Sadiq El-Mahdi Government

The rivalry between Sadiq El-Mahdi, head of the Ummah Party, and his uncle Hadi El-Mahdi, head of the Ansar religious sect, ultimately led to the fall of the Sadiq government. As the following article shows, while the conflict was basically a personal power struggle, there were differences over Islamic ideology as well. [8]

▶ ▶   With the fall of the government of Sadiq El-Mahdi on May 15, Sudan has been plunged into the most serious political crisis ever since the overthrow of the country's military regime at the end of 1964.

Ironically enough the crisis was precipitated through a long-standing and bitter dispute within the powerful Mahdi family leaders who exercise

---

[8] From *Muslimnews International*, vol. 5, no. 12 (June, 1967), pp. 9–10. Used by permission.

considerable influence over the ruling Ummah Party. The two main characters in the quarrel are conservative-minded Imam al-Hadi al-Mahdi — leader of the strong Mahdist (Ansar) religious sect — and his 31-year-old Oxford-educated and reform-minded nephew, Sayyid Sadiq-El-Mahdi who became Prime Minister nine months ago in the government formed by a coalition of his own Ummah party and the National Unionist Party led by President Ismael el-Azhari. Then also the Imam opposed his nephew for [the] Prime Ministership and tried to swing the Ummah Party against him. Sayyid Sadiq, however, won convincingly but the family feud lingered on.

The dispute between Sayyid Sadiq and the Imam developed into an open crisis when the latter publicly withdrew his support from his nephew as, in his opinion, his government was "a complete failure because of its weakness." He called upon his followers to withdraw their support in Parliament from Sayyid Sadiq and work for a new political association with National Unionists — the main opposition party and the junior partner in the coalition. This is likely to benefit President Ismael el-Azhari who viewed Sayyid Sadiq as a potential rival for the future presidency provided for by the new constitution due to be passed by the Constituent Assembly in June, as the Imam has committed the whole weight of his religious prestige behind El-Azhari. . . .

Among the key issues in constitution-making is the question whether Sudan will be an Islamic Republic as desired by the traditionalists, or a secular one which the modernists and radicals wish to see. This provided another reason for the clash between the Imam and Sadiq El-Mahdi because the former supported the traditionalists' view whereas the latter desired to establish a modern political system in his country. This makes the clash between the two as not only one of personal ambitions but also of two diametrically opposite attitudes to the country's political and social issues.

THE CHRISTIAN DEMOCRATIC PARTY IN CHILE

With his 1964 electoral victory, Eduardo Frei became president of Chile and head of the first Christian Democratic government in Latin America. The PDC (Partido Demócrata Cristiano) had its origins in Catholic Action, a lay movement, and the Conservative Party, the traditional Catholic party from which it broke off in 1938. The Christian Democrats gradually elaborated an ideology based on the social encyclicals (*Rerum Novarum*, 1891, and *Quadragesimo Anno*, 1931), which contained trenchant criticisms of laissez-faire capitalism, and also the writings of Jacques Maritain and others on "integral humanism." In general terms, one can say that Christian Democracy constitutes a kind of Catholic socialism (see IX.7, 8, and 9 for more radical forms).

In his public pronouncements, Frei sought to establish the complete independence of the PDC from the Catholic hierarchy. However, in the crucial 1964 elections in which he faced a Marxist coalition, FRAP (Frente de Acción Popular, or "People's Action Front"), effective use was made of a 1962 pastoral letter in which the Chilean bishops condemned Marxism in the harshest terms. It was abundantly clear that for all intents and purposes the PDC was indeed a Catholic party (although not *the* Catholic party, nor a clerical party) and that it had the solid backing of the church. With a Marxist victory the only alternative, it could hardly be otherwise.

9. PDC Not a Catholic Clerical Party

In this article Eduardo Frei, after giving a lengthy exposition of his party's philosophical base, attempts to refute the charge that the PDC (Partido Demócrata Cristiano) is the Catholic party in Chile.[9]

▶ ▶   The Christian Democratic Party is not a confessional or clerical party, as some believe. The currents that reflect this [Christian Democratic] inspiration, in Chile and throughout the world, have proved that they are not motivated by such purposes. This is a fact which anyone can verify. In the field of theory there have been frequent polemics with the more traditional sectors of opinion over this non-confessional and non-clerical character of Christian Democracy. The impassioned debates over Maritain have revolved around precisely these points.

Christian Democracy has never sought to implement a policy of ecclesiastical privileges, far less to impose religious belief or to establish Catholicism as the official doctrine of the State. It would take long to argue this position fully, but it would not be difficult for anyone to find a vast Christian Democratic literature on the subject. This matter has been pondered and discussed much by various authors such as Maritain, Lebret, Mounier, Ducatillon, Athayde and others.

Nor is Christian Democracy a Catholic or confessional party that expects its active members to be believers, or that in fact or by right seeks to assume the representation of the Church or of Catholicism.

Absolutely not.

[9] From Sergio Guilisasti Tagle, *Partidos políticos chilenos*, 2nd ed. (Santiago: Editorial Nascimento, 1964), pp. 218–21. Used by permission. Translated by the editor.

We have spent a lifetime proclaiming that no party has the right to call itself "Catholic party," to assume the representation of the Church, or to regard itself as the only "orthodox" vehicle for Catholics who are active in political life.

We could hardly now fall into the same error ourselves.

It is possible that the name Christian Democracy leads to misunderstanding. It does not refer to an exclusive democracy, only for Christians; not even to a democracy controlled by Christians.

We have already said [in a previous passage] that Christian Democracy wants to implement the principles of integral humanism, and we have summarized these principles. Well, then, Christian Democracy as a party works to mobilize or channel both Christian energies and democratic energies toward the realization of these ideas. The party is therefore open to all who, believers or not, share its principles regarding the temporal order and political conduct. In fact it always happens that among the active members of Christian Democracy there are Catholics, Protestants, and men without religious beliefs.

Christian Democracy is the re-encounter of Christians with democracy or, if you will, of Christians with the people. Such is its deepest significance and, at the same time, the explanation of its name. . . .

For Christian Democracy, society in its own life approaches or moves away from Christian values to the degree that it approaches or moves away from a human community informed by love, which is the supreme law of Christianity. We do not seek to create a "decoratively Christian" state, full of ostentation and religious symbols, like some that presently exist, but a State that is integrally Christian.

Nothing is further from our spirit than the revival of the religious struggles of the past.

Our political action has always made it clear that the sphere of religion must be distinguished from the sphere of the temporal. We have argued that Catholics can hold different and even contrary opinions on temporal or political affairs. The formation of alignments such as that of Catholics against non-Catholics in the political field is an absurdity. We have done everything in our power to transcend these struggles of the past and we will not be the ones to revive them. This attitude of ours is connected to the very roots of our thought, so that it naturally springs from the exposition that I have been formulating here.

The Chilean Church long ago secured a position for itself outside partisan political disputes, and thus has won the respect of all. Therefore, we seek no innovations in the existing legal framework enshrined in the Constitution with respect to relations between Church and State.

10. The Bishops of Chile Speak

While the leadership of the Christian Democratic Party (Partido Demócrata Cristiano) was anxious to establish its independence from the Catholic Church, an official pronouncement of the episcopate attacked the ideas of the PDC's opponents on both right and left, reserving its strongest blasts for the Marxists. *Social and Political Duty in the Present Hour*, published in 1962, was an opening statement in the ideological conflict which became polarized in the 1964 elections.[10]

▶ ▶   All the countries of Latin America, we can say, are passing through a period of great difficulties which especially affect the economic, political and social order. They are the index of dangerous tensions and of situations which do not correspond to the order desired by God. . . .

Our fervent wish, dear sons and daughters, is that once more in the history of our continent, Chile may give an example of intelligence and civic maturity, impelling a clear and certain evolution toward stability and economic prosperity, which will offer to the international grouping of which it is a part, the Christian solution to the problems which afflict the region.

On the difficult crossroad we travel, there are powerful entities which propose solutions, but there are other groups which do not accept the possibility of solutions and would like to maintain the status quo.

In the face of the reality which cannot be hidden, and the many facts which reveal to us the general unrest, we must make our sons see clearly that the solutions will either be energetically impelled and proposed by us Christians, or will be imposed on us against our will, in forms which will harm our most cherished interests.

For this reason, because the hour in which we live is the time for action and the moment in which a new country is coming into being, we want you to hear the voice of the Church.

We have the right and the duty to intervene, indicating the moral principles, natural and religious, which should guide you in these difficult circumstances.

The High Pontiffs have recovered this right for the Church on many occasions, not offering technical solutions for the working of the social

---

[10] From *Los Obispos de Chile Hablan: El Deber Social y Político en la Hora Presente* (Santiago, Chile: Secretariado General del Episcopado de Chile, 1962), pp. 7–9, 18–25. Translated by the editor.

order, but rather stating the moral norms on which it is founded to determine "whether the bases of a particular social order are in accord with the immutable order which God, the Creator and Redeemer, has manifested through natural law and Revelation." [Pius XII].

It is also evident "that the health or illness of souls depends on and in turn affects the form which is given to society, conforming or not to divine laws." [Pius XII].

There are social forms which favor Christianity and there are others which greatly impede it.

We believe furthermore that the noble Christian principles of love for God and country and respect for the eternal values of man should orient us in this difficult enterprise to make us choose those solutions which are in accord with our historical tradition and which permit us to conserve the spiritual heritage received from our elders and jealously guarded by the Chilean people throughout their glorious history.

We now desire to address all men of good will in our land, for political passions in all their violence have not yet been kindled and our voice, without being distorted by uncontrollable special interests, can be heard calmly, finding the path marked by intelligence and feeling, and moving all to fruitful and saving action.

We are obliged also to voice the conviction that a considerable section of the Chileans finds it difficult to see what is going on around them.

In a country seriously affected by anguish and misery, there are those who pass on the other side of the suffering without seeing it, unless fear opens their eyes. And fear alone can distort the Christian vision of reality.

It is not possible for selfishness or vested interests to obscure the truth and keep us from seeing the poverty that surrounds us and is perpetuated among us. [pp. 7–9]

In our developing countries the political function has, if possible, even greater importance than in other nations, imposing structures which may or may not agree with the Christian concept of man and his destiny.

Thus is understood the duty which the Church feels to orient the Chilean Catholics in this decisive political moment, without exceeding the limits of its competence and without taking from them the full responsibility for the decisions which they must make.

In the most serious present situation through which our country, and one could say the entire world, is passing, many citizens are asked to give their support to international communism, which promises the definitive solution to the problems of present-day society.

We cannot let the opportunity pass without giving a clear orientation with respect to this matter. We do not do so with a negative or polemical vision, but because we are thoroughly convinced that this system does not produce the remedy to the evils which we wish to extirpate.

Communism is diametrically opposed to Christianity. "It holds that there exists only one reality, matter, which by a blind evolution becomes plant, animal, man. In this doctrine there is no room for the idea of God. . . ." [Pius XI, *Divini Redemptoris*]

From these premises are clearly deduced the concept of religion which communism holds: it is a purely human, bourgeois and retrograde institution, the opium of the people, which should be persecuted and annihilated for opposing their plans. [Here follows a catalogue of communist errors.]

Why is it that such a system has been diffused so rapidly throughout the world? Here are some of the reasons for its successes.

(a) Communism in the democratic countries hides its true face; it does not present itself immediately with all its demands. It does not clearly manifest its opposition to God and the Church, nor to the country, human freedom, the right of property, the family, or the authority of parents. It only proclaims itself as the redeemer of the working class, something which the people in large part believe.

(b) The real abuses produced by the liberal [capitalist] economy. . . .

(c) We do not want to overlook the fact that the weakness and ineffectiveness of democratic governments, the lack of decisive action to solve the grave problems of the present hour, and the undue prolongation of an unjust and intolerable situation, has brought a large part of our people, even against their will, to seek the remedy for their sad state in the communist doctrine.

(d) "A truly diabolical propaganda, such perhaps as the world has never before known. . . ." [Pius XI, *Divini Redemptoris*]

(e) The disunion and inner struggles among those who do not share communist ideas, but who by making such ideas plausible, or by seeking to obtain or keep political or economic situations of privilege, lend themselves to the Marxists' game and favor their rise to power. . . .

(f) Like all error, communism contains some truth. It wants to better the conditions of the working class, suppress real abuses and obtain a more just distribution of wealth. It is also true that it has contributed no little to shaking men and institutions out of their long inertia, and has undeniably achieved material and scientific successes. . . .

Collaboration with communism is not possible. What collaboration, what possibilities of union exist with a political system or party which has as its basic presupposition the destruction of all ideas and institutions that oppose it? . . . It should come as no surprise that the Church declares that whoever betrays the sacred rights of God, of the country and of man, collaborating in an action directed against these great values, foundation and basis of all Christian civilization, is not in communion with Her. . . .

But this should not make the Catholics forget that the Church has condemned the abuses of capitalist liberalism. Furthermore, the Church concretely cannot accept the maintenance in Chile, as we have already said, of a situation which violates the rights of the human person and therefore Christian morality. . . .

Before the urgency of a situation so opposed to the principles of Christian morality, there exists the obligation and urgency to support effective solutions to poverty, although these solutions are not the perfect and complete ones which would be desirable.

This work of transformation must be sincere and look toward an authentic and real economic, social, cultural, political and spiritual elevation and development of the world of labor, and not be oriented toward a negative anticommunism which seeks the defeat and elimination of the adversary in order to preserve better and longer the present economic and social order, nor limit itself to a "paternalism" more inclined to charity than to justice. [pp. 18–25]

11. The 1964 Election Campaign: A Marxist Comment

The political editor of *El Siglo*, the communist newspaper of Santiago, here comments on the role of the bishops' pastoral letter, and the religious question in general, in the election campaign which resulted in the victory of Eduardo Frei and the PDC (Partido Demócrata Cristiano). [11]

▶ ▶   It became known early that a basic weapon of Frei's campaign would be psychological terror. An asphyxiating propaganda machine set up with the help of North American social psychologists was given the task of proving that the triumph of Allende would bring in its train the end of the world. Sociological questionnaires indicated the weak points to those who had to direct the attack in each sector and social stratum. The heaviest headlines were used to massively frighten the women with the

[11] From Eduardo Labarca Goddard, *Chile Invadido: Reportaje a la Intromisión Extranjera* (Santiago, Chile: Editora Austral, 1968), pp. 65–66. Used by permission. Translated by the editor.

supposed horrors of communism and a FRAP ("People's Action Front") government. Small businessmen and artisans were told that the regime of Allende would seize their businesses and shops. It was announced to the landless peasants that the communists were going to take away their hens, and to the small landowners that their property would be given to the landless peasants.

The Chilean Catholic Church permitted itself to be led into this field. Two years before the election and with the help of the Jesuit [Rev. Roger] Vekemans, the pastoral letter entitled "Social and Political Duty in the Present Hour" was elaborated and subscribed to by the cardinal and all the bishops. Dated September 18, 1962, the pastoral letter was read in masses in all the churches and chapels of the country. Its call was not to peace, but to war.

"From the triumph of communism in Chile, the church and all her sons can expect only persecution, tears and blood," the bishops affirmed. The letter reproduced the most virulent paragraphs against communism subscribed to by Pope Pius XI, who established a cordial collaboration of the Vatican with the Fascist government of Mussolini in Italy. One of them, taken from the encyclical *Divini Redemptoris*, affirmed: "The family, according to communism, has no reason to exist; it is a bourgeois creation upon which present-day society is built, and must be weakened and destroyed. Communism suppresses every tie which links the woman with her family and her house; it denies to parents the right to the education of their children; and it places in the hands of the collectivity the care of the home and the offspring; the woman is thrust out into public life and into work, however hard it might be, the same as the man."

The bishops cried out for a vast unity against FRAP: "Disunity and internal struggles among those who do not share communist ideas . . . lend themselves to the Marxists' game and favor their ascension to power." Less than two years later the crusaders grouped themselves in the legions of Frei's campaign.

The bodies supporting Frei's candidacy distributed hundreds of thousands of copies of an eight-page pamphlet with extracts from the pastoral letter, with the title, "Collaboration with Communism is Not Possible." An enigmatic note said: "Printed privately by citizens without political affiliation, in order to diffuse its content more widely."

Seven months after the pronouncement of the Chilean church, on April 19, 1963, Pope John XXIII proclaimed a diametrically opposed doctrine in his encyclical *Pacem in Terris*. The Pope denied the importance of religious and philosophical differences when dealing with "initiatives of an economic, social, cultural or political nature."

The Chilean Catholic Church, however, continued acting throughout the election campaign in accord with the old style. Apart from some exceptional cases, it turned a deaf ear to the voice of the Vatican. Thus, on Sunday, May 3, 1964, in the parish of Cauquenes, the religious marriage ceremony was refused to a Chilean who introduced the president of the Allende forces of that city as his best man.

VII
The Politics of Religious Pluralism

The extent of religious pluralism and the political importance of the religious minorities are questions of major importance in attempting to study any political system. In the Third World, however, they take on added significance, for religious group identities may well have a greater effect on political behavior than secular ideologies, economic interests, or membership in voluntary associations.

In seeking to explain the interactions between religion and politics, the fact of religious pluralism often explains much more than the systemic characteristics of the religions in interaction. Thus, in attempting to understand politics in India during the period from 1937 to 1947, the most important facts were that the population, although predominantly Hindu, was twenty-five percent Muslim, plus the Sikhs, Christians and smaller minorities. The nature of Hinduism and Islam as religious systems tells us little about the politics of this period; the facts of religious pluralism tell us much.

We have already touched on the communal political parties and communal grievances (VI. 1) which reflect situations of religious pluralism. We have also noted the factor of religious pluralism as a deterrent, whether effective or not, to efforts to make the majority faith the state religion (I.5) One very important phenomenon considered in this chapter is the anomic communal conflict which has become endemic in parts of the Third World. While the Hindu-Muslim massacres at the time of the partition present the most dramatic examples, there have been many others. We here include excerpts from a report on Buddhist-Muslim riots in Burma.

Religious pluralism poses a serious challenge to national integration, or nation-building in the sense of creating a national identity which all citizens share. As we have seen, religion provided an important unifying element for many anti-colonial nationalist movements (IV. 1–5). After independence, some new states have attempted the same strategy to achieve national integration. Sizeable minorities have been either ignored or urged to conform to the majority pattern as much as possible. It seems safe to say that the option of forcible conversions to achieve national unity, practiced in the not-too-distant past in the West, is no longer open to governments.

Attempts to impose the majority religion and culture on the minorities, or the fear of such attempts, have given rise to separatist movements in which minorities have sought some measure of political autonomy, whether an independent Muslim state (Pakistan) or a Sikh state within a federal union (Punjab in India).

Another strategy for dealing with religious pluralism is that found in Lebanon, where the different confessional groups receive fixed quotas of cabinet posts, parliamentary seats, and government jobs, roughly in proportion to the numerical strength of each group. Finally, some governments have adopted the principle of a secular state, which officially ignores all religious differences in its policies. India has pursued this strategy. Despite innumerable difficulties, the experience of the West suggests that secularism is indeed the answer, in the long run, to the problem of religious pluralism.

ANOMIC COMMUNAL CONFLICT

Violent conflict between religious groups is not a defunct phenomenon in the West, as amply demonstrated by protracted Protestant-Catholic conflict bordering on civil war in Northern Ireland in 1969–70. The violent demonstrations, spontaneous riots, organized street fights, and barricaded boundaries of segregated residential districts in Belfast all have very close parallels in South and Southeast Asia.

Communal violence has frequently been sparked by reports of insults to religion by members of the other community. Numerous Hindu-Muslim riots in India have followed the alleged killing of cows by Muslims, or noisy Hindu processions passing by mosques at times of prayer. Frequently the members of clerical groups in either or both religious communities take the lead in inflaming communal passions (the Rev. Ian Paisley in Northern Ireland, Buddhist monks in Burma).

The religious symbols, however, frequently stand most importantly for group self-esteem, and underlying them are conflicting social, economic, and political interests. It is the intense competition for scarce resources in the essentially secular areas of life which underlies most communal conflict, and religious group identities have been manipulated fairly easily by interested parties. In some cases, of course, violent conflict has served to dramatize the valid grievances of both minorities and majorities.

1. Report on Buddhist-Muslim Riots in Burma

In this lengthy report on the 1938 riots, much attention was paid to the underlying social and economic causes of communal tensions. In the following passages, the main emphasis is on the role of the press and that of the Buddhist monks in precipitating the outbreak of violence. [1]

▶ ▶   We have already referred in our Interim Report to the part played by the Burmese Press for a long time in fostering in Burma a condition of communal ill feeling between Burmans and Indians which was not only historically almost unknown in the country but which was, and actually still is, wholly inconsistent with the Burmese character. These efforts have been assisted by political developments and economic influences. But none of us is prepared to believe that, whatever the weight of these developments and influences may have been, they would have resulted in the deliberate hunting down of Indians that occurred in many places in July and August, and the equally deliberate campaign to drive them from Burma that has developed since and the social disorders which have resulted, but for the mischievous incitement of the Burmese Press and of other political and social agitators. It was, we think, a case of the deliberate sabotage for political reasons of the traditional relations of tolerance and goodwill which had hitherto existed in the country. And not its least danger lies in creating for the first time a communal problem in Burma which in its results must be disastrous to the country as a whole.

----

[1] From *Final Report of the Riot Inquiry Committee* (Rangoon: Government Printing and Stationery, 1939), pp. 7–8, 10, 12–13, 277–278.

We have, therefore, to see how the political and communal themes were interwoven into the contributions of the Burmese Press from the 19th until the 26th of July [1938] when the actual rioting started. The first notice of Maung Shwe Hpi's book in the Burmese Press was, we believe, taken on the 19th of July.

On that day the Rangoon *Sun* (we shall, for short, hereafter call it the *Sun*) published an article by Ledi U Uithokdasara of the Theingyi *Kyaung*, Shwedagon Pagoda. It drew attention to the book "Moulvi Yogi Awada Sadan" and its second publication and it urged all Buddhists to take "urgent action" against the book. It set out a resumé of the objectionable passages from it which it referred to as "injuring the interests of the Buddhist religion and of the Burmese people." As we have said before, the book was an unpardonable piece of folly and bad taste but it is absurd to suppose that, by itself, it could have affected by one iota either the great religion of Buddha or the national interests of the Burmese people. . . .

On the 21st of July the pace quickened. The *Sun* published a highly intemperate article over the name of U Keittima of the Theyettaw Kyaungdaik. It is a highly improper contribution attacking Muslims in general, referring to them as the people who have "taken possession of the wealth of the Burmese people and also their daughters and sisters" and as having levelled insults at the Burmese in spite of the fact that they had dispossessed them of their property. It observed that communal trouble was likely to emerge and exhorted all Burmese Buddhists to join together and to contribute newspaper articles denouncing Islam as a false religion. In the same issue of the *Sun* appeared an article contributed by U Paduma, of the Publicity Bureau of the Thathana Mamaka Young Sanghas' Association of Rangoon, in which he denounced the book and intimated that it has been brought to the notice of the General Council of that Association and that the Council proposed to take strong measures about it. A similar announcement, also over the name of U Paduma, was also made in the *New Light of Burma* on the same day. The Indian Press contented itself on the 21st of July, through the *Daily Sher*, by deploring in the editorial column the continuance and spread of ill feeling toward Indians in Burma. [pp. 7–8]

On the 23rd of July notices announcing the same meeting at the Shwedagon Pagoda appeared in the *Sun*, *New Light of Burma* and *Progress*.

The *Myanma-Uzun* referred to the offense given by the book and the *Sun* published three letters, among them one from Maung Nyunt Tin warning Maung Shwe Hpi, and another urging the raising of funds to take "necessary" action. Moreover, the *Sun* published a cartoon of the book being thrown at the head of a Burman Buddhist whilst a policeman, designed to represent the Coalition Government, stood passively by. A photographic reproduction of the cover of the book was included in the issue and a report of the preliminary meeting of the Thathana Mamaka Young Sanghas' Association held on the 21st of July. Lastly, a correspondent in this issue appealed to all Buddhist newspapers to publish in bold type every day the words:

"BUDDHISM HAS BEEN INSULTED.

TAKE IMMEDIATE STEPS." [p. 10]

That brings us to the morning of the 26th of July. We have already referred to the meeting upon the platform of the Shwedagon Pagoda convened for that day. That had been decided upon, and the agenda settled, at the meeting of the All Burma Council of the Thathana Mamaka Young Sanghas' Association as early as the 21st of July and it had been given, as we have shown, great prominence in the Burmese Press. On the 24th of July leaflets of the agenda of the meeting were widely distributed throughout Rangoon by the Shwedagon Pagoda Upasaka Association and the same Association on the same day held a preliminary meeting on the platform of the Pagoda resolving that Burmans should thenceforth have no dealing with Muslims and that the twenty thousand leaflets should be distributed in order "to acquaint the public with the disparaging remarks of Maung Shwe Hpi against the Buddhist religion." On the same evening members of the Association drove through Kemmendine calling upon all Buddhists to come to the mass meeting on the 26th. Meanwhile, the All Burma Muslim League had held two meetings — one on the 24th and one on the 25th to express their profound regret at the publication of the book and completely dissociating themselves from it. That then was the position on the morning of the 26th of July.

The 26th of July was a Tuesday during an unusually fine spell in the South-West Monsoon. The meeting was timed for about one o'clock on the platform of the Shwedagon Pagoda. We think we have already said enough to show, not only that the tone of the Burmese Press from the 19th of July onwards was both bitter and violent, but also that a deliberate attempt was being made to create on the pretext of Maung Shwe Hpi's book a demonstration of no ordinary significance. It had been organized, and its agenda had been carefully settled, by the General Council of the Thathana Mamaka Young Sanghas' Association and it had been advertised widely in the Press and by leaflet throughout Rangoon.

We are told that the meeting was attended by no less than ten thousand people of whom fifteen hundred were *pongyis* [monks]. It lasted from about 1 P.M. until 3:45 P.M. and was presided over by the Thadu Sayadaw as Chairman and Tharrawaddy U Nyeya as Secretary. Among those prominent at the meeting were representatives of the Thadu Taik and of the Bagaya *Kyaung* [monastery] at Kemmendine, the Executive Members of the General Council of the Thathana Mamaka Young Sanghas' Association at Rangoon, representatives of the Thayettaw *Kyaungdaik* [cluster of monasteries] and other Rangoon *Kyaungdaiks*, a number of representatives of various Dobama Asi-Ayon Associations and representatives of the *Sun*, the *New Light of Burma* and *Progress*. We have a record of some twelve speeches made. There is no reason why we should perpetuate them, by preserving a record of them here. It is sufficient to say that on the whole they constituted a bitter attack on Muslims. As we have said before, the Buddhist religion was not in the least jeopardy from Maung Shwe Hpi's book and there was no occasion to defend it. The tone of the meeting developed in a crescendo of vituperation and abuse against Muslims in general. Of the violent speeches made, that of U Teza, an Executive Member of the General Council of the Thathana Mamaka Young Sanghas' Association, was outstanding. Scarcely less abusive and violent was that of U Sandawuntha of the Thayettaw *Kyaungdaik*. It was noticeable that, throughout, the speeches dwelt upon the Burmese-Muslim marriage question. There was an attempt by one speaker to move a boycott of all Muslims in Burma. . . . Finally, the climax was reached when, after the close of the meeting, U Kumara of the Thayettaw *Kyaungdaik*, the President of the Rangoon Central Thathana Mamaka Young Sanghas' Association, provoked the audience to form the procession. He suggested that a procession should be taken out along the Pagoda Road to the Soortee Bara Bazaar as soon as the meeting was over "in order to show the real blood of the Burmese people who would not tolerate any insult to their race and religion." [pp. 12–13]

In our evidence we have a mournful record of these so-called *pongyis, upazins* and *koyins* [ranks of monks] up and down the country promoting meetings in their *kyaungs* for political or subversive ends, participating in rioting and, arms in their hands, leading or accompanying crowds of hooligans, committing assaults, looting and even murder and in general breaking the civil laws of the country and the laws of their own country and it must, by the encouragement it has given to the forces of disorder, be classed as one of the causes of the riots and of the general atmosphere of disturbances which has followed them. The influence of the yellow robe, whoever may wear it, is great in Burma and is on that account the more dangerous when it is misused. Its influence may be gauged by the indignation — some of it genuine — which the people have expressed to us in almost every case in which a *pongyi* has been injured, or even arrested, in these riots, no matter how dreadful his conduct may have been. We do not wish to pursue this matter, for the facts speak for themselves. We have in the course of our investigation taken specific evidence in which we have been told that in nearly fifty cases armed *pongyis* were among the crowds, in an equal number of such cases *pongyis* themselves were seen to commit assault, in nearly twenty cases *pongyis* were found looting, in eight cases they were found committing arson, and in four committed murder. We must not be taken to mean that all these cases have been judicially proved before us. On the other hand they are only those of which we have received specific evidence or to which there is a reference in official records. They are, we think, only a few of the cases that actually occurred. They are enough to show the danger in which society, and the reputation of Buddhism itself, stands at this moment at the hands of a minority of *pseudopongyis* whose influence the Sangha itself is no longer strong enough to withstand. [pp. 277–78]

MINORITY SEPARATIST MOVEMENTS

In South Asia, nationalist movements proceeded on the assumption, largely accepted in Europe after World War I, that if a group of people could be shown to constitute a *nation*, it was morally entitled to a state. Leaders of the Congress, therefore, expended much intellectual energy to prove that the Indians, despite their many religious, caste, and linguistic differences, were essentially one nation, and, hence, entitled to an independent state. The Pakistan demand, first articulated in 1940, proceeded on the same basic assumption, but found that India was not one nation but two — Hindu and Muslim. While language was the dominant factor in determining nationhood in Europe, in India religion was the dominant factor. The Muslim nation, however, was concentrated in two areas of northern India separated by a thousand miles of Hindu-majority territory, and this became the shape of the Pakistan created in 1947.

Proceeding on similar assumptions, the leaders of the Sikhs first staked out a claim to a separate state in 1946. This much smaller minority, however, was in no position to press its claim. Furthermore, after independence, Nehru and the Constituent Assembly enunciated the principle of a secular state, and the Sikh demand, even for a separate state within the Indian Union, was denounced as communal and antinational.

However, after the 1956 reorganization of states, largely on a linguistic basis, the Sikhs changed their demand to one for a Punjabi-speaking state. After much agitation, the demand was conceded to by the central government in 1966, thus achieving essentially the same goal sought by the Sikhs since Indian independence.

2. The Demand for a Separate Muslim State

In his famous presidential address to the Muslim League in 1940, Muhammad Ali Jinnah first stated the case for the creation of what was to become the state of Pakistan seven years later. The central ideological assertion was that the Muslims of India constituted a nation and, hence, were entitled to a state of their own.[2]

▶ ▶   The British government and Parliament, and more so the British nation, have been for many decades past brought up and nurtured with settled notions about India's future, based on developments in their own country which has built up the British constitution, functioning now through the Houses of Parliament and the system of cabinet. Their concept of party government functioning on political planes has become the ideal with them as the best form of government for every country, and the one-sided and powerful propaganda, which naturally appeals to the British, has led them into a serious blunder, in producing the constitution envisaged in the Government of India Act of 1935. We find that the most leading statesmen of Great Britain, saturated with these notions, have in their pronouncements seriously asserted and expressed a hope that the passage of time will harmonize the inconsistent elements of India.

A leading journal like the London *Times*, commenting on the Government of India Act of 1935, wrote: "Undoubtedly the differences between the Hindus and Muslims are not of religion in the strict sense of the word but also of law and culture, that they may be said, indeed, to represent two entirely distinct and separate civilizations. However, in the course of time, the superstition will die out and India will be molded into a single nation." So, according to the London *Times*, the only difficulties are superstitions. These fundamental and deep-rooted differences, spiritual, economic, cultural, social, and political, have been euphemized as mere "superstitions." But surely it is a flagrant disregard

[2] From Jamil-ud-din Ahmad, ed., *Some Recent Speeches and Writings of Mr. Jinnah* (Lahore, Pakistan: Sh. Muhammad Ashraf, 1946), vol. 1, pp. 174–80. Used by permission.

of the past history of the subcontinent of India as well as the fundamental Islamic conception of society vis-à-vis that of Hinduism to characterize them as mere "superstitions." Notwithstanding a thousand years of close contact, nationalities, which are as divergent today as ever, cannot at any time be expected to transform themselves into one nation merely by means of subjecting them to a democratic constitution and holding them forcibly together by unnatural and artificial methods of British parliamentary statute. What the unitary government of India for one hundred fifty years had failed to achieve cannot be realized by the imposition of a central federal government. It is inconceivable that the fiat or the writ of a government so constituted can ever command a willing and loyal obedience throughout the subcontinent by various nationalities except by means of armed force behind it.

The problem in India is not of an intercommunal character but manifestly of an international one, and it must be treated as such. So long as this basic and fundamental truth is not realized, any constitution that may be built will result in disaster and will prove destructive and harmful not only to the Mussalmans but to the British and Hindus also. If the British government are really in earnest and sincere to secure [the] peace and happiness of the people of this subcontinent, the only course open to us all is to allow the major nations separate homelands by dividing India into "autonomous national states." There is no reason why these states would be antagonistic to each other. On the other hand, the rivalry and the natural desire and efforts on the part of one to dominate the social order and establish political supremacy over the other in the government of the country will disappear. It will lead more towards natural good will by international pacts between them, and they can live in complete harmony with their neighbors. This will lead further to a friendly settlement all the more easily with regard to minorities by reciprocal arrangements and adjustments between Muslim India and Hindu India, which will far more adequately and effectively safeguard the rights and interests of Muslims and various other minorities.

It is extremely difficult to appreciate why our Hindu friends fail to understand the real nature of Islam and Hinduism. They are not religions in the strict sense of the word, but are, in fact, different and distinct social orders, and it is a dream that the Hindus and Muslims can ever evolve a common nationality, and this misconception of one Indian nation has gone far beyond the limits and is the cause of most of your troubles and will lead India to destruction if we fail to revise our notions in time. The Hindus and Muslims belong to two different religious philosophies, social customs, and literatures. They neither intermarry nor interdine together and, indeed, they belong to two different civilizations which are based mainly on conflicting ideas and conceptions. Their aspects on life and of life are different. It is quite clear that Hindus and Mussalmans derive their inspiration from different sources of history. They have different epics, different heroes, and different episodes. Very often the hero of one is a foe of the other and, likewise, their victories and defeats overlap. To yoke together two such nations under a single state, one as a numerical minority and the other as a majority, must lead to growing discontent and final destruction of any fabric that may be so built up for the government of such a state.

History has presented to us many examples, such as the union of Great Britain and Ireland, Czechoslovakia, and Poland. History has also shown us many geographical tracts, much smaller than the subcontinent of India, which otherwise might have been called one country, but which have been divided into as many states as there are nations inhabiting them. [The] Balkan Peninsula comprises as many as seven or eight sovereign states. Likewise, the Portuguese and the Spanish stand divided in the Iberian Peninsula. Whereas under the plea of the unity of India and one nation, which does not exist, it is sought to pursue here the line of one central government, we know that the history of the last twelve hundred years has failed to achieve unity and has witnessed, during the ages, India always divided into Hindu India and Muslim India. The present artificial unity of India dates back only to the British conquest and is maintained by the British bayonet, but termination of the British regime, which is implicit in the recent declaration of His Majesty's government, will be the herald of the entire break-up with worse disaster than has ever taken place during the last one thousand years under Muslims. Surely that is not the legacy which Britain would bequeath to India after one hundred fifty years of her rule, nor would Hindu and Muslim India risk such a sure catastrophe.

Muslim India cannot accept any constitution which must necessarily result in a Hindu majority government. Hindus and Muslims brought together under a democratic system forced upon the minorities can only mean Hindu rāj [rule]. Democracy of the kind with which the Congress High Command is enamored would mean the complete destruction of what is most precious in Islam. We have had ample experience of the working of the provincial constitutions during the last two and a half years and any repetition of such a government must lead to civil war and raising of private armies as recommended by Mr. Gandhi to [the] Hindus of Sikkur when he said that they must defend themselves violently or nonviolently, blow for blow, and if they could not, they must emigrate.

Mussalmans are not a minority as it is commonly known and understood. One has only got to look around. Even today, according to the British map of India, four out of eleven provinces, where the Muslims dominate more or less, are functioning notwithstanding the decision of the Hindu Congress High Command to noncooperate and prepare for civil disobedience. Mussalmans are a nation according to any definition of a nation, and they must have their homelands, their territory, and their state. We wish to live in peace and harmony with our neighbors as a free and independent people. We wish our people to develop to the fullest our spiritual, cultural, economic, social, and political life in a way that we think best and in consonance with our own ideals and according to the genius of our people. Honesty demands and the vital interest of millions of our people impose a sacred duty upon us to find an honorable and peaceful solution, which would be just and fair to all. But at the same time we cannot be moved or diverted from our purpose and objective by threats or intimidations. We must be prepared to face all difficulties and consequences, make all the sacrifices that may be required of us to achieve the goal we have set in front of us.

3. The Demand for a Sikh-Majority State

This pamphlet published by the Sikh Youth Federation put forth the arguments for Punjabi Suba, a Punjabi-speaking state. With considerable frankness, it describes the change from a Sikh communal demand to an ostensibly secular linguistic one.[3]

▶ ▶   For quite some time before India attained independence, the British regime in India was sustained by communal dissension. Communal differences were more pronounced in the Punjab than anywhere else in India, because India's three main religious communities were comparatively evenly balanced in that area, in contrast with other parts of the country. Here, communalism was deliberately nursed, and people tended increasingly to move to the narrow communal grooves from the open ground of the common national life. They wanted to prove that they constituted distinct nationalities, with different cultures and separate languages. The mother tongue of the whole of the Punjab was Punjabi. However, in the years preceding partition, the Muslims declared that their mother tongue was Urdu, and the Arya Samajist Hindus declared

[3] From *The Demand for the Punjabi Suba: A Most Crucial Challenge to Indian Secularism* (Calcutta: The Sikh Youth Federation [n.d.]), pp. 17–20, 32–33.

that theirs was Hindi. The Sanatanist Hindus maintained a position of neutrality. That left the Sikhs alone to champion Punjabi, the mother tongue of all Punjabis.

In 1946–47, while the Congress wavered on the question of the partition of India, the one leader and the one community that strongly opposed partition were Master Tara Singh and the Sikhs. On the eve of the independence, in the midst of fierce communal riots, the Hindus and Sikhs of the Punjab chose Master Tara Singh to be their dictator for the organization of defense against riots. This looked like a happy augury for the growth of amity between the Hindus and the Sikhs of the Punjab. Nevertheless, as soon as India became free, fresh communal tensions rose, and matters came to [a] head with the census. Inspired by the Arya Samajist reaction, large numbers of Hindus declared Hindi as their mother tongue even though 80 percent of the Hindus could not speak two correct sentences in Hindi. The Government realized the futility of recording the mother tongue in the census papers, and ordered that the mother tongue column would not be filled.

The concerted attempt of Punjabi Hindu organizations to make Punjabi Hindus furnish false particulars of their mother tongue, intensified the Sikh fears, which had taken root even before partition, and had been aggravated by the stunning losses of private property and important religious shrines in Pakistan. Despite this fact, the Sikhs had voluntarily accepted the dispensation that obtained. They had been given an option, and they had made a deliberate choice. They had declared that their destiny lay with India, whose secular leadership had promised to guard their interests. In the united Punjab, the Sikhs could have held a balance of power between the Hindus and the Muslims; in the partitioned Punjab, they were reduced to the position of a hopeless minority. They fondly hoped that the Congress leadership at the Centre would, in consonance with its declared ideals, be generous to minority and would carve out an area in the Punjab where the Sikhs would have unrestricted opportunity of growth and development in accordance with their special genius. Had not Mr. Nehru said at the beginning of 1947 that there was nothing wrong in conceding a political area in North India where the Sikhs might also freely experience the glow of freedom?

But the plea for a Sikh homeland within the Indian Union was decried as communal, and the Akali Dal, which has since proved to be the sole representative organization of the Sikhs, put forward an alternative demand, which it thought would not be repugnant to India's secularism — the creation of a Punjabi-speaking State. At the time the demand was made, the Sikhs constituted just 45 percent of the population in the area that was then contemplated to be included in the Punjabi-speaking State. However, the merger of PEPSU [Patiala and East Punjab States Union] tipped the balance in favor of the Sikhs, who now form 55 percent of the population of the Punjabi-speaking region of the Punjab. . . .

With the formation of Andhra on October 1, 1953, the demand for the linguistic redistribution of State boundaries gathered momentum. In deference to the growing sentiments of the people, the Government of India constituted a States Reorganization Commission in December, 1953. [The Commission, however, rejected the arguments for a Punjabi-speaking State.] [pp. 17–20]

One argument advanced against the Punjabi Suba with irritating frequency is that the demand for it is communal. No one, however, has cared to ask: If the demand for a Punjabi Suba is communal, what is the opposition to it? *Blitz* [a leftist weekly] . . . puts the case squarely under the heading, "Punjabi Hindus, Not Sikhs, Communal!" "What is communal," says *Blitz*, "is the opposition of the Punjabi Hindus (to the Punjabi Suba)." The Punjabi Hindu, it goes on to say, "has ever been in the forefront of communalism. He is denying his mother tongue and native script."

Taking the worst view of the matter: the demand for a Punjabi Suba is communal as also the opposition to this demand. Is it fair that the Government should align itself with the opposition to this demand, and that too in disregard of the following vital principles:

1. The principle of demarcation of State boundaries on a linguistic basis, accepted and implemented everywhere else in India;
2. The principle of generous treatment to minorities in a secular democracy;
3. The principle of secularism, by which we in India swear.

While the first two principles do not require any elaboration, the third one may be discussed at some length, because the opposition to the demand for a Punjabi Suba is a breach of our deeply cherished secular ideals.

Secularism, in the context of Indian conditions, means not allowing communal biases to determine or sway State policy — irrespective of whether these communal biases are Hindu, Muslim, Sikh, or Christian. Under this scheme of things, if there is a disagreement between two sections of the people over certain issues, we must let the decision of the majority prevail. In respect of the Punjabi-speaking region of the Punjab, however, the wishes of 45 percent of its population (the Hindus, even conceding that all Hindus in that region are opposed to the formation of a

Punjabi-speaking State, which of course, is not true) are allowed to prevail against the wishes of the 55 percent of its population (the Sikhs). [pp. 32–33]

IDEOLOGIES OF MAJORITY DOMINANCE

In Asia, as in the West, ideologies have been formulated which glorify the virtues of the dominant religion and culture and justify the suppression of minorities. In American history, the normative assertion that this is a "Protestant nation" was not conclusively rejected until the election of John F. Kennedy in 1960, and vestiges of the notion of a "Christian nation" still linger. Paradoxically, the Hindu communalists who vociferously opposed the partition of India propounded precisely the same religious view of nationality as the leaders of the Muslim League. Thus, Golwalkar's theory of the Hindu nation was remarkably congruent with Jinnah's two-nation theory. Golwalkar's purpose, however, was to provide a rationale for the suppression of all non-Hindu elements of the national culture.

After the formation of Pakistan, somewhat similar assumptions prevailed with respect to the Hindu minority in the eastern wing of the country. As the *raison d'être* of Pakistan is the existence of a state not only controlled by Muslims but informed by Islamic ideology, the Hindu minority should either make the necessary psychological adjustments to the situation or leave. The Muslim tradition of tolerance of minorities would be followed, but institutions which perpetuated minority separateness in the political sphere, such as separate electorates, would be continued because the *majority* community wanted them.

4. The Hindu Nation Concept

In a small book first published before partition, M. S. Golwalkar, leader of the extremist Rashtriya Swayamsevak Sangh (RSS), expounded his views on the Hindu nation. Note particularly his recommendations on the treatment of the minorities.[4]

Now we shall proceed to understand our Nationhood in the light of this scientific concept. Here is our vast country, Hindustan, the land of Hindus, their home country, hereditary territory, a definite geographical

---

[4] From M. S. Golwalkar, *We or Our Nationhood Defined* (Nagpur, India: Bharat Prakashan, 1947), 4th ed., pp. 48–49, 51–53, 55–56. Used by permission.

unity, delimited naturally by the sublime Himalayas on the North side, the limitless ocean on the other three sides, an ideal piece of land, deserving in every respect to be called a Country, fulfilling all that the word should imply in the Nation idea. Living in this Country since pre-historic times is the ancient Race — the Hindu Race, united together by common traditions, by memories of common glory and disaster, by similar historical, political, social, religious and other experiences, living under the same influences, and evolving a common culture, a common mother language, common customs, common aspirations. This great Hindu Race professes its illustrious Hindu Religion, the only Religion in the world worthy of being so denominated, which in its variety is still an organic whole, capable of feeding the noble aspirations of all men, of all stages, of all grades, aptitudes and capacities, enriched by the noblest philosophy of life in all its functions, and hallowed by an unbroken interminable succession of divine spiritual geniuses, a religion of which any sane man may be justly proud. Guided by this Religion in all walks of life, individual, social, political, the Race evolved a culture, which despite the degenerating contact with the debased "civilizations" of the Mussalmans and the Europeans, for the last ten centuries, is still the noblest in the world. The fruit proves the worth of the tree and the common mind of a people the value of its culture. The spirit of broad catholicism, generosity, toleration, truth, sacrifice and love for all life, which characterizes the average Hindu mind not wholly vitiated by Western influence, bears eloquent testimony to the greatness of Hindu culture. And even those, spoiled by contamination with foreign in-fluences, do not but compare favorably with the best in the rest of the world. Not only has this culture been most markedly effective in molding man after the picture of God, but in the field of learning (we distinguish learning and knowledge) also, it has produced, to the im-mortal glory of the Race, intellectual giants, outshining the greatest savants of the modern Scientific world. . . . [pp. 48–49] The last, language, seems to present some difficulties, for in this country every province has its own language. It appears as if the linguistic unity is want-ing, and there are not one but many "Nations," separated from each other by linguistic differences. But in fact that is not so. There is but one language, Sanskrit, of which these many "languages" are mere off-shoots, the children of the mother language. Sanskrit, the dialect of the Gods, is common to all from the Himalayas to the ocean in the South, from East to West and all the modern sister languages are through it so much interrelated as to be practically one. . . . There is thus no doubt regarding the existence in us of the fifth component of the Nation idea —

language. Thus applying the modern understanding of "Nation" to our present conditions, the conclusion is unquestionably forced upon us that in this country, Hindustan, the Hindu Race with its Hindu Religion, Hindu Culture and Hindu Language (the natural family of Sanskrit and her offspring) complete the Nation concept; that, in fine, in Hindustan exists and must needs exist the ancient Hindu Nation and nought else but the Hindu Nation. All those not belonging to the national, i.e., Hindu Race, Religion, Culture and Language, naturally fall out of the pale of real "National" life.

We repeat: in Hindustan, the land of the Hindus, lives and should live the Hindu Nation — satisfying all the five essential requirements of the scientific nation concept of the modern world. Consequently only those movements are truly "National" as aim at rebuilding, revitalizing, and emancipating from its present stupor, the Hindu Nation. Those only are nationalist patriots, who, with the aspiration to glorify the Hindu Race and Nation next to their heart, are prompted into activity and strive to achieve that goal. All others, posing to be patriots and willfully indulging in a course of action detrimental to the Hindu Nation are traitors and enemies to the National Cause or, to take a more charitable view if unintentionally and unwillingly led into such a course, mere simpletons, misguided ignorant fools.

If, as is indisputably proved, Hindustan is the land of the Hindus and is the *terra firma* for the Hindu Nation alone to flourish upon, what is to be the fate of all those, who, today, happen to live upon the land, though not belonging to the Hindu Race, Religion and Culture? This question is too very common and has its genesis in the generous impulse of so many Hindus themselves, that it deserves at least a brief answer.

At the outset we must bear in mind that so far as "Nation" is concerned, all those who fall outside the five-fold limits of that idea can have no place in the national life, unless they abandon their differences, and completely merge themselves in the National Race. So long, however as they maintain their racial, religious and cultural differences, they cannot but be only foreigners, who may be either friendly or inimical to the Nation. . . . [pp. 51–53]

From this standpoint . . . the non-Hindu peoples in Hindustan must either adopt the Hindu culture and language, must learn to respect and hold in reverence Hindu religion, must entertain no idea but those of glorification of the Hindu race and culture, i.e., they must not only give up their attitude of intolerance and ungratefulness towards this land and its agelong traditions but must also cultivate the positive attitude of love and devotion instead — in one word they must cease to be foreigners, or may stay in the country wholly subordinated to the Hindu Nation, claiming nothing, deserving no privileges, far less any preferential treatment — not even citizen's rights. There is, or at least should be, no other course for them to adopt. We are an old nation; and let us deal, as old nations ought to and do deal, with the foreign races, who have chosen to live in our country. [pp. 55–56]

5. The Ideological Islamic State

After the military coup of 1958 and the abrogation of the constitution, a commission was appointed to recommend the structure of a new constitution. In its 1961 report, the commission strongly recommended separate electorates, a device which would keep the Hindus as a separate political entity, despite the fact that the Hindu leaders themselves preferred a joint electorate which would encourage the development of a sense of common Pakistani citizenship. [5]

▶ ▶   It cannot be denied that Pakistan is based on Islamic ideology, nor can there be any doubt that the main bond between the two wings of Pakistan is this ideology. This state cannot be, in the nature of things, secular, as Islam prevades the life of a Muslim in all its aspects and does not allow politics to be kept apart from ethics, as is the case in countries with secular constitutions. The moment it is stated that Pakistan is an ideological, and not a secular, State, our critics at once think of theocracy which, in its widely accepted sense, is rule by priests in the name of God; but there is no priesthood in Islam and we are for a representative form of government. We are, therefore, theocratic only to the extent that we hold that real sovereignty belongs to God, which no non-Muslim of Pakistan disputes. Those who are anxious for establishing a classless society based on social justice should not be scared away by the malicious propaganda made against Islam, and by indiscreet and fanatical statements made by some of the doctrinaire Mussalmans, giving the general impression that a non-Muslim is at a disadvantage in a Muslim State; for, the very basis of Islam, the Qur'an, has given a charter of equal civil liberties to humanity whereunder merit and not birth counts. A distinction no doubt exists between subjects loyal to the State and those who are not, but this obtains in a secular form as well. History is replete with instances of non-Muslims having received just and generous

---

[5] From *Report of the Constitution Commission, Pakistan, 1961* (Karachi: Government of Pakistan Press, 1962), pp. 72–76.

treatment in Islamic countries. It cannot be denied that there were some instances of persecutions of non-Muslims in some stages of Muslim history, but they were mostly for political purposes. Muslim rulers have been more tolerant and just to non-Muslims than other rulers have been to those who did not belong to their faith. Arnold in *The Preaching of Islam* points out: "The very existence of so many Christian sects and communities in countries that have been for centuries under Muham-madan rule is an abiding testimony to the toleration they have enjoyed, and shows that the persecutions they have from time to time been called upon to endure at the hands of bigots and fanatics, have been excited by some special and local circumstances rather than inspired by a settled principle of intolerance." . . . The minorities in Pakistan have been quite happy and there has been no interference with their rights or liberty. As Cantwell Smith in his book, *Islam in Modern History*, points out, the rights and treatment accorded to any minority or nonpowerful group in any state depend on the ideals of those in power. A mere enumera-tion of the rights in the constitution and a declaration that the state is secular, by itself, is not a practical guarantee of the rights of the minorities. The minorities in Pakistan cannot complain that they have, in any way, been tyrannized over by the majority community. Whether the minorities felt secure, or not, depends on the attitude of the majority toward them and no non-Muslim in Pakistan can, with justification, complain that the attitude of the majority has not been one of friendliness.

It thus being our duty to safeguard the rights of the minorities, it is necessary to take into consideration their wishes in deciding whether we should have separate, or joint, electorates. One would normally expect the minorities, especially in a country where people are basically religious, to ask for separate electorates and that was what we did when we were a minority in undivided India. When Pakistan came into being, the minorities in West Pakistan asked for separate electorates and, though the National Assembly, acting under the late Constitution, once granted their demand at the end of 1956, it ultimately decided in favor of joint electorates for the whole country, mainly because, in East Pakistan, the caste Hindus were for joint electorate and the then prime minister apparently did not like to displease them, and it was considered that it would not be proper to have separate electorates in one part of Pakistan and joint in the other. As regards East Pakistan the speeches delivered in the National Assembly at its Dacca session of 1956 give the impression that the entire Hindu population of East Pakistan was desirous of having a joint electorate, but . . . [the fact is that] the scheduled castes asked for an electorate separate from that of the Caste Hindus. . . . . That the scheduled castes form a decided majority of the non-Muslim minorities in East Pakistan is clear from the figures of the last census and, considering the social disabilities of this class of Hindus owing to caste restrictions, we think that they, in the nature of things, would like to have separate electorates and not reduce the number of their representatives in the House by advocating the system of joint electorate.

The demand for a joint electorate by the minorities in East Pakistan, which, as we have indicated, is not natural, was explained by the then prime minister as due to a high sense of citizenship and a keen desire to merge themselves in the majority; it was also said that, because in the past the Hindus of undivided India denied to the Muslims the right of separate electorates demanded by them as a minority community, the Hindu members of the Assembly felt that they should not demand a similar protection, although their offer to merge themselves in the nation would cause them disadvantage by reducing the number of their representatives in the House. . . . The speeches made in favor of joint electorate by the minority members, we take it, represented mainly the Congress point of view. It is significant that when the Muslim League members pointed out that several members of the minority community were living alone in Pakistan, keeping their families in India, and that, consequently, they were not reconciled to the idea of Pakistan, a Caste Hindu member of the Assembly, while asking for joint electorate, gave an explanation which is hardly convincing. He said that they kept their families in India as their sons had no chance of getting employment in Pakistan. To quote his own words: ". . . brilliant young men who are coming out of the University, have no avenues for careers for themselves in East Bengal. They are not getting any employment here. Should they remain here and roam about in the streets to be clapped in jail as communists? Naturally, they go to other places. The whole of the world is open to them; and every citizen of a country has got the right to go out of his country if that is necessary for procuring employments. . . ."

One would pause at this stage and ask whether it is natural for any person entertaining such feeling about Pakistan, which imply not only its inability but also its unwillingness to provide employment for his sons, to have, at the same time, a burning desire to form [a] single nation in this country. On the other hand, under the circumstances as stated by him, he should, if he is prudent (we have no reason to doubt that he is), be anxious for separate electorates so that there may be a sufficient number of the representatives of the minorities who could speak in the House for these brilliant young men who are anxious to serve Pakistan and yet do not get employment, but on the other hand, run the risk of being clapped in jail branded as communists. As a matter of fact, it appears to us that these "brilliant young men" are not anxious to work for Pakistan.

There have been, we understand, cases of persons of the Hindu community who had been abroad on scholarships earned in Pakistan, going away to India after being fully qualified. This indicates that these young men are not seen in employment in our country not because they are unable to secure it, but because they are not desirous of serving this country. They apparently do not feel happy here, which indicates that they are not reconciled to the idea of Pakistan. Soon after the abrogation of the late constitution, when the present regime took effective steps against persons evading income-tax and foreign exchange restrictions, a Caste Hindu judge of the Dacca High Court, who had gone to West Bengal for the vacation, failed to return and ultimately resigned. A Hindu CSP officer, who was transferred to West Pakistan, left the country and settled down in India. As long as these members of the minority community have the feeling that their families will not be happy in Pakistan, it cannot be said that there should be only one electorate, sharing with us our advantages and disadvantages. . . .

In these circumstances, their demand for joint electorate seems clearly to be for some ulterior purpose other than the welfare of Pakistan. Some of the witnesses, while referring to this aspect of the matter, stated that the Caste Hindus who lived in Pakistan, leaving their families in West Bengal, are under the influence of that part of India, and that their demand was due to a desire to influence the elections against the ideology of Pakistan. Having regard to the course of probable human conduct, we are not prepared to say that this view is not amply justified. As for the fact that in other Muslim countries there are joint electorates, which was one of the points urged for a joint electorate in the Assembly debates, it appears to have been overlooked that, by the time a representative form of government, requiring elections to be held, came into force in those countries, the minorities there had for centuries settled down as the nationals of those countries and had no reason to look for guidance from outside. They have, generation after generation been living, with their families, and their young men have been serving in those countries. But, in Pakistan, the tendency of the Caste Hindus has been otherwise, and, until we can reasonably be certain that they have reconciled themselves to the continuance of Pakistan, it does not appear safe to have joint electorate, apart from the fact that the majority of scheduled castes are not in its favor. Another reason given by one of the advocates of separate electorates — an experienced politician — is that, in case joint electorate is adopted, there is likelihood of the Muslims doing propaganda against Hindus being elected, which might lead to communal friction. In our opinion, there is considerable force in this view. [pp. 72–76]

THE POLITICS OF COMMUNAL EQUILIBRIUM

Various constitutional and legal devices have been elaborated to solve the problems generated by religious pluralism. In a sense, the *millet* system of the Ottoman Empire dealt with the religious minorities by making each community a little state within a state. Great autonomy in legal (see III. 1), educational, social, and economic matters was exercised by each religious community. Each minority was protected by being sealed off from the rest of the population and was free to develop its own institutions. However, this option is clearly not open to a state also committed to modernization.

In British India, one important step was taken in this direction by granting separate electorates to the Muslim minority in 1909. A certain number of seats was reserved for the Muslims in the legislature, and only Muslims could vote for candidates for these seats. This institutional device, extended to other minorities also in 1919 and 1935, recognized religious communities as separate political units. Separate electorates were abolished by the Indian constitution of 1950, but as we have seen (VII. 5), in Pakistan the device was continued. The most elaborate system of communal quotas still in use, however, is found in Lebanon.

6. The National Pact in Lebanon

In the following article, George Dib, an official in the Lebanese Ministry of Foreign Affairs, traces the background of the National Pact and provides an English translation of extracts from Premier Riadh es-Solh's speech in Parliament in 1943 when the pact was concluded. This peculiarly Lebanese solution to the problem of religious pluralism has achieved a kind of static justice between the Muslim and Christian communities, but at the cost of a more dynamic process of political development.[6]

---

[6] From George Dib, "Selections from Riadh Solh's Speech to the Lebanese Assembly [October, 1943] Embodying the Main Principles of the Lebanese 'National Pact'," *Middle East Forum* (Beirut), vol. 35, no. 1 (January, 1959), pp. 6–7. Used by permission.

▶ ▶   The Lebanese National Pact of 1943 about which there has been so much talk during the recent crisis is almost wholly based on a statement of policy delivered by the late ex-premier Riadh es-Solh in the Lebanese Parliament in October, 1943. What follows is a brief introduction to a translation of the most important parts of Solh's speech, which has not, as far as I know, ever been published in English.

Perhaps the best way to understand the National Pact of 1943 is to liken it to a marriage contract. This simile suggests not only the nature of the Pact but also the most curious thing about it, namely that it has never been written down. For, just as a marriage contract is really based on the moral qualities of the individuals who compose it, so the Pact of 1943 is based on the moral qualities of the groups that composed it. Indeed, much disappointment might have been avoided if people had realized that the Pact could not go further nor become more effective than the state of the country generally would allow.

The origin of the National Pact of 1943 goes back to 1920 when General Gouraud, the French High Commissioner, established by decree the state of Greater Lebanon, in which certain areas previously Syrian were included. This act of annexation was contested, legally and politically, by the nationalists of Syria and by a group of Lebanese, mainly Muslims, who were known at the time as the "Negativists"; most prominent among them were Riadh es-Solh, Abdul Hamid Karami (father of the present Premier of Lebanon), Omar Beihum, Amin Erslan, as well as many others. Legally, the action was contested on the ground that France was not empowered by her Mandatory position to annex Syrian territory to Lebanon; politically, they regarded it as an imperialist plot designed to add to the divisions of the Arab countries.

With time, however, the Syrians began gradually to give up their demand for the return of the annexed territories, with a view to making Syrian independence easier to obtain. This change of attitude was reflected in a similar change amongst the "Negativists" of Lebanon for very much the same reasons. From then on they began to take a more active part in Lebanese political life, instead of boycotting elections as they had done previously. . . .

At the same time another group of Lebanese (mainly Christians), led by Michel Zakkour, Bishara el-Khoury, and Youssef es-Soda, was emerging. This group aimed at getting closer to the "Negativists" whose aims, perhaps, were simply to get rid of the foreigners. And as early as 1926, Youssef es-Soda founded a party with the name "The Pact" (the words "pact" and "convention" are the same in Arabic: *mithaq*) which called for an understanding amongst all Lebanese, no matter what their religion. This was in fact the first Lebanese party with a national basis.

These trends of thought grew little by little and took form with time until, in 1943, they became political principles strong enough to motivate Lebanese society. Thus, in 1943, Bishara el-Khoury and Riadh es-Solh, the two men who emerged as the leading representatives of these principles, came to an agreement on the following lines: First, the Christians gave up the idea of an isolated Lebanon and accepted an independent and sovereign Lebanon within the Arab world. The Muslims, in return, gave up the idea of giving back to Syria the territories which had been annexed to Lebanon and also the aim of uniting Lebanon with the Arab world. Not only were the Lebanese agreed on this point; the other Arab countries were ready to accept it, as is proved by the fact that the Arab League Pact of 1945 guaranteed the independence of Lebanon in its present form. Secondly, the Christians gave up the idea of foreign protection, either by way of occupation, military outposts or the concluding of treaties with the Western Powers. (Hence the Opposition's resistance to Lebanon's accepting the Eisenhower doctrine in January, 1957). In return, the Muslims agreed to stop working to make the Lebanon submit to Syrian or Arab influence. Thirdly, the number of seats in Parliament was to be distributed in such a way as to ensure a majority to the Christians. Also, the President of the Republic was always to be a Christian, while the Premier in the Government was always a Muslim. So came into existence the confessional system of government which Lebanon has kept to this day. It is based, as I have said, not on any written constitution, but on certain agreements and understandings between leading politicians of the period in which Lebanon's independence was forged.

SELECTIONS FROM RIADH ES-SOLH'S SPEECH

Our foremost duty is, to organize our independence in such a way as to make it a living reality and a blessing to be shared by all Lebanese. . . . We, together with you, are going to take the initiative and modify the Lebanese constitution so that it becomes in full accord with the true meaning of independence. You know, gentlemen, that in the Lebanese constitution there are certain Articles which put a limit on our full right to exercise our independence; they give to non-Lebanese a hand in conducting our nation's affairs. My government will ask the parliament, instantly, to introduce into the constitution modifications which will liberate it from the ties that were put on it so that it becomes the constitution of a fully independent state. . . .

Independence should not only be a mere national selfishness and a satisfaction answering the pride of a national soul; it should also be a blessing enjoyed by all the people. For this reason, my government, which understands independence in this manner, wants every Lebanese to enjoy the advantages of this era of constitutional independence and wants its traces to appear in all walks of life. This is the spirit which my government will impart everywhere and on its basis it will introduce various modifications into the machinery of government and to the public life of the nation.

My government will not follow the narrow politics which used to concentrate the attention of the Lebanese on small local matters and which planted amongst them divisions and hatred; it will carry them away from these things and open to them wider horizons which befit their well-known intelligence and indefatigable activity. This government, of which I have the honor to be the premier, wants to elevate every Lebanese and to have him share, in mind and in deeds, in a noble policy based on the prosperity, progress and the strength of the Lebanon. It will work in all seriousness and sincerity to unite everyone and to remove hatred, especially hatreds which came to a head during this election campaign, so that our strength and energy can be poured into the service of the highest interests of the nation. . . .

One of the bases of the reformation which the highest interests of Lebanon necessitates is the handling of confessionalism and the eradication of its evils. For confessionalism does not only hinder the progress of the nation and give it a bad reputation; it poisons relations between the several different groups which go to make up the Lebanese people. And we have witnessed how confessionalism, most of the time, was used as an instrument for personal profit as well as an insult to our national life in Lebanon, an insult from which others benefited. We are confident that when people are filled with the national feeling which grows with independence, under a popular system of government, they will willingly and confidently abolish the confessional system which weakens the nation.

The hour in which the abolishing of confessionalism becomes possible will be a blessed hour of full national awakening in the history of the Lebanon. We shall do our utmost to reach this historical hour at the earliest possible moment, if God permits. And it is only natural that to organize this demands preparation and planning in many different directions. . . .

What holds true of confessionalism holds true also of provincialism which, when intensified, makes many nations out of one nation.

PART THREE

Religion and Socio-Economic Change

VIII

The Religious Legitimation of Change

Beyond its significance for the individual, the dominant societal role of religion in traditional societies was the legitimation of existing structures. Not only government and law but the whole network of socio-economic relationships tended to become sacralized. One of the most important qualities of the sacred was that it was unchanging. The saying attributed to the Prophet Muhammad, "All innovation is the work of the devil," has its counterparts, stated or unstated, in the Hindu, Buddhist, and Catholic traditions as well.

Once-sacred polities have undergone profound secularization over the past century, and the governments of the contemporary Third World now find thrust upon them the weighty responsibility, new in human history, of directing a process of hopefully massive socio-economic change. The question which concerns us here is whether religion, the function of which in the past was to legitimize prevailing socio-economic systems, can now be reinterpreted to give positive ideological support to secularized political systems committed to basic social change. To go one step further, we must ask whether religion can not only legitimize but *motivate* and *initiate* change.

For the most part, thus far significant change has required the expansion of the polity at the expense of traditional religion. If "sacred"

197

meant "unchanging," it was necessary to secularize law, for example, in order to eliminate polygamy or introduce other changes in family patterns. (See Chapter III.) Such efforts have always divided religious opinion, the traditionalists insisting that sacred law admitted of no change, the modernists arguing that only the most general principles were unchanging and that in their application to evolving social needs "sacred" meant "dynamic."

In some of the readings in this and later chapters, however, the religious interpreters go beyond defensive positions to declare the moral imperative of basic change, even without reference to the probable adverse effect of such change on institutionalized religion itself. In aligning themselves on the side of socio-economic change, some of the interpreters are perfectly aware that the comprehensive secularization of culture is an almost certain concomitant of modernization.

In this chapter, we shall consider three problems which are crucial for almost all the countries of the Third World: economic development, land reform, and family planning. In examining the positions on these problems taken by the religious interpreters of the various traditions, we can see the possibilities, at least, of religion as a source of ideological support to governments with programs of modernization. It must be noted, however, that some of these statements are little more than the views of individuals, particularly in the Asian religious systems lacking coherent ecclesiastical organization.

ECONOMIC DEVELOPMENT AS A RELIGIOUS VALUE

With the exception of Islam, the major religions have on the whole tended to place a low value on the material aspect of life. This tendency is strongest in Buddhism, which exalts the withdrawal from mundane concerns into the monastic life; the highest religious values are realized by reducing one's material possessions to the barest minimum. While Hinduism posits the pursuit of *artha* (wealth) as a valid aim of life, this is ideally only for man in the householder stage of life, after which he withdraws by two stages to seek the ultimate religious goal, *moksha* (release from rebirth).

In Catholicism, the praise of poverty, as a condition more conducive to the realization of spiritual values in this life and the bliss of heaven throughout eternity, has been a major theme until very recently and was repeated in Pope Paul's address to Colombian peasants in 1968. The attempt to establish economic development as a religious value in its own right, therefore, represents a significant change in doctrine. Previously, despite the social encyclicals, the emphasis was on paternalistic charity; the new emphasis is on economic growth and more equitable distribution as a matter of justice.

1. On the Development of Peoples

In 1967, Pope Paul VI issued his well-known encyclical, *Populorum Progressio*. While liberals in the Latin American church felt it did not go far enough, the document served to focus attention on, and stimulate discussion of, the vital question of development.[1]

▶ ▶   *1. Development of Peoples*

The development of peoples has the church's close attention, particularly the development of those peoples who are striving to escape from hunger, misery, endemic diseases and ignorance; of those who are looking for a wider share in the benefits of civilization and a more active improvement of their human qualities; of those who are aiming purposefully at their complete fulfillment. Following on the Second Vatican Ecumenical Council, a renewed consciousness of the demands of the Gospel makes it her duty to put herself at the service of all, to help them grasp their serious problem in all its dimensions and to convince them that solidarity in action at this turning point in human history is a matter of urgency.

2. Social Teachings of the Popes

Our predecessors in their great encyclicals, Leo XIII in *Rerum Novarum*, Pius XI in *Quadragesimo Anno*, and John XXIII in *Mater et Magistra*, and *Pacem in Terris* — not to mention the messages of Pius XII to the world — did not fail in the duty of their office of shedding the light of the Gospel on the social questions of their times.

3. The Principal Fact

Today the principal fact that we must all recognize is that the social question has become worldwide. John XXIII stated this in unambiguous terms and the council echoed him in its pastoral constitution "On the Church in the Modern World." This teaching is important and its application urgent. Today the peoples in hunger are making a dramatic appeal to the peoples blessed with abundance. The church shudders at this cry of anguish and calls each one to give a loving response of charity to this brother's cry for help. . . .

[1] From *New York Times*, March 29, 1967.

9. *Increasing Awareness*

At the same time social conflicts have taken on world dimensions. The acute disquiet which has taken hold of the poor classes in countries that are becoming industrialized is now embracing those whose economy is almost exclusively agrarian: farming people, too, are becoming aware of their undeserved hardship. There is also the scandal of glaring inequalities not merely in the enjoyment of possessions but even more in the exercise of power, while a small restricted group enjoys a refined civilization in certain regions, the remainder of the population, poor and scattered, is "deprived of nearly all possibility of personal initiative and of responsibility and oftentimes even its living and working conditions are unworthy of the human person." [*Gaudium et Spes*]

10. *Conflicts of Civilizations*

Furthermore, the conflict between traditional civilizations and the new elements of industrial civilization break down structures which do not adapt themselves to new conditions. Their framework, sometimes rigid, was the indispensable prop to personal and family life: Older people remain attached to it, the young escape from it, as from a useless barrier, to turn eagerly to new forms of life in society. The conflict of the generations is made more serious by a tragic dilemma: whether to retain ancestral institutions and convictions and renounce progress, or to admit techniques and civilizations from outside and reject along with the traditions of the past all their human richness. In effect, the moral, spiritual and religious supports of the past too often give way without securing in return any guarantee of a place in the new world.

11. *Conclusion*

In this confusion, the temptation becomes stronger to risk being swept away toward types of messianism which give promises but create illusions. The resulting dangers are patent: violent popular reactions, agitation toward insurrection and a drifting toward totalitarian ideologies. Such are the data of the problem. Its seriousness is evident to all. . . .

23. *Property*

"If someone who has the riches of this world sees his brother in need and closes his heart to him, how does the love of God abide in him?" It is well known how strong were the words used by the fathers of the church to describe the proper attitude of persons who possess anything toward persons in need. To quote St. Ambrose: "You are not making a gift of your possessions to the poor person. You are handing over to him what is his. For what has been given in common for the use of all, you have arrogated to yourself. The world is given to all, and not only to the rich." That is, private property does not constitute for anyone an absolute and unconditioned right. No one is justified in keeping for his exclusive use what he does not need, when others lack necessities. In a word, "According to the traditional doctrine as found in the fathers of the church and the great theologians, the right to property must never be exercised to the detriment of the common good." If there should arise a conflict "between acquired private rights and primary community exigencies," it is the responsibility of public authorities "to look for a solution, with the active participation of individuals and social groups."

24. *Use of Revenue*

If certain landed estates impede the general prosperity because they are extensive, unused or poorly used, or because they bring hardship to peoples or are detrimental to the interests of the country, the common good sometimes demands their expropriation. While giving a clear statement on this, the council recalled no less clearly that the available revenue is not to be used in accordance with mere whim, and that no place must be given to selfish speculation. Consequently it is unacceptable that citizens with abundant incomes from the resources and activity of their country should transfer a considerable part of this income abroad purely for their own advantage, without care for the manifest wrong they inflict on their country by doing this.

25. *Industrialization*

The introduction of industry is a necessity for economic growth and human progress; it is also a sign of development and contributes to it. By persistent work and use of his intelligence, man gradually wrests nature's secrets from her and finds a better application for her riches. As his self-mastery increases, he develops a taste for research and discovery, an ability to take a calculated risk, boldness in enterprises, generosity in what he does and a sense of responsibility.

26. *Liberal Capitalism*

But it is unfortunate that on these new conditions of society a system has been constructed which considers profit as the key motive for economic progress, competition as the supreme law of economics, and private ownership of the means of production as an absolute right that has no limits and carries no corresponding social obligation. This unchecked liberalism leads to dictatorship rightly denounced by Pius XI as producing "the international imperialism of money." One cannot condemn such abuses too strongly by solemnly recalling once again that the economy is at the service of man. But if it is true that a type of capitalism has been the source of excessive suffering, injustices and fratricidal conflicts whose effects still persist, it would also be wrong to attribute to industrialization itself evils that belong to the woeful system which accompanied it. On the contrary, one must recognize in all justice the irreplaceable contribution made by the organization of labor and of industry to what development has been accomplished. . . .

29. *Urgency of the Task to Be Done*

We must make haste: Too many are suffering, and the distance is growing that separates the progress of some and the stagnation, not to say the regression, of others. Yet the work required should advance smoothly if there is not to be the risk of losing indispensable equilibrium. A hasty agrarian reform can fail. Industrialization, if introduced suddenly, can displace structures still necessary, and produce hardships in society which would be a setback in terms of human values.

30. *Temptation to Violence*

There are certainly situations whose injustice cries to heaven. When whole populations destitute of necessities live in a state of dependence barring them from all initiative and responsibility, and all opportunity to advance culturally and share in social and political life, recourse to violence, as a means to right these wrongs to human dignity, is a grave temptation.

31. *Revolution*

We know, however, that a revolutionary uprising — save where there is manifest long-standing tyranny which would do great damage to fundamental personal rights and dangerous harm to the common good of the country — produces new injustices, throws more elements out of balance and brings on new disasters. Real evil should not be fought against at the cost of greater misery.

32. *Reform*

We want to be clearly understood; the present situation must be faced with courage, and the injustices linked with it must be fought against and overcome. Development demands bold transformation, innovations that go deep. Urgent reforms should be undertaken without delay. It is for each one to take his share in them with generosity, particularly those whose education, position and opportunities afford them wide scope for action. May they show an example, and give of their own possessions as several of our brothers in the episcopacy have done. In so doing, they will live up to men's expectations and be faithful to the spirit of God, since it is "the ferment of the Gospel which has aroused and continues to arouse in man's heart the irresistible requirements of his dignity. . . ."

2. The Spirituality of Economic Development

The Chilean bishops, in their well-known 1962 letter, "Social and Political Duty in the Present Hour" (see also VI. 10), illustrated the fundamental shift in Catholic thought from other-wordly to this-wordly preoccupations and interpreted the struggle for economic development in terms of spiritual values. [2]

▶ ▶   The Christian, to be one truly, has to take a position with respect to these reforms, in order to achieve social structures which permit lower income strata a greater participation in the fruits of the productive process. "The economic wealth of a people does not consist only in the total abundance of its goods, but also and even more on real and effectual distribution, according to justice." [John XXIII, *Mater et Magistra*]

Therefore, the Christian must support institutions of social renewal and, if the opportunity exists, participate in them. He will also have to support institutional changes such as an authentic agrarian reform, the reform of private enterprise, tax reform, administrative reform and others. . . .

But the Christian's action cannot stop with the exclusively re-distributive aspect. A wider distribution of opportunities, products, capacities and responsibilities can have a great influence on the increase of the total product and therefore, in the satisfaction of global needs. For this reason the disciple of Christ, impelled by love of neighbor, must concern himself directly with the increase of the quantity of goods and services which the economy of the country places from year to year at the disposal of the national community. In other words, love of neighbor implies a serious responsibility for economic development. . . .
[pp. 15–16]

[2] From *Los Obispos de Chile Hablan: El Deber Social y Político en la Hora Presente* (Santiago, Chile: Secretariado General del Episcopado de Chile, 1962), pp. 15–16, 18. Translated by the editor.

This is not an unworthy task for the Christian, but a necessary implication of love for our neighbor in need. This is not a shameful concentration on the material aspect of life but a response to the situation of underdevelopment in which we find ourselves. We do not hesitate to speak of a true "spirituality of economic development." [p. 18]

3. Allah Expects Industrialization

In this article, a Muslim scholar interprets technological and economic development as man's major task on earth, assigned to him by God. Active participation in developmental efforts, not other-worldly preoccupations, characterize the life lived in obedience to the divine will. [3]

▶ ▶ *God Is the Owner of the Earth*

The seminal principle or even the real basis of Islamic economics states that the earth is God's own property. This principle, however, is not a newly devised theory reached by toil and labor. It is rather an elementary fact, or a self-evident truth, since God did create it out of nothing. God, thus, is the owner of the earth. Nobody whosoever can arrogate its possession to himself, or claim that he was the creator, for it is older than the human race itself. Human flesh and blood have been created and are still being created of its very dust, "From the (earth) did we create you, and into it shall we return you."

"And God has produced you from the earth, growing (gradually). It is He who hath produced you from the earth and settled you therein."

If labor, from the purely economic viewpoint is the only means of production and consequently the chief means of possession it is, then, all the more correct to assume that God is the owner of the earth. But labor which entitles people to the right of possession is different from God's labor, since he created it out of nothing and molded it in the form of an unprecedented ideal. This was stated by God in his holy Qur'an in such verses as:

"Yea, to God belongs the dominion of the heavens and the earth." "For the earth is God's." "Say: To whom belong the earth and all beings therein? (Say) if ye know! They will say, To God."

---

[3] From Al Bahay Al Kholi, "On Property and Ownership Between God and Man," *Minbar Al-Islam* (Cairo, English ed.), January 1962, pp. 24–26.

The Earth Is God's Gift to Man

It is, therefore, an obvious fact based on the realities of our actual life on earth that God did not create it with all its treasures for his personal use, but ultimately for Man.

God gave us the earth which is easy to exploit and which is prepared to yield its riches to man if he only knows how to handle them, with the definite end of Man's prosperity. This, as a matter of fact, was stated in the holy verses.

"So the earth is God's gift to Man," and Muhammad, his Prophet says, "Adian Land is God's own and his Prophet's. . . . It is, thereafter yours." An Adian piece of land is usually a waste, originally cultivated or not. In Arabic, it is common to call an ancient building or a waste land, "Adian" in ascription to the Adian monarchy which perished in olden times as a punishment for violating God's laws. The purport of the Prophet's statement, nevertheless, is obvious: the earth is originally owned by God and is his gift to man.

Civilization: Profane Ends and Lofty Ideals

But why, shall we ask, did God give us the earth?

Apparently there are two ends: the one is tangible and temporal while the other is spiritual and eternal, i.e., to worship God, may He be exalted, through using his gifts. This noble end impregnates profane life with exalted meanings and gives rise and significance to noble values which make our life worth living. These noble ends illuminate the very depths of one's soul, and make life logically proceed to a reasonable end. Life would really be insignificant if man was merely destined to eat, drink, multiply and die.

These noble ends have to be stressed because they stipulate man's dignity and the significance of life. The earth with all its blessings serves man's ideals and gives substance to the practical side of his faith in God. But this is another question and should be treated elsewhere.

The tangible end, on the other hand, is to cultivate the earth and to establish various and magnificent civilizations, with a full exploitation of the riches of the earth for Man's prosperity and happiness. But all of this must be considered as a means of achieving the above-mentioned spiritual end.

The Laws of Man's Thought Are the Keys of the Earth's Treasures

Reflecting on the condition of the earth from all points of view, one can easily see how vast are its resources of animal, agricultural and mineral wealth. It has also other potential resources which can multiply this wealth and increase prosperity. Apart from this, man is endowed with intelligence and other intellectual faculties by which he can exploit these natural resources and invest the treasures of the earth for his own good. It is the will of God, therefore, to make man exploit the riches of the earth and establish civilizations as great and magnificent as anything can ever be.

If God had never meant the earth to be civilized, he wouldn't have provided it with these resources or endowed man with any faculties. The earth would have been a desert with palm trees here and there, and man could still have been an animal looking merely for dates.

It would really have been strange if man was not equipped with faculties which enable him to exploit the treasures of the earth and understand its mysteries. It could even have been said that the earth was created for another master, definitely not man, who has not yet appeared.

The Vocation of Man between the Law of His Being and the Law of God

This appropriateness of Man's faculties to the earth's resources displays a remoter part of God's wisdom, "who both ordained laws, and granted guidance, He who gave to each (created) thing its form and nature, and further, gave (it) guidance."

He created everything according to a pre-planned design. It also gives a valid proof that God exists, but this is another question and should be left to another treatise. What concerns me here is the perfectly harmonious correspondence between the laws of Man's thought and the natural laws of the earth. Much can be understood if one reflects on this correspondence, the least of which is Man's responsibility. For being endowed with these faculties indeed means that man is responsible for investing earth's resources and establishing magnificent civilizations. We can thus conclude that these intellectual gifts constitute the laws of Man's being that determines his vocation, the main part of which is to establish vast civilizations on earth. In the holy Qur'an we find verses which translate this law of Man's being into a law of God, asking the same thing of man, "It is He who hath produced you from the earth and settled you therein." The settlement of man on earth implies, as most of the outstanding commentators maintain (such as El-Kortoby and El-Gassas), Man's responsibility as to peopling and investment of the earth which leads definitely to civilization.

Towards Industrialization

Constructive work, in the light of modern science, is not confined to agriculture or architecture only; it also means the full exploitation of the mineral wealth and the expansion of industry. This, in consequence, leads to an inevitable increase in commercial activity. From the holy verse, "And We sent down Iron, in which is (material for) mighty war, as well as many benefits for mankind," we can infer that God points to industrialization, refers to the advantages of iron and asks man to extract iron ore. God knows that man is always interested in what is useful to him so he referred to the element of utility in "iron" when he said "In which is (material for) mighty war, as well as many benefits for mankind." For that would make man extract it.

Industrialization thus can be realized and, as we know, it is the major factor in establishing great civilizations.

Extracting iron, as a matter of fact, is only an example to be followed in the vast industrial field. Mining is important because without the mineral resources no constructive work in the fields of architecture and industry can be carried out. God referred also to this when he mentioned the prophet Solomon, Peace be upon him. "And to Solomon (we made) the wind (obedient): its early morning (stride) was a month's (journey); and its evening (stride) was a month's (journey); and we made a font of molten brass to flow for him; and there were jinns that worked in front of him, by the leave of his Lord, and if any of them turned aside from our command, We made him taste of the penalty of the blazing fire. They worked for him as he desired, (making) arches, images, basins as large as reservoirs, and (cooking) cauldrons fixed (in their places): Work ye, sons of David, with thanks! But few of my servants are grateful!" Out of all this, one can easily conclude that civilization, in this wide sense, is a heavenly commandment and a duty exacted by Islam in direct and clear words.

LAND REFORM AND SOCIAL JUSTICE

Agrarian reform has been or is on the agenda of the vast majority of Third-World states. And religious institutions have been prominent among the large landholders in the Hindu, Buddhist, Muslim, and Catholic countries alike. Land reform programs in South India have had to deal with the fact that vast tracts of land, encompassing many villages, were owned by the presiding deity (a juridical person) of a Hindu temple. In Ceylon, land reform legislation has exempted from its scope the temple lands managed by monasteries. And the Catholic church continues to be counted among the largest landlords in a number of Latin American countries.

Religious institutions thus have usually opposed land reform legislation in the defense of their vested interests. In some cases, however, they have been able to disengage themselves from the economic power structure sufficiently to speak to the entire society on the moral imperatives of radical agrarian change. Thus the Chilean bishops, in a passage not included in reading VIII. 4, declared their intention of redistributing a sizable portion of their land to the workers, which intention was indeed carried out. Individual leaders like Vinoba Bhave in India have been able to address themselves to the general problem of land reform without the embarrassment and encumbrances of ecclesiastical vested interests in the status quo.

To the modernizers, secular and religious alike, agricultural land owned by temples and churches is most decidedly not sacred. If an element of sacredness is to be found anywhere, it is in the relationship between the land and the man who works it.

4. The Catholic Church and Land Reform in Chile

In 1962, the Chilean bishops issued a collective pastoral letter entitled "The Church and the Problem of the Peasantry." Redefining the right of personal property, the bishops sought to justify land reform measures which entailed the compulsory acquisition of land by the state for the purpose of a more equitable redistribution. [4]

▶ ▶   The conditions in which the peasant sector finds itself at present, as we have seen, cry out urgently for a profound transformation of the rural structure. On this matter there is an almost unanimous consensus.

The base on which it is necessary to build a better ordering has to be respect for the moral and spiritual principles which inhere in the created order, in which the human person constitutes the greatest of values, by virtue of being the image of God. (And the common good has to become the result of the most essential social virtues inaugurated in the world by Christianity: justice and love.)

Only a fully incarnated Christianity, concrete, present throughout the length of our life's journey, of our existence, of our generation, will dispel the temptation to abandon to other ideologies the valorization of the land and the humanization of the man on the land in this Latin America which is Christian by birth and destiny.

---

[4] From *La Iglesia y el Problema del Campesinado* (Santiago, Chile: Secretariado General del Episcopado de Chile, 1962), pp. 20–25, 32–33. Translated by the editor.

We consider it a grave and urgent duty, therefore, that all who find themselves linked to the land, whether as managers, proprietors or workers, form a completely Christian perspective on this subject, which will then lead them to act efficaciously, in collaboration with all persons of good will, until achievement of the goal that the relations desired by God between the land and man constitute a true factor of the common good.

We want to remember the basic Christian principles which must orient the passage from the present conditions toward a social order more in conformity with the will of the Creator and with the nature of things. These were given by God to all men so that they could provide for their material needs and, consequently, no one can be excluded from the fundamental right to use the material goods of the earth. "The fundamental point of the social question," says His Holiness Pius XII, "is that the goods created by God for all men be shared equitably by all, according to the principles of justice and love." There exists no other right capable of annulling "the natural end of material goods, and (the right of property) could not be made independent of the first and fundamental right of its use which corresponds to all, but rather must serve it to make possible the achievement of its ends."

"The church, as it has always defended the legitimacy of private property, with no less energy has insisted on its social function, remembering the necessity that the goods created by God for all men flow in an equitable manner toward all."

The right of private property, including the goods of production, is so intimately connected to the development of the person and the securing of his liberty that it is one of the most fundamental rights of man; it is based on the ontological priority and the finality of individual beings over society. The exercise of the right of property, however, is not absolute, but is conditioned by the social function of material goods, as His Holiness John XXIII once more reaffirms in his encyclical *Mater et Magistra.* . . .

We cannot forget that society has its own end, different although not opposed to that of individuals, namely, the common good. Property must be structured in such a way that, without ignoring the rights mentioned earlier, it attends in a preferential way to this common good. "It is the responsibility of the state, custodian and promoter of the common good, to keep watch so that the juridical forms which property assumes fulfill both their individual function and their social function. The state, whose reason for being is the realization of the common good in the temporal order, cannot remain absent from the economic world; it must be present in it to promote with opportunity the production of a sufficient abundance of material goods, the use of which is necessary for the exercise of virtue, and to care for the rights of all citizens, above all, of the weakest, who are the workers, the women, and the children. It is also its undeniable duty to contribute actively to the improvement of the living conditions of the workers. . . ." [*Mater et Magistra*]

If it is the duty of each citizen, in proportion to his responsibility, to form a sound judgment, to express it freely creating a climate of opinion around him, and to act in conformity with the basic orientations which we have tried to expound in this pastoral letter according to Christian Doctrine, it is certainly the duty of the state as an important factor to carry out the reforms which are necessary today for a better structuring of agriculture. . . .

As a pretext against the idea of reforming agrarian structures, the opposition often points to the consequent decrease in production. In the goal to be reached, however, next to the elevation of the peasantry to a higher level of life, is the better rendering of service by agriculture to the community. To have as a point of view the increase of production has always been the goal of the landowners. To leave the more just juridical ordering of property and its social function as a secondary problem is to encourage an exaggerated individualism with disregard for the human element, respect for which requires that moral values be accounted higher than material values, in this as in every other human activity. It is precisely in this that the action of Christians against the inertia of worldly materialism, the enemy of God's plan, must consist.

If the Christian message, which revolutionized the concept of the ancient world, has still not been fulfilled totally, it is reserved to our generation to take a step forward, toward a goal for which Catholics have the right and duty to march in the vanguard. [pp. 20–25]

It is the function of the state to provide, by all means at its disposal, agricultural land to all who ask for it, in conformity with set requirements of capacity, guarantee of work, rural occupation, etc. Its first action must be to distribute those lands which are its property, as it is doing at present. We praise the diverse initiatives taken in this regard.

However, in view of the magnitude of the rural problems which we have made known, this work of a social character does not seem sufficient by any means. It seems that the expropriation of those agricultural properties which have certain characteristics and which can be divided up for redistribution has become legitimate, for this signifies a greater service to the common good.

It is a grave responsibility of the technicians, in carrying out this reform in the agricultural structure, that they bear in mind that the goods of the earth must serve the common good of society, and that in the expropriation the principles of justice and equity must be respected, to the absolute exclusion of private or partisan interests.

It must be borne in mind, furthermore, that violent occupations of land, which are illegal, can never confer titles to property. [pp. 32–33]

5. Fatwa on Land Reform in the United Arab Republic

A year after the 1961 agrarian reform law was promulgated by the Nasser government, the following *fatwa* providing the necessary Islamic legitimation was published. The argument based on the three (or four) essentials of life is a recurrent theme in Muslim writings on the subject and has close parallels in Catholic and Hindu thought as well.[5]

▶ ▶ *Question:* Some of my fellow citizens have asked me whether, as was broadcast by some Islamic States, the socialist laws issued by the United Arab Republic in July, 1961 are adverse to the spirit of Islam?

Answer: To tell the truth, I was surprised to hear such allegations broadcast by an Islamic state. All matters related to religion should never have been dismissed so lightly. Any one taking the responsibility of seeking the judgement of God in any religious question should be equipped with definite proofs from the Holy Book, the Prophetic Traditions (Sunnah) and the spirit of Islamic jurisprudence. The general rule is that which is allowed by religion is clear, that which is forbidden is also clear but in between there are dubious matters. In view of all this I had to spend a long time studying these laws in the light of what I know of Islamic rulings on similar matters. I have been led to the following:

1. Islamic jurisprudence respects private property which is obtained by lawful means and prohibits any infringement of it; whoever spoils the property of another should pay him either in kind or in terms of real value.

2. Islamic jurisprudence ordains that the proprietors should recognize in their property certain rights for others by which it seeks to attain social adjustment and realize a sense of brotherhood which binds all Muslims. Thus *al-zakat* (the poor due) is one of the essentials of Islam. It is imposed on all able Muslims who must pay it in money, goods or

---

[5] From "The Mufti Answers Your Questions," *Minbar Al-Islam* (Cairo, English ed.), July, 1962, pp. 56, 58–60.

crops out of their own accord. If not, the ruler is to exact it and spend it in the ways prescribed by Islam. . . . [p. 56]

3. Private ownership is legitimate in the eyes of Islamic jurisprudence as long as the owner observes the ordinances of Allah concerning his wealth. But if he does not abide by them, the ruler is entitled to devise the laws and regulations which force him to adhere to the commandments of God. For instance, if a father refuses to spend on his children or his grown-up sons who are poor and unable to earn their living the ruler has the right to force him to do so'even and if it means confiscating enough of his money to cover their expenses. . . .

4. Money, according to Islamic jurisprudence, is good and a Muslim should acquire it by work and through legitimate means. A Muslim should not secure it by means prohibited by God such as usury, misappropriation of other's property, bribery or larceny. God says: "And do not eat up your property among yourselves for vanities, nor use it as bait for the judges, with intent that ye may eat up wrongfully and knowingly a little of (other) people's property."

5. In the eyes of God money is God's property. For God — glorified and blessed be His name — is the creator of everything, and it is He who enables man to gain money. He has made him his vicegerent on earth to exploit it for his benefit and the benefit of others. . . .

6. Ownership in Islam is permissible only as long as the owner alone will bear the consequences. Thus Islamic jurisprudence prohibits the monopoly of food and suchlike materials necessary for the sustenance of people. Books of the Sunnah state that the Prophet said: "All people partake in three things: water, fodder [or pasture], and fire." Some other texts add: "and salt." This is so because these elements are fundamental to all people. Hence these fundamentals should not be owned by a single person or a group of persons lest they should bar access to other people on the pretext that these things belong to them exclusively and should not be used by others without their authority and approval. Private ownership in such essentials should be banned in order to guarantee the necessities of life for all people. *Faqihs* — Jurists — have unanimously prohibited the monopoly of people's food and the necessities of their daily life. The prohibition safeguards the interests of the people and is in accordance with the aforementioned tradition — *hadith*.

Thus we can sanction the nationalization of public institutions indispensable to everyday life such as the institution established to secure water, electricity and easy transport.

In the light of these rulings supported by proofs from the Qur'an, the Sunnah and the behavior of the Prophet and his companions, we can proceed to study the contents of the socialist laws issued by the United Arab Republic in July, 1961. We came out with the following conclusions:

These laws have not abolished private ownership which Islamic jurisprudence has allowed and which it has made the cornerstone of many individual interrelations. They did not aim at robbing the owner of his property, but rather at amending the law of agrarian reform issued in 1953, making one hundred feddans — acres — the maximum of landownership instead of two hundred as was specified in the 1953 law. Moreover the proprietor is to be compensated for whatever land he loses and will be paid by the Government the value of his land within an appointed time. He is to be given also a certain percentage of interest to compensate for his exploitation of land while it remained in his possession. Restriction of land-ownership has been initiated by the desire to enable cultivators and farm-workers to own land, because much of the cultivable area was in the possession of a small, select group of people who would never sell a finger's breadth of it except to other proprietors. Even if they sold it, it would be at prices beyond the paying capacity of most farmers. This act is undoubtedly sanctioned by Islamic jurisprudence. Early Muslims recognized this, Al-Awzary said that Caliph Omar and the Prophet's companions agreed to let the cultivators of Syria and Iraq continue to possess their land and pay its Kharaj tax — and prohibited anyone to buy it either by the will of its original owner or by coercion. The reason was that the land should remain in the hands of its proper cultivators and should never pass to any one else no matter who. Restriction of land ownership has no other objective than to realize public good through allowing small farmers who own nothing [the] chance to own something. Moreover, for the land to remain in the possession of a few people whose only concern is to exploit efforts of those who till the land, to secure profits only for themselves, never to sell except at highly exaggerated prices — this shows an attitude which runs contrary to social justice. Can anyone then assume that the restriction of land ownership is adverse to Islam, or opposed to its commandments? Surely it is not. Surely it accords with the spirit of Islamic jurisprudence and with what Omar and his companions have ruled. For Omar did not consent that land should be taken from its owners who cultivated it and be given to the invaders who had nothing to do with husbandry. Add to this argument the fact that the socialist law of agrarian reform stipulated a fair compensation for the land confiscated by law.

The law of agrarian reform has yielded its fruits. It raised the standard of living of farmers and peasants and assured them of a decent way of earning their living from land owned by them which they can cultivate. They are no longer brutally exploited to satisfy the avarice and greed of others. This act has a precedence in what the Prophet has done with the wealth of Beni Al-Nadir when he took it from the Jews. In this connection God says: "What God has bestowed on His Apostle (and taken away) from the people of the townships, belongs to God, to His Apostle and to kindred and orphans, the needy and the wayfarer; in order that it may not (merely) make a circuit between the wealthy among you. So take what the Apostle assigns to you, and deny yourselves that which he withholds from you. And fear God; for God is strict in Punishment. . . ."

Thus the distribution of wealth between the poor and the rich so that it may not be circulated among the rich only, is a procedure approved of by Islamic jurisprudence; because it ensures justice among individuals. [pp. 58–60]

6. Vinoba Bhave on Land Reform in India

One of Gandhi's closest associates, Vinoba Bhave, began his remarkable *Bhoodan* (land gift) movement in 1951 as an answer to Communist-led agrarian disturbances. Later known as the "walking saint," Vinoba's technique was simply to walk from one village to another and appeal to wealthy landlords to give him one-sixth of their land for redistribution to the landless. [6]

Through *Boodan-yajna* [land-gift sacrifice], I intend to solve the land problem, which is the main problem for the whole of Asia. If we try to solve this problem through violence, the feeling of hatred among our own people would be on the increase. In this scientific age, its consequences would not be beneficial. If, on the contrary, we are able to solve this big problem through non-violence, love and peace, then cooperation among the people and strength of the whole community will grow and people will be happy. Some people ask me, "Why is it that you go on walking for nothing? Why do you exert yourself so much for the Bhoodan work? Why don't you get the work done through legislation? That would be easy and everything would be achieved." But how can everything be achieved through legislation? Suppose an act were to

---

[6] From Acharaya Vinoba Bhave, *Revolutionary Sarvodaya* (Bombay: Bharatiya Vidya Bhavan, 1964), pp. 38–39, 42. Used by permission.

be passed confiscating land from the present owners. If an agriculturist then were to refuse to part with his land, he would be imprisoned. That is all that law can do. The sanction behind any law is the coercive power of the state which implies the power of the army. That is why what we expect to happen, after preparing people's minds for it, would be voluntary action. If there is no cooperation of the people and if a reform is thrust on them through legislation, it would not only fail to achieve its objective but there would be widespread violence and hatred in society.

There is a place for law alongside of non-violent effort. If a particular reform is voluntarily adopted by a number of individuals and if that voluntary action prepares the public mind for the change, then whatever little work is left to be done could be achieved through the process of law. Thus even in non-violence there is a place for legislation. But that place comes last. The effort that is at present being made for the solution of the land problem through non-violence is itself a great power in this age of science.

Yet I consider it a small achievement that the problem of land is being solved through Bhoodan and Gramadan. What is of greater importance is that the level of thinking gets elevated as a result of this movement. People of an entire village would constitute themselves into a family. Air, water and land — which all are just gifts of God to man — would be shared by all. The villagers would take to cooperative endeavor. A villager will begin to think, "I shall work not for myself but for the society. I shall care not only for myself but for the whole village community." When we adopt such an attitude, the entire moral plane is changed. That is the reason why I experience so much vigor and enthusiasm in conducting this movement. I am now rather advanced in age and yet I do not feel any fatigue. The reason is that I have within me an extraordinary feeling of bliss. . . . [pp. 38–39]

If we use bad means for a good end, then problems would continue to crop up in India. But if we use non-violent means for solving our problems, there would be no problems at all in the world. This is the reason why I want to solve the land problem peacefully. I am asking people to donate land in Bhoodan. I am not begging alms. . . . When a demand is being made by me in my capacity as a representative of the *Daridra Narayan* — the God in the form of the poor — it is not alms I am asking for; I am thereby imparting to the people instruction in the rudiments of social obligation. In other words it is *deeksha* — initiation — and not *bhiksha* — alms. I have, therefore, come to this conclusion that the noble work which God wanted to get done through the Buddha has now been entrusted to a weakling like me. [p. 42]

THE POPULATION EXPLOSION AND FAMILY PLANNING

As the magnitude of the population problem has come to be understood, government-sponsored birth control programs have proliferated throughout the Third World. The question of the congruity or conflict of contraception with the religious values of the major religions has thus become a matter of some concern. Planned parenthood programs have encountered very little religious opposition in the Hindu and Buddhist countries. Their limited success thus far is largely explained by traditional attitudes of conservatism toward a new idea, calculations which make many sons an economic asset, and other factors.

In the Muslim world, particularly in Pakistan, some conservative *ulama* have denounced birth control as un-Islamic. Note, however, the *fatwa* issued by the Grand Mufti of Jordan strongly supporting it (XIII. 7). In the Catholic world, of course, the issue has divided the church right down the middle, particularly since Pope Paul's 1968 encyclical, "Of Human Life." Both liberal and conservative responses to the encyclical revealed at least as much concern over the definition of papal authority in the church as over the issue of birth control.

7. Fatwa of the Grand Mufti of Jordan

In this authoritative legal opinion issued in 1964, the highest-ranking interpreter of Islamic law in Jordan upheld the validity of contraception and even abortion. As stated in the *fatwa*, it was issued partly in response to questions posed by officials, and it is likely that governmental policies had some effect on the formulation of the statement.[7]

▶ ▶   In the name of God, the Merciful and the Compassionate. Fears of the world from the increase of population have assumed serious proportions everywhere, and experts have come to regard this as a portent of woe, ruination, and dire consequences. In their consideration how the world can be protected against this towering evil and grave menace, they have been led to think that "restriction of procreation" is one of the greatest measures. They know, however, that most people do not follow this course unless the ruling of religion in this respect has been made clear to them. Therefore, Muslims have looked up to reliable religious

[7] From "Family Planning in Islam: Statement by the Grand Mufti of Jordan, December, 1964." Distributed by The Pathfinder Fund, 1575 Tremont Street, Boston, Mass.

divines to state to them the ruling of religion on the subject. Questions converged on us for this purpose, including questions from official sources. This is our Statement on this matter.

It is acknowledged that the liberal Islamic law accommodates itself to nature and to human condition. God says: "Set thou thy face then, as a true convert, towards the faith the nature made by God in which he has made men; there is no altering of God's creation."

One of the natural things inherent in human beings is marriage. But the purpose of marriage is procreation for the perpetuation of the species. This divine Qur'anic verse refers to that and regards it as one of the blessings bestowed upon God's servants. God says: "God, too, has given you wives from among yourselves and has given you sons and grandsons from your wives, and supplied you with good things." Therefore, marriage has been one of the Islamic religious ways and procreation has been one of its desirable and gratifying aims. Even the law-giver views multiplicity with favor, for multiplicity implies power, influence and invulnerability. This is why, in one of the traditions of the Prophet, marriage with an affectionate prolific woman is strongly urged. The tradition says: "Marry the affectionate prolific woman, for I shall be proud of you among the nations."

Nevertheless, the law-giver made marriage with a prolific woman and marriage for procreation conditional upon the availability of means and the ability to bear the costs of marriage and meet the expenses of child education and training, so that children may not go to the bad and develop anti-social ways. And according to the Islamic religious rule (laws change as conditions change), marriage should be disallowed if the would-be husband is incapable of meeting the expenses of married life. To this, reference is clear in the Qur'an and in the Traditions. The Qur'an says: "And let those who do not find a match live in continence until God makes them free from want out of his bounty." The Tradition says: "O young men, whoever of you is capable financially let him marry, and whoever is not capable let him fast, for fasting is preventive." From the foregoing verse and the tradition, the definite inference is that "restriction of procreation" is legal a fortiori; because to stop procreation altogether is more serious than to limit it. It is a cause for much wonder that those who urge celibacy should at the same time hesitate to allow family planning.

Moreover, there are genuine traditions which allow methods for restricting procreation, such as coitus interruptus. For instance, in the two most reliable collections of traditions, Abu-Said is reported to have said that in one of the raids, he and others captured a number of women, and they used to practice coitus interruptus. He also said that they asked the Prophet about that and the Prophet said: "Indeed, do that," and repeated it three times, and continued: "No creature to be created from now till the Day of Judgement will not but be created." Another report has it that a man said to the Prophet: "I have a young wife, I hate that she should be pregnant, and I want what men want; but the Jews claim that coitus interruptus is minor infanticide." The Prophet replied, "The Jews lie. If God wishes to create the child, you will not be able to divert him from that." In the two reliable collections of traditions, it is stated that Muslims used to practice coitus interruptus during the lifetime of the Prophet and during the period of the Qur'anic revelation. It is also reliably reported that Muslims used to practice coitus interruptus during the lifetime of the Prophet: the Prophet knew of this, but he did not prohibit it. . . .

The jurists also state that it is permissible to take medicine for abortion so long as the embryo is still unformed in the human shape. The period of this unformed state is given as 120 days. The jurists think that during this period the embryo or the foetus is not yet a human being. A report says that Omar (The Second Caliph) does not regard abortion as infanticide unless the foetus is already past the limit.

Malik, the founder of the Maliki Orthodox Way, says that the husband should not practice coitus interruptus with his wife unless she permits it. Al-Zarqani, in his comment on this, says that the practice is lawful if the wife allows it. Permission or prohibition of coitus interruptus may serve as a guide in deciding the question of abortion before the foetus is animated. If it is to be allowed or prohibited, it is the more reason that abortion is allowed. Then Al-Zarqani says: "A corollary of this is the use of contraceptives by a woman to eliminate pregnancy altogether."

All this shows that there is agreement among the founders of the four Orthodox Ways that coitus interruptus is allowed as a means for contraception. Religious servants inferred from this that contraceptives might be used, and even medicines might be used for abortion.

Accordingly, we hereby give our judgment with confidence in favor of family planning.

8. Humanae Vitae

In 1968, Pope Paul VI issued his long-awaited encyclical letter on the regulation of birth. The encyclical, on the face of it, seemed to offer little room for liberal interpretation, so unequivocal was its reaffirmation of the traditional Catholic teaching against all artificial means of contraception.[8]

▶ ▶ The most serious duty of transmitting human life, for which married persons are the free and responsible collaborators of God the Creator, has always been a source of great joy to them, even if sometimes accompanied by not a few difficulties and by distress.

Marriage is not, then, the effect of chance or the product of evolution of unconscious natural forces; it is the wise institution of the Creator to realize in mankind His design of love. By means of the reciprocal personal gifts of self . . . husband and wife . . . collaborate with God in the generation and education of new lives.

In relation to physical, economic, psychological and social conditions, responsible parenthood is exercised, either by the deliberate and generous decision to raise a numerous family, or by the decision, made for grave motives and with due respect for the moral law, to avoid for the time being, or even for an indeterminate period, a new birth.

God has wisely disposed natural laws and rhythms of fecundity which, of themselves, cause a separation in the succession of births. Nonetheless the Church, calling men back to the observance of the norms of the natural law, as interpreted by their constant doctrine, teaches that each and every marriage act . . . must remain open to the transmission of life.

In conformity with these landmarks in the human and Christian vision of marriage, we must once again declare that the direct interruption of the generative process already begun, and above all, directly willed and procured abortion, even if for therapeutic reasons, are to be absolutely excluded as licit means of regulating birth.

Equally to be excluded . . . is direct sterilization, whether perpetual or temporary, whether of the man or of the woman.

The Church on the contrary does not at all consider illicit the use of those therapeutic means truly necessary to cure diseases of the organism, even if an impediment to procreation, which may be foreseen, should result therefrom, provided such impediment is not, for whatever motive, directly willed.

[8] From *New York Times*, July 30, 1968.

9. A Mexican Response to Humanae Vitae

A group of Catholic clergy and laity organized by the Pastoral Center of Cuernavaca concluded their discussions on the encyclical by issuing the following "pastoral note." The bishop of Cuernavaca, a leading liberal in the Mexican hierarchy, later commented favorably on the note. [9]

▶ ▶ Every encyclical must be applied in the different local churches by considering concrete pastoral situations. This is the duty of local pastors, who on the other hand must also maintain obedience and unity in the church.

Our "Note" must be understood purely at the pastoral level, and concerns the classification of consciences with regard to the moral prescriptions contained in the encyclical *Humanae Vitae*. It responds to the problems in the minds of many Mexican Catholics, as a result of the discussion — above all in private — occasioned by the prohibition of artificial means of contraception. We seek to contribute something positive to the pastoral application of the encyclical, in terms of our circumstances, which requires a more complex reflection than the pure enunciation of principles. We do it in a spirit of collaboration with the hierarchy, with the will to participate at our level, but in a spirit of communion and dialogue, pending their eventual official instructions. Our intention is to be in complete conformity with traditional Catholic doctrine.

We believe that in this case the following points should be considered as elements in a right formation of the individual conscience:

1. The papal decision is in its own right an expression of the ordinary teaching authority (Magisterium) of the church, and therefore requires adherence on the part of Catholics, because of our faith in the charisma of the Spirit which attends the teaching authority.

2. Adherence to the teaching authority admits of degrees, from an absolute adherence which may lead to martyrdom, to a loyal conditioned adherence. This last, at which level the points of the encyclical which concerns us are found, refers to pronouncements which are in themselves fallible, which does not mean that it is necessarily so.

---

[9] From Espinosa Mireles *et al.*, "Humanae Vitae: nota pastoral," *Correo del Sur* (Cuernavaca, Mexico), November 17, 1968, reprinted by Centro Intercultural de Documentación (Cuernavaca, Mexico), doc. 68/113, pp. 1–4. Used by permission. Translated by the editor.

3. The greater or lesser degree of conditioned adherence depends on objective doctrinal criteria. When the teaching authority expresses a truth or norm of action as contained in Revelation, its requirement is maximal and the teaching can be even infallible. At another level, at times the teaching authority expresses itself on something which is not directly revealed, but necessary and good so that man in his actual cultural context can live fully the faith and the law of Christ: theological truths that lead to faith, the exposition of norms of morality and necessary applications to live the moral life in its fullness. At this level there exists the possibility of erring, or at least, of not reaching all of the truth. It is at this level that some moral norms of *Humanae Vitae* are found.

4. Together with this, the pastoral efficacy of an act of the ordinary teaching authority may be greater or less according to the form of its exercise: more or less collegial, more or less expressive of a consensus in the church.

5. In any case, the norm which emanates from the teaching authority is in itself, in conscience, the norm of conduct for Catholics. (In our case, the moral conclusions of *Humanae Vitae*.) This means that the Christian, in forming his conscience in a concrete situation, cannot fail to refer to the teaching of the Pope, and furthermore, in our case, to the exhortation of the Mexican episcopate.

6. This reference to papal teaching, nevertheless, is not absolute (point 2 above). That is to say, in the concrete situation of a married couple this teaching — or rather, its application — can coincide or even conflict with a reference to other moral values, of natural or evangelical law, which the couple are also solemnly obliged to maintain (the equilibrium of mutual love, assuring the development of the children, the wife's health, etc.).

7. This coincidence or conflict of values occurs in concrete pastoral contexts. In Mexico it occurs in a largely underdeveloped population, in which the number of children in poor families reveals an irresponsible parenthood, in which the number of abortions on the other hand is considerable, in which there is a lack of information and education on these subjects, in which the level of foresight, discipline and organization of life on the purely human plane (without considering the ascetic plane) is chronically deficient.

8. In their decision married couples act as adults before God. The pastoral teaching of the church accompanies them only to the threshold of their decision, giving them the light of its teaching authority, to which they should always adhere on their own, even when in a concrete case this is not the only motive of their decision, inasmuch as they are also under

the light and requirements of other solemn values, and eventually may have to opt for a lesser evil. These situations will help to mature both the proper exercise of pastoral authority and the responsibility of Christian obedience.

9. The progressive education of consciences and wills toward the moral ideal, by means of teaching and the sacraments, is the work of the pastoral ministry. This should create an internal dynamism, a yearning toward greater perfection, and not immobilize the Christian in static norms. It must know how to respect the slow maturation and the formation of convictions. It must know that a proposed norm is not always assimilated automatically by a Christian conscience, and that it is necessary to give time for the Gospel to "penetrate." It must know how to distinguish between the matrimonial values which the church promotes constantly and universally, and the means which it proposes to cultivate and secure these values, but subject to the cultural or moral level of Christians in concrete situations.

10. The sacramental life is not a prize for those who have reached an ideal, but a support for those who with good will seek it. Finally, the Christian life is dominated by the mystery of the Cross and by the supreme law of love.

IX

Religion
and
Marxism:
Ideological
Interaction

From the early nineteenth century until the end of World War II, the dominant idea which represented change in the Third World was liberalism. Its emphases on individual freedom and a de-sacralized view of human society were revolutionary. Since the postwar emergence of many new states, however, a much greater emphasis has been placed on economic problems, and today the dominant idea which represents change is socialism. For this reason the ideological interaction of Third-World religions with Marxism has become a significant question.

It is hardly surprising that Hindu, Buddhist, Islamic, and Catholic versions of socialism have emerged from this interaction. The reconciliation has been promoted by forces on both sides. The religious reformer and apologist sees in its affinities with socialism the proof of his tradition's validity and relevancy to modern life. The linking of Islam with socialism, for example, is used partly to establish the modernity and adequacy of the former. On the other hand, the Marxists and democratic socialists, despite their secularist predispositions, are fully aware of the powerful legitimizing potentiality of religion when linked to political ideologies. If socialism makes religion relevant, religion makes socialism legitimate, especially in still largely traditional societies.

Relevancy and legitimacy have in part been quite consciously pursued by the religious and ideological reinterpreters, but the process has also been one of which the reinterpreters themselves have not been completely aware. There has been an element of deliberate manipulation of ideas, but also an element of unconscious response to the intellectual environment.

The formulations range from the simple proposition that religion and socialism are not in conflict, but are compatible and complementary (IX. 3), to the much stronger statement that socialism uniquely expresses the values of religion in socio-economic structures (IX. 7). Religious reinterpreters, especially the Catholics, are aware of the dangers of sacralizing and absolutizing a new set of socio-economic structures, as religion in the past had done with respect to traditional and capitalist structures. However, the intensity of the theological support for socialism as the best answer *under present conditions* in the Third World is nevertheless impressive.

Ideological formulations of religious socialism have been most prominent in the cases of Islam and Catholicism, the religious systems rooted in strong concepts of the reality and meaning of human history. The Hindu-oriented Sarvodaya movement, of Gandhian inspiration, has given much greater importance to history than traditional Hindu thought. The problem of relating Buddhism positively to history and social change, however, has still received relatively little attention from Buddhist scholars.

SARVODAYA: HINDU SOCIALISM

Gandhi developed his theory and technique of *satyagraha* (nonviolent resistance) primarily to bring about political change, namely, Indian independence (see IV. 2). He did employ *satyagraha* in socioeconomic conflicts concerning untouchability and labor-management problems, but as a technique of nonviolent social change it was not elaborated further. The neo-Gandhian Sarvodaya movement launched by Vinoba Bhave, in contrast, addressed itself primarily to socioeconomic change, particularly in the crucial area of land reform. Vinoba's idea of *Bhoodan* (land gift) came to him in 1951 as a direct response to Communist-led agrarian disturbances in the state of Hyderabad.

As we shall see, Vinoba found important areas of agreement between Marxism and Sarvodaya as social philosophies committed to radical social change. In emphasizing the need for fundamental changes in men's values as necessary to sustain structural changes, the Sarvodaya movement attracted to its ranks a leading socialist, Jayaprakash Narayan.

1. Bhave on Communism and Sarvodaya

In this remarkable address, Vinoba used the same categories to analyze the two movements and found unexpected similarities. He also identified some of the Marxists' inconsistencies with considerable insight. [1]

▶ ▶ Many people feel that the Communists are a destructive force. No doubt we have differences of opinion on many points. Communism by itself is not destructive. By itself Communism is an ideology worth consideration. The communist ideology has something in it which was not in the world before it. I do not want to go into details. I have written a brief introduction on Communism. In that I have called Marx a *Mahamuni* (great sage). By reading the works of *Mahamuni* Marx, innumerable people in the world have changed their views. What is, however, amazing is the fact that even when the heart of the Communists have been converted by Marx, they do not themselves believe in change of heart. It is clear that we differ from them. I told them that "My friends, you yourselves are an example of change of heart. Then how can you say that change of heart is not possible?" So far as the Communists' objective is concerned, I regard it as a good thing. The main point is how that objective is to be achieved.

No Communist, in the final analysis, believes that man is not essentially good. They accept that after a certain stage, the State will disappear. I say that a person who has this conviction undoubtedly entertains in himself a faith in human nature. In the absence of such faith, nobody can believe that State will finally wither away.

Some people say that in *Satya Yuga* [the golden age] the State was not necessary and there really was no State at that time. There are others who say that there never was a *Satya Yuga* in human history but it will come at some subsequent date. So those who believe that there was a *Satya Yuga* are *Puranavadis* (who believe in Puranas). Those who believe that *Satya Yuga* will come at a later stage are the Communists. And so these *Puranavadis* and Communists are both *Satya Yugavadis*. One says that there had been a *Satya Yuga* and the other says that a *Satya Yuga* will come. What do we say? We say that neither the past nor the future is in our hands. We have only the present in our hands and we want to bring *Satya Yuga* in the present. That is the only difference. The Puranist

---

[1] From William Theodore de Bary, ed., *Sources of Indian Tradition*, Vol. II (New York: Columbia University Press, 1964). Used by permission.

is a past *Satya Yugavadi* and the Communist is a future *Satya Yugavadi*. But the Sarvodayite is a present *Satya Yugakari*. Please note that I have not used the word *Vadi* [believer] but *Kari* [doer]. Now for us both these can have sympathy. Many Jan Sangh people met me and said: "Why do you talk of *Ahimsa* [nonviolence] in this *Kali Yuga*; you cannot practice *Ahimsa* work in *Kali Yuga*." These Puranists believe that nonviolence obtained in *Satya Yuga* and they believe that it cannot work today. So they oppose it.

Communists also oppose it sometimes and say that we are Utopians. They say that today, if it is necessary, we should be prepared to take to violence, but ultimately, of course, we will have nonviolence. In other words, for the ultimate establishment of nonviolence, they want that today we must have the courage to take to violence. But I believe that today if the heart is bent upon violence and if after this you expect that nonviolence will appear at a certain stage in the future, the possibilities are that it will never come. These are some of the basic differences. There are, however, no differences in so far as the conception of *Satya Yuga* is concerned. There are hardly any differences about the concept of an ideal society. I do not want to go into minute details. The picture of heaven which the Puranists present before us and the dream of heaven which the Communists place are hardly different. And we ask the Puranists: "Your picture of heaven is undoubtedly attractive, but will you tell us — which is the ladder for ascending to that place?" We also ask the Communists: "Your dream of heaven also appeals to us, but which is the ladder for reaching there?" The Communists reply that today we will have to be prepared for the fullest violence. And so, in effect, one says that we will achieve heaven after our death and the other says that we will achieve it after killing others. Both these concepts become difficult to digest.

Now they also find difficulty with us. They say that you give very good sermons, but then are you the only ones who have sermonized like this? There have been innumerable saints and you have read all their works and you repeat the same things. But can you hope to succeed where Christ and Buddha failed to succeed? Is there any dearth of teaching regarding nonviolence in the Bible? I have heard that the Bible has been translated into 1,000 languages of the world, and at present it is being translated into many other languages. And when soldiers die in the battle field, they have a Bible in the pocket. Nevertheless, violence continues. These followers of the Bible take the name of God, read the Bible every Sunday and forget it for the remaining six days of the week? And so they ask us: What special thing can be achieved through these sermons? Do you really believe that we can bring about a transformation through such sermons? If you do this well and good. But we do not have faith in it."

Thus, in effect, their difficulty with regard to us is that even though they like our idea, they cannot accept it. But why should we enter into controversies? We have to understand that if we sincerely believe that our ideas have in themselves the seeds for creating a new power in the world, then we have actually to create that power. When without any previous knowledge I had the great experience at the village of Pochampalli [where the first gift of land was made in 1951], for the whole night I meditated on the event. I wondered whether it had the hand of God behind it. Now along with my faith in God, I also have a little faith in mathematics. I made a rapid calculation. I understood that the problem will be solved only when we can get 5 crore [a crore is ten million] acres of land as donation. But then this huge figure created doubts and fears in my mind. It appeared almost impossible to believe that we will get 5 crore acres of land, and so when I became doubtful I thought of the Communists. They were also doing some work in that area. And then I thought that if I cannot believe that we shall get enough land through love and persuasion, then there is no alternative for me but to have faith in the Communist ideology. If this work of nonviolence and Sarvodaya has no effect, then you will have to take to Communism. Such is the nearness between the two ideologies. I thought that the last two points in a circle are nearest to each other. And this nearness begins where the circle ends. In other words, that which is the farthest is the nearest. Communism believes in violence but there can be no doubt that it is generated by compassion. This is a strange paradox. There is inspiration from compassion but at the same time there is faith in violence. . . .

What do we find today? We see that some people who are always talking of peace in actual effect believe in *status quo*. They are afraid of a change in human society. As against this, people who want a social revolution do not want to confine themselves within the four walls of *Ahimsa*. They actually do not believe either in violence or in nonviolence. They are in a sense compassionate, and so the contradiction visible in a compassionate people taking to violence is nothing new and is not surprising. This contradiction has been there. But then they say where do you find a logic in life? Life is full of contradictions. Which place is there where contradiction is not to be seen? And so they say for once let us attack this contradiction, and keep aside your nonviolence for a time and accept violence. They say violence is after all as old as the world, and has been coming down to us from ancient times, but, of course, ultimately we will have to bring about nonviolence.

In other words, they say that after one big spate of violence, we will establish nonviolence which will continue to the very end. And so their advice is that [you should] keep faith in nonviolence but have some weapons in your hands. And they ask: Have you no compassion for the poor? The poor are being crushed and oppressed and for their redemption get ready to commit some violence. If you do not agree to this violence, you in effect become incompetent. We have to answer this objection. It is said that those who stand for peace actually maintain the *status quo*, and the revolutionaries take to violence. But what are we? We are revolutionaries but we work peacefully. On us lies the responsibility to show to the world that any problem of this world can be solved through peace. I want to lay down before this gathering its responsibilities. The experience of the last six years has been the development of great hope that we will be able to bring about a peaceful revolution. Thus, innumerable people who have believed that we can have a peaceful revolution have now developed a faith in these possibilities. I regard it as our great success which we never anticipated.

2. From Socialism to Sarvodaya

Jayaprakash Náráyan, a leading socialist once regarded as the probable successor to Nehru as prime minister, gave up his work in party politics (in the Praja Socialist Party) in 1954. He here traces the events which led him to devote his life to the Sarvodaya movement.[2]

▶ ▶ This process of reexamination and reevaluation that I have briefly traced above was a collective experience of those who were working in the CSP [Congress Socialist Party] and old Socialist Party. The conclusions that I have indicated above were also collective in nature, the emphasis on democracy, the need for decentralization, the realization that means must be morally consistent with the ends — these were the common conclusions drawn from a common experience. Thus the Marxist-Leninist CSP, through several incarnations, developed into the democratic-socialist PSP [Praja Socialist Party].

Thus far I travelled together with my colleagues in happy comradeship, the memory of which will sweeten the remaining part of my life. But some years back my journey took a turning where we parted

---

[2] From Bimla Prasad, ed., *Socialism, Sarvodaya and Democracy: Selected Works of Jayaprakash Narayan* (New York: Asia Publishing House, 1964), pp. 151–53, 160–61, 165–67. Used by permission.

company. That parting began with what has come to be grandiloquently known as *Jeevandan* [dedication of one's life] (1954), but which was no more than a decision on my part to withdraw from party-and-power politics and to devote the rest of my life to the *Bhoodan* and Sarvodaya movement.

The same old beacon lights of freedom, equality, and brotherhood that had guided the course of my life and brought me to democratic socialism, drew me onward around this turning of the road. My regret is that I did not reach this point in my life's journey while Gandhiji was still in our midst. However, some years back it became clear to me that socialism as we understand it today cannot take mankind to the sublime goals of freedom, equality, brotherhood and peace. Socialism, no doubt, gives promise to bring mankind closer to those goals than any other competing social philosophy. But I am persuaded that unless socialism is transformed into Sarvodaya, those goals would remain beyond its reach; and just as we had to taste the ashes of independence, so future generations may have to taste the ashes of socialism.

My final break with Marxism, though not with politics, had come during the three weeks fast at Poona (1952). It was then that a long process of questioning started by the Russian purges came to an end, and it became clear that materialism as a philosophical outlook could not provide any basis for ethical conduct and any incentive for goodness.

If man and his consciousness and the society and culture which he has built up are mere manifestations of matter — howsoever dialectically active — I can see no reason why in such a society anyone should try to be good, that is, be generous, kind, unselfish. Why should then one feel sympathy with those who are weak, poor or sick? What is matter will dissolve into matter after death. So what incentive can there be for moral behavior? Lust for power or wealth, or desire to win the acclaim of the people, or the regard of one's peers, may be incentives to action. But such incentives can have no concern with valuations of right or wrong. Ethical ideas have no doubt a history and a social origin, but when the individual begins to question his inherited standards of conduct and asks himself why he should act ethically, materialism offers him no answer. . . .

The Marxists (and the materialists generally), having reduced consciousness to a behavior of matter, naturally knocked the bottom out of ethics. They talk a good deal no doubt of revolutionary ethics, but that is nothing more than the crassest application of the theory that the end justifies the means. Once an individual persuades himself, sincerely or otherwise, that he is on the side of the revolution (or the

Party or the People) he is free to commit any infamy whatsoever. [pp. 151–53]

As questioning about politics was not confined to the party system alone, fundamental questions arose in my mind as to the place and role of the State in human society, particularly in relation to the goals of social life that had fixed themselves before me. Perhaps my schooling in Marxism, with its ideals of a stateless society, made these questions more pointed and troublesome. Though I had given up the basic postulates of Marxism, because they did not promise to lead me to my goals, I continued to feel strongly that human freedom could be fully and wholly realized only in a stateless society. I was, and am, not sure if the State would ever wither away completely. But I am sure that it is one of the noblest goals of social endeavor to ensure that the powers and functions and spheres of the State are reduced as far as possible. I became at this time, and still am, an ardent believer, like Gandhiji, in the maxim that that government was the best that governed the least. The test of human evolution for me became man's ability to live in amity, justice and cooperation with his fellowmen without outward restraints of any kind. That is why I have considered the human and social problem to be at bottom a moral problem.

With this conception of the role and place of the State in society at the back of my mind, I viewed with very deep apprehension the march of the State to greater and greater glory. Democratic socialists, communists, as well as welfarists (not to speak of the fascists), are all statists. They all hope to bring about their own variety of the millenium by first mastering and then adding to the powers and functions of the State. . . .

The only remedy for this that I could think of took me farther away from politics and toward Sarvodaya. The remedy obviously is, as I have said above in the context of internal and external discipline, to make it possible for the people to do without the State as far as practicable and to run their affairs themselves directly. Speaking as a socialist, I would put it thus: the remedy is to create and develop forms of socialist living through the voluntary endeavor of the people rather than seek to establish socialism by the use of the power of the State. In other words, the remedy is to establish people's socialism rather than State socialism. Sarvodaya is people's socialism. [pp. 160–61]

During Gandhiji's lifetime, in spite of the fact that I was gradually drawing close to him, as I have recounted above, I could not see how this nonviolent technique could bring about a social revolution. I had seen how that technique worked during the national revolution, but how feudalism and capitalism could be abolished by the same means and a new society created was not at all clear to me. I had, no doubt, read Gandhiji's writings on revolution through change of heart. But in the absence of a direct demonstration, those ideas seemed impractical in the extreme. During my Marxist days, I had written a vehement critique of the theory of trusteeship; and though I had moved considerably away from Marxism by the end of Gandhiji's life, I was not prepared to accept that trusteeship could be a social, as distinguished from individual, norm of behavior. . . .

I was in this frame of mind when an event of great significance took place. In a remote village of Telengana, *Bhoodan* was born. My first reaction to the event was of the usual sort: it would take hundreds of years in this manner to redistribute all the land in the country, I thought. . . .

About this time, the old Socialist Party had decided that it should turn its urgent attention to the question of redistribution of land which it considered to be the most vital question of economic reform before the country. In a resolution on this subject which I had sponsored, the Pachmarhi Party Conference (1952) had made a brief reference to Bhoodan, welcoming it and promising support. Some time afterwards, I went to see Vinoba when he was in the Banda district of U.P. to discuss this question of land redistribution. I saw that he was serious about the problem and his economic outlook was revolutionary in a basic way. I decided to join Vinoba's movement. But I had a three weeks' fast impending, which completed, I plunged into the Bhoodan "Ganga" [the Ganges river] in the Gaya district of Bihar. My brief experience was exhilarating beyond expectation. Within a week nearly seven thousand acres were obtained as gifts — most of them spontaneous and from small holders — announced at my meetings.

As the movement progressed it took on new forms. Already in 1952 it had disclosed an aspect which was startlingly attractive. In the village Mangroth of the district Hamirpur in U.P., *gramdan* [village-gift] had been announced. Vinoba has a great talent for coining words and investing old words with new meanings. Thus *dan* in his vocabulary does not mean gift, but "sharing together." That is his rendering of Shankar's definition, *danam sam vibhagah*. *Gramdan* was equitable sharing together of the lands of the village by the people of [the] village. *Bhoodan* signified distribution of land to the landless, *gramdan*, on the other hand, meant communization of the land: institution of community, in place of individual, ownership of land. It became evident that *Bhoodan* had within it the germ of total agrarian revolution. [pp. 165–67]

BUDDHIST SOCIALISM

In the area of social, political, and legal thought, Buddhism has produced strikingly little compared with the other three religions. Springing up out of a complex Indian civilization which had already evolved answers to these questions, Buddhism was essentially a new doctrine of individual salvation. Even when it spread over South and Southeast Asia, and independent Buddhist kingdoms emerged, many of the associated political ideas as well as court rituals were of Brahmanical origin.

In the contemporary Buddhist world, however, many intellectuals find themselves drawn to both Buddhism and Marxism, and various approaches have been taken to reconcile the two doctrines. Some, like U Ba Swe in the following article, emphasize the idea that they operate in two very distinct spheres, the spiritual and the temporal, so that each doctrine can reign supreme in its own sphere without ever coming into conflict. Others, like D. C. Vijayavardhana, emphasize the positive similarities such as the common value of egalitarianism and the monastic order as a communist society in miniature.

3. Buddhism and Marxism Are Complementary

In a 1951 speech U Ba Swe, then Minister of Defense and Mines, declared categorically that Marxism was the ideology of the Burmese revolution. Marxism and Buddhism could both guide the individual's life, each in its own sphere. [3]

▶ ▶   In point of fact the vital force that creates a revolution or establishes an era cannot be personified. Ideology alone is the genesis of revolution. Whatever be the program of work or whatever be the kind of revolution, it is ideology which acts as a guide to action. Human beings are but players in the drama of revolutionary process, always taking their cue from ideology. . . .

Let me be plain. Marxism is the guide to action in our revolutionary movement, in our establishment of a Socialist Burmese Society for workers and peasants. Our revolution can only be achieved with Marxism as a guiding principle. Only Marxism can pave the way for the attainment of the goal to which we look forward. Our revolution is impossible without Marxism as a guide. . . .

[3] From U Ba Swe, *The Burmese Revolution* (Rangoon: Pyidawsoe Printing Works, 2nd ed., 1957), pp. 11–12, 14–15, 25.

When I insist on the acceptance of Marxism as a guide to action in our revolutionary movement, I do not mean the acceptance, *in toto*, of the carbon copy of the Russian or the Chinese revolutionary pattern. No doubt, as I have said, Marxism must be a guide to action in our revolutionary movement. But when it is actually put into practice, we must take our environment into account. It must be adapted to suit our own surroundings. It is not for us to do only according to what the text says, or to what a leader dictates, or to what a country is doing. . . . [pp. 11–12]

Let me pause here to explain what Marxism actually is. Marxist philosophy rejects the theory of creation. In point of fact, Marxist theory is not antagonistic to Buddhist philosophy which also rejects the theory of creation. These two are, frankly speaking, not merely similar. In fact, they are the same in concept.

But if we want to have the two distinguished, one from the other, we can safely assume that Marxist theory occupies the lower plane, while Buddhist philosophy occupies the higher.

Marxist theory deals with mundane affairs and seeks to satisfy material needs in life. Buddhist philosophy, however, deals with the solution of spiritual matters with a view to seek spiritual satisfaction in life and liberation from this mundane world.

Both these two philosophies are correlated. I dare say that you will agree with me regarding this statement when you study the two closely.

I declare that I have implicit faith in Marxism, but at the same time I boldly assert that I am a true Buddhist. In the beginning, I was a Buddhist only by tradition. The more I study Marxism, however, the more I feel convinced in Buddhism. Thus I have become a true disciple of Lord Buddha by conviction, and my faith in Buddhism has grown all the more. I now believe that for any man who has deeply studied Buddhism and correctly perceived its tenets there should be no obstacles to become a Marxist. [pp. 14–15]

But then you might ask whether this satisfaction of material needs like food, clothing and living space is the be-all and end-all of life. In that respect we may differ from the view of the Communists. They may prefer to hold the view that satisfaction of material needs is the ultimate consummation of life. But I don't see it in that way. . . . Marxist theory . . . may be able to give us the satisfaction of all material needs. But still there are spiritual needs that remain to be satisfied.

Vexed by anxieties and fears in respect of food, clothing and homes, human minds cannot dwell on old age, disease and death. But with the satisfaction of men's material needs, men can boldly face these three phenomena. Marxism cannot provide an answer to spiritual liberation. Neither can science do [so]. Only Buddhist philosophy can. Only where there is a satisfaction of spiritual needs can we find solace in life. Only then can we find our way to the liberation from this mundane world.

It must, however, be conceded that material satisfaction of life can be attained only through Marxism. [p. 25]

4. Buddhism and Socialism Are Congruent

In *The Revolt in the Temple*, which emphasizes the close association of Buddhism with the Sinhalese nation (see IV. 3), we also find a strong statement of the congruence of Buddhism with the universalistic ideology of socialism.[4]

Buddhism demands for the attainment of happiness a new mentality detaching men from possessions, controlling the passions, losing themselves in something greater than themselves, and directing thought towards moral and intellectual perfection. As a model of this ideal society, the Buddha set up His Sangha, consisting of a minority within the State to live voluntarily a selfless life, non-attached to possessions or social position, and communally sharing whatever necessaries of life they received; for more than this He could not do since He had not, nor desired, absolute power within the State. The problem of applying this Socialist way of life to a wider community the Buddha left to His followers; and today, in Marxian Communist countries, the experiment is being tried to make their entire populations live this kind of life under State compulsion and direction. . . .

Marxism accepts the factor of struggle, of the battle for life, as one of the fundamental principles of human evolution; it is the struggle of classes and not the struggle between individuals or between nations. This struggle in society has as its aim, according to the principles of Marxian Communism, the destruction of all classes and the establishment of the classless society, the completely equalitarian and non-attached community. This establishment of the community without differences of classes and non-attached to possessions, or fame, or power, or social position, can be realized only through a social revolution. The Marxist revolution ends with the establishment of a dictatorship; and this

[4] From D. C. Vijayavardhana, *The Revolt in the Temple: Composed to Commemorate 2,500 Years of the Land, the Race, and the Faith* (Colombo: Sinha Publications, 1953), pp. 593–97, 603–04. Used by permission.

dictatorship, according to Marxist theory, is only temporary. The dictatorship of the proletariat is established for a certain period only, until the moment at which the new social machinery of a completely equalitarian and non-attached community without classes is definitely established. Afterwards, in the opinion of militant Communists, the equalitarian non-attached society will attain peace and happiness — in other words, the highest Buddhist ideal, an all-encompassing Arahat-world, is expected to come into being. . . .

Buddhism does not accept the Marxist conception of the class struggle, the Marxist theory of revolution and temporary dictatorship based on class divergencies, nor the theory of the domination of one class by another — neither the working class by the bourgeoise nor the bourgeoise by the working class. But, if there is no doubt that the divergencies between individuals and classes practically do exist, there is again only the Buddhist method which must be used for harmonization between the classes and the progressive disappearance of inequalities. That means the evolutionary method — the method of democracy: discussion, cooperation, agreement. It means also in a certain sense a struggle, but between human beings we must try always to solve these problems by the human, non-violent, non-sanguinary means and methods. That is Buddhism. . . .

The early Sangha, as established by the Buddha, comprised real Communists whose precept and practice have virtually disappeared from the earth. They were a classless community every member of which was equal (*sama samaja*) and equally free. They individually owned no property, all possessions being held by the community. This ideal of communal ownership of property is emphasized in the *Mahaparinibbana Sutta* where it is said: "So long as the Brethren shall divide without partiality and share in common with the upright and the holy, all such things as they receive in accordance with the just provisions of the Order, down even to the merest contents of a begging bowl, so long may the Brethren be expected, not to decline but to prosper." Here, as far as it was humanly possible, was realized the true Communist ideal of a classless, equalitarian and non-attached society.

Communism, in its orthodox theoretical form, is thus not at all inconsistent with the Communism of the original Sangha. And, although in practice, in Russia and elsewhere, modern Communism exhibits many and marked divergences from the orthodox theory, it still remains true that the ideal Buddhist way of life and a genuine Communism can be thoroughly consistent with each other. There are many Buddhists who are convinced that there is much more in common between Buddhism and Communism than between Buddhism and capitalism. The Buddhists, therefore, should avoid an indiscriminate condemnation of Communism, which would compel many, especially of the younger generation, to feel that they must choose between Buddhism and Communism. [pp. 593–97]

Marx, who made Communism a classic doctrine in the history of economic theory, was an idealist insufficiently equipped with knowledge either of natural or human history; he saw man only as part of an economic process, and his path to progress was the path of conflict; only through hatred, violence and revolution could mankind realize itself. The Buddha saw man as a conscious part of Nature, and his path to happiness was a moral and intellectual one; only by raising his ethos to a higher level could man achieve progress culminating in perfection.

Marx taught that a man is what environment makes him and no more; the Buddha taught that a man is what he makes himself. Change the structure of society, said Marx, and you change the man. Change yourself, said the Buddha, and you will help to change the structure of society.

The moral of these comments should be obvious. The *thesis* of traditional Buddhism and the *antithesis* of Marxian Communism are incomplete. They contain both merits and defects. The Buddhist tends to regard the perfecting of the individual as the essential task of religion, and thus to ignore the need for constructing a better order of society; the Communist tends to assume that a change of system is sufficient and that the conversion of the individual is irrelevant.

The Buddhist hides from the realities behind a barrier of well-meaning phrases, and concentrates his attention so largely on the need for Love and Kindness that he ignores the inevitability of conflict with the reactionary elements; the Communist is concerned so exclusively with the struggle that he tends to become ruthless and intolerant in his outlook.

. The Buddhist is so entangled in the claims of tradition that he is a stranger in the world of current politics; the revolutionary is so impatient towards traditional claims that he ignores the values contained in the past order, and is accordingly crude in his criticism of religion and apt to disregard the cultural assets of religion.

The Buddhist believes that truth can be discovered in the realm of pure theory, delighting therefore in speculative thought and ready to make irrelevancies the cardinal issues of his religion; the Communist regards action as the sole essential, thus excluding from consideration any question of the existence of absolute principles, and so rendering his case opportunistic.

These examples, though roughly stated, may help to indicate that we have reached a stage when a *synthesis* is necessary. The first step towards such a synthesis must be the frank realization that politics cannot be divorced from ethics. [pp. 603–04]

ISLAMIC SOCIALISM

There is a long history of ideological formulations of Islamic socialism, going back at least to the great Pan-Islamist leader Jamal al-Din al-Afghani in the 1890s. Like many later interpreters, Afghani emphasized the institution of *zakat* (a tax for the relief of the poor) and the prohibition of interest-taking in Islam as demonstrating its socialistic character.

Islam undoubtedly has egalitarian values, a strong concept of social justice, an emphasis on the solidarity of the community as opposed to the individual, and a basic assumption that the ruler must intervene in the affairs of his subjects to ensure justice. All of these elements would seem to place Islam closer to a socialist than to a capitalist view of society. However, Islamic notions of social justice, such as the prohibition of interest, became embedded in a highly static system of law, the *shari'ah*, which is far removed from the dynamic spirit of modern socialism.

It is still not clear to what extent the interpretations of Islamic socialism have influenced behavior in support of socalist policies in the United Arab Republic or elsewhere. The *fatwas* of the *ulama* may succeed in legitimizing socialism, to their satisfaction, but the deeper question is whether religious fervor can be channeled into developmental action.

5. Islamic Socialism of the Masjumi Left Wing

By the 1960s, there were many efforts to formulate an ideology of Islamic socialism in the Middle East. Indonesia, however, had a much longer tradition of Marxist-Islamic ideological interaction, and the following statement was produced by the left wing of the Muslim Masjumi Party in 1948. [5]

▶ ▶ What is the aim of our national revolution? The aim is the unity of the Indonesian people and the realization of social justice and prosperity

[5] Reprinted from George McTurnan Kahin, *Nationalism and Revolution in Indonesia* (Ithaca, N.Y.: Cornell University Press, 1952) pp. 309–10. Copyright 1952 by Cornell University. Used by permission of Cornell University Press.

for our people. Therefore the abolition of the colonial system alone is not enough. We need an economic and political structure which can guarantee the realization of social justice, and this could not be realized in the Dutch time which was colonialistic and capitalistic in nature.

Our constitution is also influenced by socialism, as is proved by article 33. However, socialism in the constitution has no spiritual connection with Marxian Socialism, because article 29, clause one, stipulates that our state is based on Religion. The followers of the constitution who are now following Marxian Socialism unconsciously pursue a wrong path.

Collectivism without individualism is like a flock of sheep which can be dispersed easily. It is Fascism if a certain ideology will impose collectivism upon the people by forcibly eliminating a class of people.

Islam forbids the forcible imposition of a certain ideology. Individualism is properly respected by Islam; each individual is responsible for himself to God. Islam calls for the reaching of agreement by means of discussion among the people. In our revolution many Muslims are forgetting the principles of Islam; they support Marxian Socialism and participate in actions which merely create troubles and hamper the revolution.

Our national revolution needs an ideology which can guarantee the realization of social justice. However, I believe that Marxism cannot fulfill the need; in addition, Marxism is contrary to the Constitution. The ideology which is suitable to our society is Religious Socialism, an ideology which is in harmony with the Constitution. Religious Socialism does not abolish individualism, individual initiative, and individual responsibility. Thus, not only the freedom of the whole nation is guaranteed but also the freedom of the individual, without closing the door for possible nationalization or socialization of certain vital enterprises. This is the ideal of our national revolution.

Therefore it is not correct to state that it is not yet the time to begin socialist revolution. On the contrary, our national revolution obviously indicates elements of socialism, which are similar to Marxian Socialism. If the elements of socialism do not exist, the national revolution means nothing to us, as it does not give new hope. However, the basis of socialism in our revolution is not the historical materialism of Marx, but its basis is the duty of man towards man and the duty of man towards God.

Therefore, the means of realizing socialism must be different from the means used by Marxian Socialism with its class struggle. According to Religious Socialism socialization is only a means to realize social justice and the people's prosperity. Therefore to achieve socialization it is not necessary to eliminate a certain class or groups, and it is also not necessary to introduce an over-all socialization; it is enough if socialization is introduced when necessary. . . .

Competition arising out of private initiative as such is not bad, but the contrary, because competition increases production and improves the quality of goods. We must not forget that the progress of production and economy in Europe and America was possible because of competition. Only at a certain stage does this liberal economy not increase production and is there a tendency to limit production. At that stage the government must intervene by nationalizing certain private enterprises or establishing enterprises itself.

Generally speaking the limitation of competition and/or socialization should not be introduced merely because of desire to realize a certain theory; the time and circumstances must also be taken into consideration. If the government organs are not yet well enough organized to carry out and supervise the regulations made by the state because of the lack of capable personnel, and if home production is not yet sufficient to supply the needs of the people, we must think twice before we introduce socialization or limit competition. Otherwise merely for the sake of realizing a certain theory, we will cause our own people to die.

6. Socialism of Islam in the United Arab Republic

In this *fatwa* on the socialist legislation promulgated in 1961 the Mufti finds ample justification for the nationalization of major sectors of the economy. While the principle of "absolute interest" he expounds would seem to allow for any legislation deemed to be in the interest of justice, some limits are specified at the end of the selection.[6]

Socialism of Islam

In the Safar 1382 issue of Minbar Al-Islam I answered the inquiry made by one of our citizens about the truth of the allegations broadcast by some of the Muslim States purporting that the Socialist Laws issued by U.A.R. in July, 1961, are adverse to the spirit of Islam.

In my answer, I explained how the restriction of land ownership to 100 feddans and the distribution of the land exceeding that area among destitute and small farmers, who own no land, is a matter conformable

---

[6] From "The Mufti Answers Your Questions," *Minbar Al-Islam* (Cairo, English ed.), April, 1963, pp. 64–65, 67–68.

with the Islamic Laws. Concluding I said: "In truth, the restriction of agricultural land-ownership does by no means contradict Islam." I also gave several examples from the tradition and conduct of the Prophet — peace and prayers of God be upon him — and his Companions in substantiation of my argument.

This time, I shall discuss the rest of the provisions of the aforesaid Socialist Laws in order to know the views of Islamic Laws towards them.

Under the Socialist Laws, some banks and commercial firms were nationalized while in the capital of others, the State had a holding interest of 50 percent. But in either case, the shareholders affected by those laws were compensated for their shares at the market rate on the day on which the nationalization was put into effect.

In the light of our knowledge concerning the rules of Islamic Law (*Shari'ah*), we can easily judge whether the nationalization conforms with those rules or not.

To me, the first mark illumining our way in this study is the view of the Islamic Law regarding the prohibition of monopoly, which is explicitly stated in the authentic *hadiths*, foremost among which is the one narrated by Muslim, Ahmad and Abu Dawoud who quoted Saeed Ibn Al Mussib as having reported that Muammar Ibn Abdulla Al Adawy heard the Prophet saying "He who resorts to monopoly is a wrong-doer." There is also the *hadith* reported by Abu Horairah through Al Imam Ahmad's "Musnad" in which the Prophet said "He who monopolizes a commodity with a view to raising its prices for the Muslims is a wrong-doer."

After narrating these two *hadiths* with others on monopoly in his book *Nail Al Awtar*, Al Imam Al Shawkany said: "The apparent meaning of those *hadiths* indicate that monopoly is prohibited without any distinction being made between the sustenance of Man and beasts or any other essential. The reference to food in certain narratives cannot restrict the absolute text, for the majority of jurists maintain that the specification of certain things cannot be considered an evidence excluding other things. Consequently, the prohibition of monopoly in connection with food does not restrict the application of the prohibition in connection with other essentials and the *hadiths* prohibiting monopoly should not therefore be restricted." . . . .

Thus, if a group of people monopolized cultivable land and the shares of companies and banks by owning hundreds of feddans or thousands of shares, thus, depriving other people of the opportunity to utilize them for earning their living, and if such people declined to sell the excess in their land or shares to those who need them at reasonable price, then such monopolizers are wrong-doers. When the case is such, the ruler can force those monopolizers to sell part of their land or shares to those who need them or to the state to be exploited in the public interest.

He who reads the explanatory note issued with the Nationalization Law No. 117 of 1961 will see that the Law aimed at nothing other than the realization of the high national interest of the country. . . .

We have already proved that nationalization is substantiated by the authentic *hadith* reported in the books on tradition in which the Prophet — may God's peace and prayers be upon him — said: "All people partake in three things: water, fodder [or pasture] and fire" and in another text "salt" as well. The rule here is not confined to those essentials alone, but it rather applies to all the likes, which are essential and indispensable for people's life.

This view was also promulgated by Dr. Mustafa El Sabai, who in the second edition of his book *Socialism in Islam*, under the title "The Nationalization of Essentials," said: "It is noticed that these things are essential for the life of people, particularly the nomads of that time. But the reference to them in the aforementioned *hadith* does not mean that the rule is confined to them alone. Under the rules of Islam, all the like essentials should not be owned by one individual or a group of people lest their monopoly should involve exploitation of other people's need to those essentials. The state should therefore look after the utilization and distribution of such necessities among the people." . . .

One of the evidences of Islamic rules approved by the majority of jurists and erudites is the "absolute interest" (the interest not stipulated in the Islamic Law), which is also a legal proof on which the legislation of rules is based. Thus, in any case about which there is no rule derived from the Islamic Law in a text from the Qur'an or tradition or by unanimity in view (*Ijma*), analogical deduction (*Qias*) or approval (*Istehsan*), the rule necessitated by the absolute interest is to be enacted. In this case, the legislation does not depend on the existence of an evidence from the Islamic Law recognizing that interest.

The following are the arguments raised by those jurists and erudites to prove the legality of absolute interests:

1. People's interests are renewable and infinite. Thus, if rules are not enacted in conformity with people's interests and the exigencies of their circumstances and social institutions, then many of those interests will be withheld at different times and different places, and legislation will no longer conform with people's interests and their development. Obviously, this does not agree with the intention of the legislator. . . .

2. Actions of the Prophet's Companions and the erudite Imams through whom the legislation of the rules governing the absolute interest was communicated, even though it was not recognized by the Islamic Law.

The first Caliph Abu Bakr Al Siddiq collected the scattered scripts of the Holy Qur'an in one place and fought those who prevented *Zakat* (poor due). He also appointed Omar Ibn El Khattab — may God be gracious to him — as his successor. Omar, too, stopped the system of distribution of *Zakat* among the newly converted Muslims, imposed land tax, organized registers for the State's affairs, established prisons and withheld the implementation of the punishment imposed on thieves during the year of famine. Osman got the Muslims to adopt one way of Qur'anic recitation. He also entitled to inheritance the wife divorced by her husband during his death sickness with the object of preventing her from inheriting [from] him.

Hanafite jurists approved the interdiction of the impudent Mufti, the ignorant physician and the bankrupt merchant. Followers of Imam Malek allowed the imprisonment of the defendant to get him to confess his crime. The Shafiites enjoined the execution of any group of people proved guilty of killing one single person. All these legislations were supported by nothing but the absolute interest.

Accordingly, if the ruler of the country found that the country's interest requires the total or partial nationalization of some banks and companies, this ruler can issue the law necessary for this need. He will be supported in this case by the absolute interest in addition to the other proofs already quoted from the Prophet's tradition and the Companions' course of action.

What is noteworthy in this connection is that the absolute interest, which is considered one of the evidences of legislation, must be real not imaginary and public not private. It must not contravene any legislation confirmed by a text from the Qur'an or tradition or by *Ijma*, *Qias* or *Istehsan*. Thus, it is not allowed to enact, for example, legislation stipulating equality between the son and the daughter in inheritance, because such a legislation would contravene an *explicit* text from the Qur'an and tradition and would contradict the view unanimously agreed upon by the Muslims.

As we are very eager to see that the legislation of laws must conform with the rules of the Islamic Law, we believe in the view adopted by the majority of jurists allowing legislation for the absolute interest while keeping in view the aforementioned conditions stipulated by those jurists. In this way, we do not close the door for the real public interest, which safeguards the good of the largest number of people. At the same time, we do not open that door for a legislation contradicting God's rules, which are proved by other evidences.

CATHOLIC SOCIALISM

There has been a strong critique of capitalism in Catholic social teaching since *Rerum Novarum* (1891). Pope Leo XIII saw laissez faire capitalism, with all its dehumanizing effects, as the economic aspect of the upheavals which had shaken Europe since the sixteenth century. Protestantism, nationalism, rationalism, liberalism, capitalism—all reflected man's revolt from the church. And communism was spawned by capitalism.

The continuing Catholic criticism of capitalism was mitigated only by the fear of communism, especially after the Russian Revolution. Up to 1960, papal and episcopal pronouncements on communism were unrelenting in their bitter hostility. But Pope John XXIII, in opening the windows of the church to the modern world, refused to keep even this one closed, and in his social encyclicals began the Catholic-Marxist dialogue. The Christian Democrats in Latin America, unlike those in Europe, had long been engaged in formulating a moderate form of Catholic socialism. But after Pope John, much more radical theses emanated from the Catholic clergy, priests and bishops alike. We shall here examine three of these radical statements.

7. Socialism Closer to the Spirit of the Gospel

In 1967, fifteen bishops from various parts of Asia, Africa, and Latin America published this statement. While described as a Third World response to and elaboration of Pope Paul VI's encyclical "On the Development of Peoples," the message propounded much more revolutionary theses.[7]

▶ ▶   As bishops of some of the peoples which strive and struggle for development, we join our voice to the anguished call of Pope Paul VI in the encyclical *Populorum Progressio*, in order to define clearly the duties of our priests and faithful, and to address some words of

---

[7] From Dom Helder Cámara *et al.*, "15 obispos hablan en pro del Tercer Mundo," *El Día* (Mexico City), September 23, 1967, reprinted by Centro Intercultural de Documentación (Cuernavaca, Mexico), doc. 67/35, pp. 2–4, 6–7. Used by permission. Translated by the editor.

encouragement to our brothers of the Third World. . . . The peoples of the Third World form the proletariat of present-day humanity, exploited by the great and threatened in their very existence by those who, only because they are stronger, arrogate to themselves the right to be the judges and the policemen of the peoples who are materially less well-off. Now then, our peoples are neither less honest nor less just than the powerful of this world.

Revolutions have been and are being produced in the actual evolution of the world. There is nothing surprising in this. All the established powers came into being in an era more or less remote from revolution, that is, a break with a system which did not secure the common good and the setting up of a new order more likely to achieve it. Not all revolutions are necessarily good. Some are no more than palace revolts and produce nothing more than changes in the oppressors of the people. Some do more harm than good, "engendering new injustices. . . ." (*Populorum Progressio*). Atheism and collectivism, to which certain movements feel they must be tied, are grave dangers for humanity. But history shows that certain revolutions were necessary and once freeing themselves from a momentary anti-religion have gone on to produce good fruits. No case proves this better than the French Revolution which in 1789 occasioned the affirmation of the rights of man (see *Pacem in Terris*). . . .

From the doctrinal point of view, the Church knows that the Gospel demands the first and radical revolution: conversion, the total transformation from sin to grace, from selfishness to love, from pride to humble service. And this conversion is not only internal and spiritual, but is directed at the whole man, corporate and social as well as spiritual and personal. It contains a communitarian aspect full of consequences for the entire society, not only for earthly life but above all for eternal life in Christ, who from heaven would bring all humanity unto Himself. Such is the Christian vision of the integral development of man. In this way the Gospel has always been, visibly or invisibly, within the Church or outside, the most powerful ferment of the profound mutations of humanity for the past twenty centuries.

Nevertheless, in its historical earthly pilgrimage, the Church has been practically always linked to the political, social and economic system that, at one moment in history, assured the common good and at least a certain social order. On the other hand, the Churches find themselves so linked to such a system that they appear to be confused with it, united in one flesh as if in marriage. But the Church has only one husband, Christ. The Church is not married to any system whatever it might be, and less to "the international imperialism of money" (*Populorum Progressio*), as it was not married to the monarchy or feudalism of the old regime, and as it will not be tomorrow with one form or another of socialism. It is sufficient to examine history to see that the Church has survived the ruin of the powers which at one time thought they should protect or could use her. At present the social doctrine of the Church, reaffirmed by Vatican II, has rescued her from this imperialism of money, which seems to be one of the forces to which she was linked for some time.

After the Council vigorous voices were raised which demanded that this temporal collusion between the Church and money, denounced on several sides, be ended. Certain bishops have already set the example. We ourselves have the duty to make a serious examination of our situation with respect to this problem, and to liberate our Churches from all servitude to the great international finance. "One cannot serve God and money."

Concerning that which the Church holds as essential and permanent, that is, her faithfulness to and communion with Christ in the Gospel, she is never identified with any economic, political or social system. The moment a system ceases to promote the common good for the benefit of the interests of a few, the Church must not only denounce the injustice but separate itself from the iniquitous system, and be ready to collaborate with another system better adapted to the needs of the time and more just. . . .

Bearing in mind the necessities for certain processes of material progress, the Church for now a century has tolerated capitalism with its loans made at legal interest and other practices in little conformity with the ethic of the prophets and the Gospel. But she can only rejoice to see another social system less foreign to this ethic appear among humanity. It will be the responsibility of the Christians of tomorrow, according to the initiative of Paul VI, to guide these currents of moral values, which are solidarity and fraternity, back to their true Christian sources (*cf. Ecclesiam Suam*). Christians have the duty to show that "the true socialism is Christianity integrally lived, in the just distribution of goods and fundamental equality" (Patriarch Maximus IV, 1965). Far from overlooking it, let us know how to embrace it joyfully as a form of social life better adapted to our time and closer to the spirit of the Gospel. Thus we will avoid the confusion of God and religion with feudalism, capitalism and imperialism which are, in fact, the oppressors of the poor and the workers. These inhuman systems have engendered others which, while desiring to liberate the peoples, oppress persons, if these other systems fall into totalitarian collectivism and religious persecution. But God and true religion have nothing to do with the diverse forms of the Mammon of iniquity. On the contrary, God and true religion are always with those who seek to promote a more equitable and fraternal society among all the children of God in the great human family.

8. Communist-Catholic Revolutionary Coalition

Father Camilo Torres, the Colombian priest-revolutionary (see V. 5–7), published the following "Message to the Communists" in his weekly paper *Frente Unido* ("United Front"). Note the long quotation from Pope John's *Pacem in Terris* which Torres applied to his United Front. [8]

▶ ▶ The traditional relations between Christians and Marxists, between the Church and the Communist Party, may cause erroneous suspicions and suppositions to arise concerning the relations which in the United Front may be established between Christians and Marxists and between a priest and the Communist Party.

For this reason I believe it is necessary that my relations with the Communist Party and its position within the United Front remain very clear before the Colombian people.

I have said that I am a revolutionary as a Colombian, as a sociologist, as a Christian and as a priest. I regard the Communist Party as having authentically revolutionary elements and, therefore, I cannot be anti-communist as a Colombian, as a sociologist, as a Christian, or as a priest.

I am not anti-communist as Colombian, because anti-communism is oriented to persecute nonconformist compatriots, Communists or not, of whom the majority are poor people.

I am not anti-communist as a sociologist, because in the Communist plans to combat poverty, hunger, illiteracy, the lack of housing, the lack of public services, we find effective and scientific solutions.

I am not anti-communist as a Christian, because I believe that anti-communism carries with it a blanket condemnation of all that the Communists defend and, among that which they defend, there are both just and unjust things. By condemning them all together, we are exposed to condemning equally the just and the unjust, and this is anti-Christian.

[8] From *Camilo Torres, Por el Padre Camilo Torres Restrepo (1956–1966)* (Cuernavaca, Mexico: Centro Intercultural de Documentación, 1966), pp. 30, 329–31. Used by permission. Translated by the editor.

I am not anti-communist as a priest, because although the Communists themselves may not know it, among them there may be many who are authentic Christians. If they are of good faith, they can have sanctifying grace and if they have sanctifying grace and love their neighbor they will be saved. My role as a priest, even though it is not in the exercise of the external cult, is to bring men to an encounter with God, and to accomplish this the most effective means is to make men serve their neighbor in accord with their conscience.

I do not intend to proselytize among my Communist brothers by trying to get them to accept the dogma and practice the cult of the Church. I do intend, definitely, to get all men to work in accord with their conscience and to seek the truth sincerely and to love their neighbor in an effective way.

The Communists must know very well that I will not join their ranks either, that I am not and will not be a Communist, as a Colombian, as a sociologist, as a Christian, or as a priest.

Nevertheless, I am ready to struggle with them for common objectives: against the oligarchy and the domination of the United States, for the seizure of power by the masses.

I don't want public opinion to identify me with the Communists and for that reason I have always wished not to appear in public with them only, but with all revolutionaries, independents and those of other persuasions.

It does not matter that the great press obstinately pictures me as a Communist. I prefer to follow my conscience rather than yield to the pressure of the oligarchy. I prefer to follow the norms of the pontiffs of the Church rather than those of the pontiffs of our ruling class. John XXIII authorizes me to march in unity of action with the Communists when he says in his encyclical *Pacem in Terris* :

It must be borne in mind, furthermore, that neither can false philosophical teachings regarding the nature, origin and destiny of the universe and of man, be identified with historical movements that have economic, social, cultural or political ends, not even when these movements have originated from those teachings and have drawn and still draw inspiration therefrom. Because the teachings, once they are drawn up and defined, remain always the same, while the movements, working on historical situations in constant evolution, cannot but be influenced by these latter and cannot avoid, therefore, being subject to changes, even of a profound nature. Besides, who can deny that those movements, in so far as they conform to the dictates of right reason and are interpreters of the lawful aspirations of the human person, contain elements that are positive and deserving of approval?

It can happen, then, that a drawing together or a meeting for the attainment of some practical end, which was formerly deemed inopportune or unproductive, might now or in the future be considered opportune and useful. But to decide whether this moment has arrived, and also to lay down the ways and degrees in which work in common might be possible for the achievement of economic, social, cultural and political ends which are honorable and useful: these are the problems which can only be solved with the virtue of prudence, which is the guiding light of the virtues that regulate the moral life, both individual and social.

When the masses seize power, thanks to the collaboration of all revolutionaries, our people will discuss their religious orientation.

The example of Poland shows us that socialism can be built without destroying what is essential in Christianity. As a Polish priest said: "We Christians have the obligation to contribute to the building of the socialist state as long as we are permitted to worship God as we wish."

9. Catholic Marxism

The author of this article, Father Francisco Lage Pessoa, is a Brazilian priest living in exile in Mexico. (See also X. 4.). He accepts the basic Marxist analysis of society and history, and even finds in Marxist atheism "the unconscious search for the ultimate consequences of redemption."[9]

▶ ▶   The few Christians who do not adhere blindly to the capitalist system attempt, often with generosity, to remedy the evils by proposing reforms which in turn are promised by the politicians; but since such reforms cannot be carried out within the capitalist setup they are always postponed, as occurred with the celebrated "revolution in freedom."

In addition to the demands made of the politicians and the rich in the name of the gospel (the classic example is the encyclical *Populorum Progressio*, rightly called "a letter to the rich"), some people endeavor to *do something*. Ten years ago, charity pure and simple was in vogue: distributing North American powdered milk, opening medical dispensaries, taking part in sanitation campaigns ("a latrine for every house"), committing oneself to intensive "social work" which became a panacea. Today, the uselessness of such measures now proved, there prevails a

---

[9] From Francisco Lage Pessoa, "Brasil: La Iglesia y el Movimiento Revolucionario," in B. Castro Villagrana *et al.*, *La Iglesia, El Subdesarrollo y La Revolución* (Mexico City: Editorial Nuestro Tiempo, S. A., 1968), pp. 160–64. Used by permission. Translated by the editor.

more sophisticated approach to the maintenance of the social *order*, through the influence of the Church. There are agencies of aid, proceeding in general from intelligent Europe, bearing elegant little Latin names (*Caritas, Misereor, Adveniat*) which, in addition to being caught up in a fever of construction, often in the center of slums, send priests and laymen in profusion to Latin America, in order to save it from *communism* (a naive person might think that it was to preach the gospel, but those in charge themselves confess that it is not for that) and everywhere open schools for leaders. Naturally the leaders are not leaders of anything, for they are chosen according to the employers' criterion of the "good worker."

The remedy, however, is nothing but a palliative, always ill intentioned, at least objectively. It is not for the Church as such to assume the role of social reformer within a system itself in the name of Christianity. This is not its mission, but rather that of preaching the gospel, which is the defense of the whole man, of all men, against all discrimination and injustice and in support of every struggle for the welfare of the peoples of the earth. The rights of God and of the Church can never be against the rights of men and of nations: and this expression (so often used to attack attempts at change) will have meaning if rightly applied. Otherwise people will always believe in the alliance, denied in words but affirmed in deeds, between the Church and every established power, whatever it be.

It is the mission of the Christian to work with freedom of option in temporal things, to secure the true justice and fraternity demanded by the gospel, making use of adequate means to establish systems that really serve the people in their search for happiness. If Christians cannot have this freedom, so highly praised since Vatican Council II, all struggle will be in vain and it would be better for the peoples if the Church did not exist, established to disfigure the true face of Christ.

Once it is recognized that capitalism is the evil par excellence in the realm of the economy and organization of society, it is necessary to do away with it, to put in its place a social system "less separated from the gospel," for the advent of which "the Church rejoices," as the few bishops of the Third World say. We would prefer the more realistic expression, "the Church *should* rejoice," because, unfortunately, we see no symptom of joy in the Church over the strengthening of socialism in the world.

But can a Catholic be a socialist? This is the question that the well intentioned will ask me. Naturally, from what I have already said, my answer is affirmative. Not only can they, but, according to the degree of their consciousness of the social problem, they have the obligation to be socialists, if the historic moment in which they live thus determines it and there is no other solution for the development and welfare of the peoples of the earth. The question, however, refers much more to an existing division between socialism and the church of the social encyclicals. No one ignores the fact that, from Pius IX to our days, not excepting John XXIII, the popes have spoken against socialism. This last-mentioned (John XXIII), spoke in a completely different manner, but, as for many people the question is understood simply in terms of a word, socialism, this is the end of the matter. Here we are face to face with a taboo: the Catholic cannot be a socialist, because the popes prohibited it. It is a pure taboo because, in the first place, the popes never bothered to explain what form of socialism they were talking about, on the contrary almost always using the emotional language of one situated "on the other side." Then too, from the texts we see that what frightens the popes (I would not say "the Catholics") is the atheistic aspect of Marxist socialism: a certain necessity of socialism to be anti-God.

We could discuss at great length the subject of atheism, which is historically a legacy of the Encyclopedists and the French Revolution. The libertarian spirits of that time felt that they had to combat the Church, or rather, the higher clergy. From there they were carried into combat by the very dynamics of polemics, from the notion itself of religion and God. When Marx came on the scene, with his stupendous vision of the workers' struggle, opening up a new era in the liberation of the peoples, he had only to approve those ideas, deepen them in a more realistic sense (religious alienation) and create modern atheism.

One could ask, at the risk of scandalizing both sides: may not that atheism be the unconscious search for the ultimate consequences of redemption? That which would signify "finding God in the heart of man" (Paul VI), "where, if He is not present He will not be anywhere" (*Galileo*, from Brecht). And that religion, that so easily allies itself to the exploiting power and becomes its plaything to put to sleep the consciousness of the poor, can it be the gospel of Christ? We are in a time when people, including Christian authors, speak of "the death of God," of the "tomb of God." May not that death be the figure of the death of Christ, who is going to announce his resurrection? I like to imagine the history of humanity as a repetition, in cycles, of the history of the God-Man. How many times will he not have died so that, after the gloomy and sometimes long Holy Saturday, he could be resurrected with a new face, not always recognizable to his old companions! . . .

It would be necessary for all to undertake a dispassionate study of

Marxism, to discover its fundamental realities (which have nothing against the true Christian) and a new reading of the gospel, in search of the genuine face of Christ. For those who believe in Christ: that that man, dispossessed of all except an enormous capacity to transform all in love, be known and analyzed. Let those who defend capitalism against communism be asked if it is that Christ they follow. And let them answer with the heart, not with property. Christ, the true Christ, cannot be an embarrassment for anyone concerned for a systematic distribution of wealth, for a revaluing of the whole man, for the struggle against his alienations toward a perspective of lasting international peace and friendship; for a socialism truly respectful of man and his rights.

X

Religion
and
Revolutionary
Change

Religion has played an important role in the overthrow of
colonial regimes (IV. 1–5), revolts against national governments
(V. 1–4), and major transfers of power through elections (VI. 1–2, 9–11).
While the word *revolution* has sometimes been applied to all of these
events, thay have not constituted revolutions in the sense used here,
namely, a major restructuring of political, social, and economic power in
society. Indeed, in most cases cited above, the only significant change has
been a purely political one: the replacement of one group of rulers by
another.

The major structural revolutions in history — the French, Mexican,
Russian, Chinese, and Cuban revolutions — have all been inspired by
secular ideologies. In the contemporary Third World, Marxism
continues to be the most influential revolutionary ideology. As shown in
Chapter IX, however, the major religions today do not necessarily stand
in opposition to Marxism, but admit of various forms of coalition or
even ideological synthesis. While such coalitions or syntheses are clearly
the work of small minorities within the respective religious systems,
their significance is still considerable.

In this chapter we examine religious statements on revolution. There
are various relationships of these ideas to Marxism. In general the

religious interpreter strives to show that the revolutionary imperative comes directly from his religious tradition. In other cases there is frank recognition that the religious revolutionary idea was discovered or rediscovered only under the stimulus of Marxism. In still other cases, some form of ideological synthesis with Marxism explicitly recognizes both as valid sources of the revolutionary impulse.

We have included one of Vinoba Bhave's strong statements on revolutionary change. The other selections in the chapter, however, all come out of Latin American Catholicism. This is undoubtedly the most important source of serious religious debate on revolution in the Third World today. The Catholic church, unlike the other religious systems, has become profoundly engaged in one form or another with the idea of revolution. With the general discussion of revolution as a religious value comes inevitably the debate over the legitimacy of violence as the means of effecting the revolution.

RELIGION MEANS REVOLUTION

The religious exponents of revolution, unlike some of their secular counterparts, are deeply conscious of the psychological changes, the revolution in men's values, which must accompany structural changes in society. Religion, in its traditional concern with internal belief, values, and motivation, may thus serve as a useful corrective to ideologies such as Marxism which view these factors as mere reflections of the economic relationships obtaining in a given society.

The religious revolutionary doubts that external coercion alone, such as the legislative power of the state, is capable of producing the revolution in men's minds. Therefore, Vinoba Bhave has adopted the noncoercive moral appeal as his primary method, in keeping with the doctrine of *ahimsa* (nonviolence). In Camilo Torres' radical thought, the revolution, even though it required violence, sprang out of the fundamental Christian ethic of "love thy neighbor." And it was abundantly clear in his own case that love for his neighbor indeed propelled him into revolutionary action.

1. Vinoba Bhave on Revolutionary Change

In this article Bhave articulates his concept of a profound social revolution based on moral revolution. Note the extensive use made of Hindu mythological themes in his exposition.[1]

---

[1] From Acharya Vinoba Bhave, *The Principles and Philosophy of the Bhoodan Yagna* (Tanjore: Sarvodaya Prachuralaya, 1955) pp. 1–3. Used by permission.

▶ ▶   Our work consists in changing the present social order from the very root. This is the secret of this *Bhoodan* [land-gift] campaign. That is why when people ask me whether this can be done by legislation alone, I reply in the negative. This is not a one-sided movement. When it succeeds the State will change, the Government will change and the life-structure will change.

To the society which we seek to build up I have given the name "Samyayogi Society." I struck at this word from the Gita which teaches us to do unto others as we do unto ourselves. We should treat others in the same manner as we want to be treated by them. So also we must behave towards society as we aspire to be treated by it. When Hanuman met Ravana he placed before him the injustice of the latter's act in having stolen Rama's consort. He told him that he [Ravana] could easily see the error of his ways since he [Ravana] was himself a *grahastha* [householder]. He asked him to visualize the situation in the event of his own wife being kidnapped. . . .

I ask the landowners to imagine from their own experience the condition of those who own no land. I ask the property owners to imagine from their experience the conditions of those who own no property. If you have any appreciation of their feeling it is enjoined upon you to distribute among them the extra that you have. This is your Dharma.

The most essential requisite of Samyayogi social structure is that all land, all property, and all wealth should belong to society. Only Vishnu [a god] can be the lord of Lakshmi [goddess of wealth], a seat which you have usurped. Bhartruhari has said that to us Lakshmi is mother, and we are her children. On the contrary, today we aggrandize ourselves as her lord. I feel this is injustice, and a denial of religion. It is not a single individual behaving thus, but the whole of society. Should somebody commit adultery it is his fault and not that of the society. But if the social structure be such that it grants the right of ownership of land to some, of ownership of property to others and so on, everybody would enjoy what he gets hold of. And all this is regarded sacred and holy! Now the priests of Vaidyanatham assaulted me. When I pondered over it I felt that they believed that we were out to destroy religion and they were out to protect it by the force of arms. Where religion enjoys such sanctions irreligion gets entrenched very deep.

What I want to inculcate among the people is that our body is made from and of society and for the service of the society. Service is thus a debt on our shoulders which we have to repay. We are distinct from our body. So when we are not the owners or masters of even our body, how dare we claim our right on other things as land and property? Ganga [the river Ganges] loves all alike. She quenches the thirst of the lion as also of the cow. Should somebody claim his right upon such a beneficient Ganga, would we accept it? If none has claim on the Ganga, how can we have on land or property?

I go on saying from village to village that if classes or differences had been dear to God's heart, He would not have provided everybody with one nose. He would have granted one nose to a poor man while ten or more to a minister. But he feels that everybody requires [a] nose and should have [an] equal right to breathe air. As none can claim ownership of air, water or sunshine, so also none can claim that of land. Should somebody claim it, that is due to [a] wrong idea which is irreligious. Hence I have given it the name of moral revolution — *Dharmapravarthan*. I want to root out the wrong ideas and erect the new society on the basis of religious ideas.

It is why I demand one-sixth of land. There are some 5 crores [a crore = ten million] of landless people in our country. For them we require five crores of acres, about one-sixth of good land available in India. In case these calculations come out to be incorrect I would demand again more land. For what I want is that there must be a complete redistribution of land and property, as also of power.

2. The Christian and the Latin American Revolution

In 1963, the well-known journal *Mensaje* ("Message"), published by the Jesuits in Santiago, Chile, devoted an entire issue to the subject "Revolution in Latin America." In an editorial introduction to this issue, the revolution is defined, and the Christian response to it is outlined. [2]

▶ ▶   At first glance the theme "Revolution in Latin America" appears to be no more than an old refrain. For many European countries the history of Latin America is reduced to a picturesque and temperamental succession of "revolutions." Generals with broad sashes and beautiful decorations snatch power from other generals. This is all, and the "revolution" is no more than a game of crafty and ambitious children who do not know how to behave like adults; a supplied and exhausted theme of operettas and vaudeville acts.

[2] From "Revolución en América Latina," *Mensaje* (Santiago, Chile), 1963, no. 115, pp. 589, 591–92. Used by permission. Translated by the editor.

Something strange, however, is taking place. That light and ironic European judgment has always bothered us. Thus we used to strive to hide or disguise our domestic revolutions and we ostentatiously paraded the continuity and democracy of our regimes. But now we ourselves speak of revolution. Desired or feared, propitiated or combated, revolution is present in the mind of all. And when we speak of revolution we are not thinking of the barrack revolts and mutinies of former years but of something new and different. Almost without wanting to do so we think of Russia, China, and Cuba.

Revolutionary winds, in fact, are blowing. An immense and ever growing majority is becoming conscious of its force, of its misery, and of the injustice of that political, legal, social, and economic "order" which it is obliged to accept; and that majority is not disposed to wait longer. It demands a change: a rapid, profound, and total change of structures. If violence is necessary, it is ready to use violence. It is the mass of the people which aspires to possess itself of power in order to achieve an authentic "common good." Logically this mass desirous of revolution is inspired by the only revolutionary ideology which it finds within reach: the Marxist ideology.

To deny this fact is to close one's eyes to a patent reality. Year by year the population of Latin America increases by millions, but what are those millions? Millions of hungry, illiterate men housed in shameful huts. Those millions mean simply that year by year desperation increases, and as a consequence, the unbreakable decision to "change," come what may. This, and nothing else, is what the "Revolution in Latin America" signifies. It is desperation which, mounting up, becomes the pressure of a mighty surge of the sea, and threatens to destroy an "order" which is order for few and disorder for many. [p. 589]

The Christian is a son of the Truth, and his attitude must be truthful. His judgment must be objective, and therefore, he has to face the facts without permitting them to be distorted by his desires or fears. He must judge on the basis of what is, and this judgment has to be his norm of action and of life. He should not tilt at windmills but neither should he hide his head in the sand like the ostrich of the fable. Neither ingenuous illusion nor fearful realism; to be Christian means to deal fairly with the truth without being frightened if its route leads to the cross.

Faced by the "revolution on the march," it is impossible to remain neutral. Either one takes a decision against it and fights it openly or covertly, or one takes a decision favorable to it; there is simply no possibility of another alternative.

. . . The great modern revolutions have sprung up from Christian soil. Liberalism as well as Marxism are "heresies," deformations of Christianity. Our great task must be to revive an authentic Christianity; to give to the revolution on the march its true and profoundest dimension: the Christian dimension.

Christianity, in fact, was in reality a gigantic revolution. Christ did not come to defend old frameworks but to make them crack open, as the old leather bottles are broken by the power of new wine; wine to break hypocritical harmonies, to shake the dross and withered leaves with the flaming wind of his Spirit. It was a revolution but, let us not forget, one impelled by an invincible love.

We do not see how an authentically Christian attitude can be reconciled with a closed anti-revolutionary attitude, opposed to the radical and urgent change of structures. The attitude which faces the fact of the revolution on the march, and strives to guide it through Christian channels, seems to us to be immensely more Christian. This attitude springs from a conviction: we are all brothers, we all have the duty and the right to accomplish our human mission and task; we must all live as humans. We must therefore re-establish a political regime, a legal, social, and economic order which effectively achieves the "common good," the good of all, even though we have to sacrifice certain "particular" goods. And this accomplishment is not to be postponed to the "last days" for it is urgent. What is required is a deep and integral change of structures, an urgent change which responds to the panting and furious yearning of the masses. Not through fear but through conviction; because it is just, because the Redemption of Christ reaches all, because for the Christian there is no noble or plebian, because we are all children of God and inheritors of eternity. We must even be disposed to renounce spontaneously not a few of our comfortable and pleasant "liberties" if it is necessary thus to assure the freedom, the "liberation" of the great majority.

Some will say that this decision to change, and brusquely, the ruling structures in order to replace them with others which make really possible the "common good" is not properly "revolution." It is utopian, they will affirm, to think that this radical change can be achieved by legal means or peacefully. There will be no lack of intransigent and closed-minded sections of the public which, under diverse pretexts, will oppose radical reforms. The only revolution in fact possible will be the revolution of the uncontrollable masses, the revolution of violence and vengeance, of plunder and the firing-squad.

We do not dare to be so categorical. In any case the Christian — child of hope — has the obligation to strive to "Christianize" the coming revolution, to channel it into human channels, to strip it of vengeance, resentment, ambition, private gain, violence, and injustice. He must struggle loyally and earnestly for the "common good," at the same time defending the sacred and inalienable character of the human person.

The revolution is on the march. Not to oppose it, still more, to propitiate it clearly involves a risk (no one can know exactly where the revolution ends), but life is risk and Christianity is not a religion of tender security but of generous madness. What is important — this has to be the imperative for the Christian of today — is sincerity, truthfulness, loyalty. Let us not use Christianity as a cosmetic or as armor! Let us not speak of "sacred" western culture! Let us avoid every commonplace and every hypocrisy! . . . Let us not forget that only linked to Christ can we "Christianize" the revolution on the march. [pp. 591–592]

3. Love of Neighbor and Revolution

In this "Message to the Christians," Father Camilo Torres explains the Christian values which motivate the revolution. (See also V. 5–7 and IX. 8.) The traditional Catholic teaching on the legitimacy of opposition to tyranny is also invoked.[3]

▶ ▶   The convulsions produced by recent political, religious and social developments have possibly brought much confusion to the Christians of Colombia. It is necessary that in this decisive moment in our history we Christians stand firm on the essential foundation of our religion.

The main principle in Catholicism is love of neighbor. "He who loves his neighbor fulfils the law" (St. Paul, Romans 13:8).

In order to be true this love must seek to be effectual. If benevolences, alms, the few free schools, the few housing projects, what has been called "charity," do not succeed in giving food to the majority of the hungry, nor clothing to the majority of the naked, nor instruction to the majority of the uneducated, we have to seek effective measures for the welfare of the majority.

Privileged minorities who have power are not going to seek those measures, because generally those effective measures compel the minorities to sacrifice their privileges. For example, in order to bring

---

[3] From *Camilo Torres, Por el Padre Camilo Torres Restrepo (1956–1966)* (Cuernavaca, Mexico: Centro Intercultural de Documentación, 1966), pp. 29/325–27. Used by permission. Translated by the editor.

about a situation in which there are more jobs in Colombia, it would be better that capital not be taken out of the country in the form of dollars but that it rather be invested internally, in sources of work. But as the Colombian peso declines in value every day, those who have money and power are never going to prohibit the export of money, because by exporting it they are free from devaluation.

It is necessary, then, to take power away from the privileged minorities and to give it to the poor majority. This, if it is done rapidly, is the essence of a revolution. The Revolution can be peaceful if the minorities do not respond with violent resistance.

The Revolution, therefore, is the way to achieve a government which feeds the hungry, clothes the naked, teaches the uneducated, which carries out works of charity, of love for neighbor not only in an occasional and transitory manner, not only for a few, but for the majority of our neighbors.

For that reason the Revolution is not only permitted but obligatory for Christians who see in it the only effective and full way to achieve love for all. It is true that "there is no authority but that which comes from God" (St. Paul, Romans 13:1). But St. Thomas says that it is the people who make the concrete attribution of authority.

When there is an authority against the people, that authority is not legitimate and is called tyranny. We Christians can and must struggle against tyranny. The present government is tyrannical because only twenty percent of the voters support it and because its decisions emanate from the privileged minorities.

The temporal defects of the church should not upset us. The Church is human. The important thing is to believe that it is also divine and that if we Christians fulfill our obligation to love our neighbor, we are strengthening the Church.

I have left the duties and privileges of the clergy, but I have not ceased to be a priest.

I believe that I have given myself to the Revolution for love of neighbor. I have ceased saying mass in order to make real that love of neighbor in the temporal economic and social field. When my neighbor has nothing against me, when the Revolution has been accomplished, I shall again offer mass if God permits. I believe that thus I follow the commandment of Christ: "If you bring your offering to the altar and there remember that your brother has something against you, leave your offering there before the altar, and go, be first reconciled with your brother, and then come and present your offering" (St. Matthew 5:23–24).

After the Revolution we Christians will have the consciousness that we have established a system oriented to the love of neighbor. The struggle is long, let us begin now. . . .

THE DEBATE OVER MEANS

Among Latin American Catholics committed to revolution, the use of violence has become the crucial question of continuing debate. In the Catholic tradition, there is no near-absolute prohibition of violence, such as is found in Theravada Buddhism. In fact, Pope Paul specifically referred to the doctrinal justification of insurrections against tyranny in "On the Development of Peoples" (VIII. 1), although his purpose was to warn against the use of violence.

The most important and very telling argument of those who opt for violent revolution has little to do with theology. It is simply that nonviolent revolution, although morally preferable, does not work. This conclusion led Camilo Torres to abandon the work of peaceful agitation and mobilization and join the Army of National Liberation. And this is the conclusion reached by Father Lage Pessoa in the next selection. On the other hand is the statement of Dom Helder Cámara, Archbishop of Recife, Brazil, who urges the "realists" to consider some of the other probable consequences of violent revolution, including armed intervention by the United States. Dom Helder concludes, somewhat like Vinoba Bhave, that the most profound revolution must begin in the minds of men.

4. Nonviolence Does Not Work

Drawing upon his long experience as a social-activist priest in Brazil, Lage Pessoa reluctantly concludes that major structural changes cannot be effected in Latin America by peaceful means. (See also IX. 9.)[4]

▶ ▶ We arrive at a crossroad; change is necessary, but by peaceful means or not? My answer will appear to be a highly existential one. I am a priest who for twenty-five years has struggled with peaceful weapons against the monstrous destroyer of all liberty and equality. Incessant preaching to all strata of society, counseling to a Catholic

---

[4] From Francisco Lage Pessoa, "Brasil: La Iglesia y el Movimiento Revolucionario," in B. Castro Villagrana *et al.*, *La Iglesia, El Subdesarrollo y La Revolución* (Mexico City: Editorial Nuestro Tiempo, S. A., 1968), pp. 164–67. Used by permission. Translated by the editor.

Action that sought to be Christian, participation in workers' strikes, mass action, organization of legal trade unions. The response, in summary, is this: having escaped a murder attempt, I was arrested and imprisoned in Brazil for more than a year, tortured, condemned to twenty-eight years in jail, forcing me to seek political asylum in Mexico, on the same day of the sentence by default. At the risk of appearing simply a bitter man, my conclusion is that no other solution remains but resort to violence. Not from my case — one example among very many others — but from the evidence of the facts, which demonstrates that peaceful means are ineffectual and even counterproductive. I, then, am on the side of violence if this expression is used in counter-distinction to the nonviolence which I professed in the first part of my life.

It will be much more important, however, to be able to justify myself fully with the apocalyptic vision of our countries: hunger, misery, unemployment, unjust wages, prostitution, and lack of respect for human life translated in all forms is the established violence, called by some bishops of the Third World "the subversion of money." Against this *state* of violence, effective *acts* of violence are necessary to save humanity from slavery. Not wishing to see it is hypocrisy or fear; both are sentiments which do not accord with the spirit of Christ. It is necessary to struggle, now with weapons in hand. To do this is, a first step, to organize soundly, with the meager means available to the poor, in order to say at the opportune hour a vigorous "it is now enough" to so much degradation.

This "now enough" will necessarily take the form of guerrilla warfare, the present name for insurrection. Pope Paul VI, in a little sentence of his letter (*Populorum Progressio*) in a pacifist context sums up with precision the Christian principle with regard to this matter: "revolutionary uprising — save where there is manifest long-standing tyranny which would do great damage to fundamental personal rights and dangerous harm to the common good of the country. . . ." *Manifest long-standing tyranny* (what more could it be in our countries, and how long has it existed?) *which would do great damage to fundamental personal rights* (this requires much less than the present circumstances, for Latin American violence is killing our poor) *and dangerous harm to the common good of the country* . . . (who does not know the spoilation that our countries suffer?) is the condition of insurrection expounded by Paul VI, a condition which, although mentioned in passing, demolishes all his reformist assertions. But the sentence was necessary, once the existence of men like Camilo Torres required it, men ready to renounce all to join the struggle of the humble, in the name of the gospel. And to die, as was the case of the young Colombian priest, "martyr of the Christ of Tomorrow" as Alceu Amorso Lima called him, when a whole Catholic tradition demanded it, a tradition which now the proponents of non-violence strive to have abolished.

In traditional ethics the problem is called, *Conditions for a Just Insurrection*. Violent action to overthrow tyranny (we summarize the manuals of the Catholic school) is legitimate, when the following four conditions are present:

1. *A Just Cause*. Here the attempt is made to define tyranny. . . . A government is not unjust for having caused particular educational or economic laws to be enacted which are judged unjust, but when in fact, the common feeling lacks any assurance that the happiness and well-being of the people are being sought.

2. *A Well-Grounded Hope of Success*. Since insurrection entails the expectation of bloodshed, more or less serious disorders and many other situations, it must have a reasonable hope of victory. Here it will be necessary to apply almost literally what the Master says about the prudence of the king who must go forth to battle only after calculating his forces in comparison with his enemy's (Luke 14:31–32). The probable triumph presupposes that the cost (human and material) of the revolution not be greater than the benefit and that the new form of government be really capable of securing the common good.

3. *That Peaceful Means Have Been or Are Ineffective*. It is necessary to exhaust the whole range of legal and extralegal means (the subject of nonviolence: pressure, demonstrations, threats). But it is evident that not all can be required; certain actions of that type under dictatorships, instead of producing results, serve only to disarm the opposition, diminishing its true capacity for the struggle.

4. *That the Means To Be Employed Be Honest*. The most just cause cannot legitimate intrinsically perverse means, according to the very concept of natural law. . . . It is legitimate to kill, because the other was the aggressor; however, it is not legitimate to kill a civilian population. It is legitimate to kill soldiers; however, it is not legitimate to torture and kill prisoners. . . .

Guerrilla warfare, in order to be effective, requires certain conditions, the most important of which is that it involve the peasants and workers. If they do not feel solidarity with the struggle, the guerrilla fighter corps is isolated and surrounded by potential adversaries everywhere. It will be appropriate to remind ourselves of the lesson that those bishops of the Third World give in the declaration cited above: "It is first for the poor peoples and the poor of the peoples to carry out their own promotion and development. That they regain confidence in themselves, that they instruct themselves . . . that they listen to those who can awaken the consciousness of the masses." They say this after affirming that "it would be an illusion to await passively a free conversion of those of whom our father Abraham warns us: *they would not listen though one returned from the dead* (Luke 15:31)."

Without the understanding of the peasants, a clear understanding which transcends the super-propaganda of the masters of the world, no effective action will be possible. Here, a great danger is foreseen: that the Catholic hierarchy, manipulated by publicity and bewitched by fear, begin to play into the hands of those who have all, against the dispossessed, the humbled and offended. It would be necessary to tell those hierarchs that, if they don't have the courage to be Christians, at least they should not pawn their pastoral office by suppressing the hunger and thirst for righteousness which consumes those who have renounced all in order to live with the dispossessed. In all, they should be guided by the yearning for a new world, considerably better than that in which half of the little ones die of starvation, in which the life expectancy of adults does not reach thirty years, such conditions as have been denounced by hundreds of Brazilian priests.

5. Nonviolent Revolution Based on Realism

While Archbishop Dom Helder Cámara makes clear his deep appreciation for those true revolutionaries who opt for violence, he states that his personal calling is to be a man of peace. Furthermore, the most basic task is to create a revolutionary consciousness in the masses, which cannot be done by guns and grenades. [5]

One first observation, fundamental to a clear understanding of the problem of violence: the entire world needs a structural revolution.

In the underdeveloped world this truth seems evident. If one looks at the underdeveloped world from any angle — economic, scientific, political, social, religious — one comes to understand that a cursory,

[5] From Dom Helder Cámara, "La Violencia: ¿ Opción Unica?" in *Informaciones católicas internacionales* (Berlin 17–103, Mexico 6, D. F., Mexico), no. 312 (May 2, 1968), pp. 4–7. Used by permission. Translated by the editor.

superficial revision will in no way suffice. What must be attempted is a revision in depth, a profound and rapid change — let us not fear the word — it must become a structural revolution.

Paul VI said: "Let us be understood well, the present situation must be faced courageously and the injustices it implies fought and overcome! Development demands audacious, profoundly innovative transformations. Urgent reforms must be undertaken without any delay. Each one must generously do his part."

From the economic point of view, who does not know that in the underdeveloped countries internal colonialism exists, that is, that there is a small group of privileged people of the country itself, whose wealth is maintained at the expense of the misery of millions of fellow-citizens? It is still a semi-feudal regime; there is the appearance of patriarchal life, but in reality the absence of personal rights, a sub-human situation and true slavery. The rural workers — true Pariahs — do not have access to the greater part of the land that the great landlords keep uncultivated for the increased value it will have tomorrow.

When this situation exists in a continent like Latin America, entirely Christian — at least in name and tradition — one can measure the enormous responsibility of Christianity there. Without forgetting the great examples of abnegation, sacrifice, and even heroism, it is necessary to recognize that for the past — and the danger persists in the present — we, Latin American Christians, are gravely responsible for the situation of injustice that exists on the continent. We accepted the slavery of the Indians and African slavery; and now, have we spoken clearly and in a loud voice to our landlords, to the big men, to the powerful? Or do we close our eyes and help them to have a clear conscience, once they have concealed frightful injustices through alms destined to construct churches (frequently scandalously large and rich, a contrast which clashes with the surrounding misery) or through alms for our social work? In practice, have we not perhaps given to Marx an appearance of being right when he presented to the outcastes a passive, alienated and alienating Christianity, truly an opiate of the masses? . . .

At the moment of asking ourselves if the structural revolution which the world needs necessarily implies violence, it must be observed that violence already exists, that it is exercised, sometimes even without knowing it, by the very ones who denounce it as a plague for society.

It exists in the underdeveloped world; the masses in their subhuman situation are subjected to violence by the small group of privileged people, the powerful. It is known that if the masses attempt to convert themselves into a people and initiate a basic education or popular culture effort, if they organize themselves in labor unions or cooperatives, their leaders are called subversives and communists. It has been very justly said: "They show themselves to be rebels against the established disorder — they are outlaws — they must disappear so that order may reign." The disorder-order!

With respect to "Law," it is very often an instrument of violence against the less powerful or else is reduced to beautiful phrases in the text of declarations, such as that of the Fundamental Rights of Man, the second decade of which the world is beginning to commemorate. A good way to celebrate this anniversary, on the part of the United Nations, would be to verify if some of these rights exist that they be truly respected in two-thirds of the world. . . .

Violence also exists in the developed world, as much on the capitalist side as on the socialist side. . . .

In view of this triple violence: within the underdeveloped countries, within the developed countries, perpetrated by the developed countries against the underdeveloped countries — one comes to understand that it is possible to think, speak and act in terms of a liberating violence, a redeeming violence.

If the powerful of the underdeveloped world do not have the courage to disengage themselves from their privileges and to do justice to millions of persons in subhuman situations; if governments draw up reforms that remain on paper, how it it possible to hold back the youth tempted by radicalism and violence? . . .

Allow me to state my position. I respect those who in conscience feel obligated to opt for violence, not the too-easy violence of the drawing-room guerrilla fighters, but those who have proved their sincerity by the sacrifice of their lives. It seems to me that the memory of Camilo Torres and Che Guevara merit as much respect as that of the pastor Martin Luther King.

I accuse those of the right or the left who wound justice and impede peace as the true promoters of violence.

My personal vocation is that of a pilgrim of peace, following the example of Paul VI; personally I prefer a thousand times to be killed than to kill.

This personal position is based on the gospel. A lifetime of effort to understand and live the gospel brings me to the profound conviction that the gospel, if it can and if it must be called revolutionary, is so in the sense that it demands a conversion of each one of us. We have no right to enclose ourselves in selfishness; we must open ourselves both to the love of God and to the love of men. And it is enough to consider the

Beatitudes — quintessence of the gospel message — to discover that the choice for Christians seems clear; we Christians are on the side of nonviolence, which is in no way a choice of weakness and passivity. Nonviolence is to believe more in the power of truth, justice, and love than in the power of war, death, and hate.

If this strikes you as moralism, wait a moment. The option for nonviolence, if it is rooted in the gospel, is also based on reality. Do you want realism? Then I say to you: If in any part of the world, but above all in Latin America, an explosion of violence should take place, you can be sure that the great powers will arrive immediately — even without a declaration of war — the Superpowers will be there and we shall have a new Vietnam. You want more realism: Precisely because we must come to the structural revolution, it is necessary to promote first, but in a new sense, a "cultural revolution." Because if mental outlooks are not changed in depth, then the reforms of structures, the basic structures, will remain on paper and ineffectual.

BIBLIOGRAPHY
Books available in paperback are marked with a star (★).

I. *Comparative Studies, and Collections Dealing with Several Religions*

Bellah, Robert N., ed., *Religion and Progress in Modern Asia*. New York: The Free Press, 1965. Chapters on Hinduism, Buddhism, Islam, and Catholicism.

Eisenstadt, S. N., ed., *The Protestant Ethic and Modernization: A Comparative View*. New York: Basic Books, 1968.

Silvert, Kalman H., ed., *Churches and States: The Religious Institution and Modernization*. New York: American University Field Staff, 1967. Chapters on Judaism, Islam, and Catholicism.

★Smith, Donald E., ed., *South Asian Politics and Religion*. Princeton, N.J.: Princeton University Press, 1966. Chapters on Hinduism, Buddhism, and Islam (India, Ceylon, and Pakistan).

★————, *Religion and Political Development*. Boston, Mass.: Little, Brown and Co., 1970. Material on Hinduism, Buddhism, Islam, and Catholicism.

★Von der Mehden, Fred R., *Religion and Nationalism in Southeast Asia: Burma, Indonesia, The Philippines*. Madison, Wis.: University of Wisconsin Press, 1963. Material on Buddhism, Islam, and Catholicism.

II. *Hinduism, Politics, and Social Change*

★Bondurant, Joan V., *Conquest of Violence: The Gandhian Philosophy of Conflict*. Berkeley, Calif.: University of California Press, 1965.

★DeBary, William Theodore, ed., *Sources of Indian Tradition*, Vol. II. New York: Columbia University Press, 1964.

Derrett, J. Duncan, *Religion, Law and the State in India*. New York: The Free Press, 1968.

Heimsath, Charles H., *Indian Nationalism and Hindu Social Reform*. Princeton, N.J.: Princeton University Press, 1964.

Luthera, Ved Prakash, *Concept of the Secular State and India.* Bombay: Oxford University Press, 1964.

Mishra, Vikas, *Hinduism and Economic Growth.* London: Oxford University Press, 1962.

Rudolph, Lloyd I., and Susanne H. Rudolph, *The Modernity of Tradition: Political Development in India.* Chicago, Ill.: University of Chicago Press, 1967.

★Singer, Milton, ed., *Traditional India: Structure and Change.* Philadelphia, Pa.: American Folklore Society, Vol. X, 1959.

————, and Bernard S. Cohn, eds., *Structure and Change in Indian Society.* Chicago, Ill.: Aldine Publishing Co., 1968.

Sinha, V. K., ed., *Secularism in India.* Bombay: Lalvani Publishing House, 1968.

★Smith, Donald E., *India as a Secular State.* Princeton, N.J.: Princeton University Press, 1963.

Srinivas, M. N., *Social Change in Modern India.* Berkeley, Calif.: University of California Press, 1966.

III. *Buddhism, Politics, and Social Change*

Benz, Ernst, *Buddhism or Communism: Which Holds the Future of Asia?* Garden City, N.Y.: Doubleday and Co., 1965.

★Evers, Hans–Dieter, ed., *Loosely Structured Social Systems; Thailand in Comparative Perspective.* New Haven, Conn.: Yale University Southeast Asia Studies, 1969.

★Mulder, J. A. Niels, *Monks, Merit and Motivation: An Exploratory Study of the Social Functions of Buddhism in Thailand in Processes of Guided Social Change.* DeKalb, Ill.: Center for Southeast Asian Studies, Northern Illinois University, 1969.

Nash, Manning, *The Golden Road to Modernity: Village Life in Contemporary Burma.* New York: John Wiley and Sons, 1965.

★————, et al., *Anthropological Studies in Theravada Buddhism.* New Haven, Conn.: Yale University Southeast Asia Studies, 1966.

★Sarkisyanz, E., *Buddhist Backgrounds of the Burmese Revolution.* The Hague: Martinus Nijhoff, 1965.

Schechter, Jerrold, *The New Face of Buddha: Buddhism and Political Power in Southeast Asia.* New York: Coward-McCann, Inc., 1967.

Smith, Donald E., *Religion and Politics in Burma.* Princeton, N.J.: Princeton University Press, 1965.

IV. *Islam, Politics, and Social Change*

Abbott, Freeland, *Islam and Pakistan.* Ithaca, N.Y.: Cornell University Press, 1968.

Ahmad, Aziz, *Islamic Modernism in India and Pakistan, 1857–1964.* London: Oxford University Press, 1967.

Anderson, J. N. D., *Islamic Law in the Modern World.* New York: New York University Press, 1959.

Berkes, Niyazi, *The Development of Secularism in Turkey.* Montreal: McGill University Press, 1964.

Binder, Leonard, *Religion and Politics in Pakistan.* Berkeley, Calif.: University of California Press, 1961.

——, *The Ideological Revolution in the Middle East.* New York: John Wiley and Sons, 1964.

Geertz, Clifford, *The Religion of Java.* Glencoe, Ill.: The Free Press, 1960.

——, *Islam Observed: Religious Development in Morocco and Indonesia.* New Haven, Conn.: Yale University Press, 1968.

Gibb, H. A. R., *Modern Trends in Islam.* Chicago, Ill.: University of Chicago Press, 1947.

Hourani, Albert H., *Arab Thought in the Liberal Age.* London: Oxford University Press, 1962.

★Jay, Robert R., *Religion and Politics in Rural Central Java.* New Haven, Conn.: Yale University, Southeast Asia Studies, 1963.

Kerr, Malcolm H., *Islamic Reform: The Political and Legal Theories of Muhammad Abduh and Rashid Rida.* Berkeley, Calif.: University of California Press, 1966.

★Levy, Reuben, *The Social Structure of Islam.* London: Cambridge University Press, 1962.

Malik, Hafeez, *Moslem Nationalism in India and Pakistan.* Washington, D. C.: Public Affairs Press, 1963.

Proctor, J. Harris, ed., *Islam and International Relations.* New York: Frederick A. Praeger, 1965.

Rosenthal, Erwin I. J., *Islam and the Modern National State.* London: Cambridge University Press, 1965.

Safran, Nadav, *Egypt in Search of Political Community.* Cambridge, Mass.: Harvard University Press, 1961.

★Smith, Wilfred Cantwell, *Islam in Modern History.* Princeton, N.J.: Princeton University Press, 1957.

★Von Grunebaum, G. E., *Modern Islam: The Search for Cultural Identity.* New York: Vintage Books, Random House, 1964.

V.   *Latin American Catholicism, Politics, and Social Change*

Camara, Helder, *The Church and Colonialism: The Betrayal of the Third World.* Denville, N.J.: Dimension Books, 1969.

D'Antonio, William V., and Frederick B. Pike, eds., *Religion, Revolution and Reform.* New York: Praeger, 1964.

de Kadt, Emanuel, *Catholic Radicals in Brazil.* London: Oxford University Press, 1970.

Guzman, German, *Camilo Torres.* New York: Sheed and Ward, 1969.

★Halperin, Ernst, *The Christian Democratic Alternative in Chile.* Cambridge, Mass.: MIT Center for International Studies, 1964.

————, *Nationalism and Communism in Chile.* Cambridge, Mass.: MIT Press, 1965.

Houtart, Francois, and Emile, Pin, *The Church and the Latin American Revolution.* New York: Sheed and Ward, 1965.

Kennedy, John J., *Catholicism, Nationalism and Democracy in Argentina.* Notre Dame, Ind.: University of Notre Dame Press, 1958.

Landsberger, Henry A., ed., *The Church and Social Change in Latin America.* Notre Dame, Ind.: University of Notre Dame Press, 1970.

Mecham, J. Lloyd, *Church and State in Latin America.* Chapel Hill, N.C.: University of North Carolina Press, 1966.

★Pike, Frederick B., ed., *The Conflict Between Church and State in Latin America.* New York: Alfred A. Knopf, 1964.

*Vallier, Ivan, *Catholicism, Social Control, and Modernization in Latin America.* Englewood Cliffs, N.J.: Prentice-Hall, 1970.

Williams, Edward J., *Latin American Christian Democratic Parties.* Knox-ville, Tenn.: University of Tennessee Press, 1967.

INDEX

INDEX